Human Rights in the New Millennium

Human Rights
in the
New Millennium

Prof. N. Sanajaoba

Manas Publications
New Delhi-110 002 (India)

Manas Publications
(Publishers, Distributors, Importers & Exporters)
4858, Prahlad Street, 24, Ansari Road, Darya Ganj,
New Delhi - 110 002 (INDIA)

Ph.: (O) 23260783, 23265523, (R) 27131660, 27143052
Fax: 011 - 23272766
E-mail: manaspublications@vsnl.com

First Published: 2004
Rs 595/-

ISBN 81-7049-115-0

Typeset at
Manas Publications

Printed in India at
R.K. Offset
and Published by Mrs Suman Lata for
Manas Publications, 4858, Prahlad Street,
24, Ansari Road, Darya Ganj,
New Delhi - 110 002 (INDIA)

Preface

The critical legal trends that set in swiftly at the threshold of the twenty-first century the - intial moments of third millennium-are the focal theme of the discourse. Interestinghly, the trends have already reached out the centrestage before we can generate a meaningful discourse. The social-political phenomena and events have in the fleeting moments overtaken the frames of reference. Institution of anticipated durability have de-constructed by giving way to their successors. Several contemporaneous institutions have been carved out by the western architects while retaining the western values, perceptions and characteristics.

The inevitable collapse of imperialism in the early part of the century and steady decay of colonialism in its multifarious manifestations have happened swiftly, only to be followed by United Nations, the rise and fall of Soviet Union and the cold war. The advantage and burden of the sole surviving-superpower has correspondingly increased.

It seems that sub-terranean oceans have intermingled and walls of national sovereignty have virtually merged with the single landmass. No body could ever imagine the wiring of the globe via the information super highway and the unity of the cyber-space. The existing twentieth century institutions are laden with information-avalanche and the semi-colonial enclaves could hardly survive the onslaught. Hence, the political seismicism in semi or neo-colonial enclaves elsewhere in the world. The impact of science and technology on the institutions is enormous. The dark side is the conversion of man to what Herbert Marcuse labelled as-'one dimensional man'

For a couple of centuries in the past, a rational discourse usually means concretisation of the western premises, not necessarily of the explicit ideology. It acquires ligitimisation by inducting of western methodology, knowledge, values and scientific rationality in the undefended rest of the world, which have been left with no choice. Constitutional and rights-discourse are deeply entreched in these trappings. The rationality that emerges from this siege-consciousness not only pre-empt other alternative forms of rationality but also espouses gleichschaltung-impact by levelling and regulating the rivals and siblings. At the stage, the communication ceased to be a dialogue and it become an effective monologue.

When the Western approaches can not cope with the objective realities and the potential of the developing world, the constitutional engineering assumes a discursive flashpoint, as the system is not fully responsive. Occasionally, the flashpoint borders around crisis—political economics or, constitutional. Western experiences are not essentially egalitatian or, perfectionist. Had they been flawless, the need for perstroika-restructuring would not have been felt. The discursive domain can not be limited by one set of agenda of other. The liberal democratic approach is inadequate.

The alternative pattern of discourse may be sought by a dialectical construction of the universal connection, the unity of opposites and the developmental process, despite the *Ideologie Kritik*- the critique of ideology. So far no rights nor constitutional discourse has been easily bailed out of the western facination. It may not have happened due to sheer choice, but due to prolonged hegemony, colonialism and imperialism over the rest of the world. The official dogma of the ruling clique has, however, immobilised the vast sea of human subject. They have been subjected to Pavlovian acculturation and they cannot yet even after decades of the culmination of imperialism, explore and *'emancipatory reason'*. A glaring demonstration of the captive reason takes this form. The Bible is ligitimate, if you and I accept the first sin unconditionally and absolutely, otherwise not. This is the rationality which gets along with other scriptures and contemporaneours political constitutions as well. Constitutions are sanctifies, whereas even the laws of Physics are altered after every revelation and the right structure remain undisturbed, because it emanates from the same holy political constitution or, the judgements of the political appointees-the common law judiciary, who are not accountable to the people.

A profound contrast can be witnessed when millions of Soviet citizens directly legislate their own statutes, by legitimation to the normative structure, which would regulate their conduct and behaviour. The banana republic—name given by Gunnar Myrdal to the Asian Republic—would consider this as impractical and paradoxically redundant. The Soviet Union had on several occasions drastically amended their constitutions by retaining the basic structure intact. The 1977 Soviet constitution had been adopted by the Parliament only after its scrutiny in 1,500,000 meetings among the people, who recommended four lakh amendments and with incorporating as many as 118 amendments in the 173 article—original draft. The left radicals in the developing countries can't even imagine such a colossal exercise, because they are not used to it. So is the fate of the people, who have been immobilised and handicapped by the top-down democratic values. The rationality behind is eugenic, selective, disisive and hierarchical.

The rights discourse - one of the two dominant American philosophical concern, the other being the 'justice'- has been similarly entrapped in the western barrack-democracy. Their vintage rationality emanates from the rationality derived from from post-nationhood, post-industrial and post-colonial society. The developing society would have to join the race from height, they have not yet reached. The concept of unequal race negates the legitimation of the rights-discourse, generated by the unequal society. Added to the polemic is the legacy of unequal philosophy in the west and the developing world. The entire gamut of western rights-discourse has been unfolded by keeping the atomistic individual at the centre, whereas the eastern society placed the social-organic whole at the centre. That is why the puritanical western democratic institutions as such could not address to the demanding rights-discourse in the developing world. The Indian elitist mind-set, therefore, has been immobilised and handicapped from looking beyond what they have been tutored in Pavlovian sense and cultivated to react in a specific way. However, an enlarged pattern of discourse would narrow down the conceptual hiatus.

Aside the domain of *Ideologic Kririk,* the critique of ideology that is, we can revisit Kritische Theorie-the critical social theory that takes the flaws of positivism and its methodology seriously. Unlike the other two approaches, the Frankfurt school social- theorists categorically explored that the political authority has used 'Reason' for oppressive purposes, snuff the communication from the oppressed people, that capitalism has anaestherisied the discontent of the exploited people and that the modern civilisation is diseased. Dogmatism has overlooked the other dimensions of humankind. The dogma explains the human situation and human situation does not happen, so as to fit in the dogma. Humanity does not surrender itself to the instrumentalities of its own making.

In the United States and European countries, deconstructionist theories like the Critical Legal Studies Movement (CLS) are found across the board. The scholarship, dons and national media would be divided in either opposing or supporting the movements. The critical approach empowers every one in the domain and activates the interactive process. An elite need not be a partisan to one form of consciousness or another in this scenario.

It triggers off and simulates an enlarged pattern of discourse, which would eventually generate unity of knowledge, multiple choice and autonomous decision making. The alternative approaches expand the multiple choice. The difficulty came up when the 'reason' has been under siege. The alternative has been offered by institutions. The *Institution fur Sozialforchung* at Frankfurt, organised by the exiled German emigres during the Nazi regime, made a point which is fundamental in the discursive voyage: we missed the 'Emancipatory Reason' and on the pressures from empiricism and positivism, reason has been bended.

The nineteen critical legal essays incorporated herein are selective and not seductive. The treatise of these essays embodies the flashpoints in the contemporary law's empire. Admittedly, the discourse does not stand to re-affirm the conventional, falsified legitimation of the doctrines, legal concepts and dominant views and it is not a clear case of *Ideologie Kritik* either. Its nearest affinity lies in the domain of Kritische Theorie, because the social theorists of the developing societies. We can not and should not be post-industrial society. If some of the propositions in this treatise of essays would prick the conscientious readers in the developing world, the author could not have asked more and he could not have done better.

The author ramains thankful to the publisher Mr.V.K. Garg, Manas Publications, forums and friends, who are prepared to differ from what the author proposes here in and also to colleagues, who would partly agree on second thoughts. I should share the moments of my children-Miss Naorem Linthoi and Mr. Naorem Kiyamba, who would usually locate their father at a home away from the home.

Prof. N. Sanajaoba

Contents

Part-I

Constitutional Discourse

Part-II

Rights Discourse

Part-III

Enlarged Legal Discourse

Part-I

Constitutional Discourse

1

The Proposed New Constitution

Idealpolitik is the impulse, found behind the hackneyed adherence of the microscopic Indian power-elite and the newly created Hindustani bourgeoisie nouveau riche to the obsolescent regimentation of post 1947 imperial India, that results in national oppression, subjugation of national entities and also to the collateral socio-economic deprivation of the legitimate classes and entities. This impulsive self or, imperial aggrandisement is recurrently legitimised by proxy reformists —time servers— who in the thick of Marxian political linguistics entrap the unleashed people's creative power so that they may remain content with the democratic leftovers of the reformists and their class alliance.

Realpolitik unleashes a continuous pattern of protest movements and political violence ranging from the classical methods of fasting, *dharna*, gherao to communal outbursts and militant exercise of the 'Right of the People to Self-Determination' and also to seeking access to militant 'National Liberation Movement' in NES (North Eastern States), Punjab and Kashmir. The ugly side of the *realpolitik* in the imperial continent of India gives testimony to a cruel form of state terrorism, hardly witnessed during the British era. A typical ingenuous Hindustani power-elite, represented by opinion leader or politician, university don or ex-serviceman (including judge ex-serviceman, media person or idea-person chooses a blind-spot in the *realpolitik* in order to morally justify the ongoing national *oppression* and socio-economic deprivation. University syllabus, moral code (*Bhakti*), the class laws and statutes or, the political process hitherto imposed upon generation after generation provides a legitimate framework for the unhygienic regimentation of the disempowered, overwhelming non-power elite — the illiterate mass.

We ask a supreme court judge or, a patronizing, uncreative university don or, unhygienic opinion—leader for a blessing or panacea for the structural malaise: his revolutionary spirit and message cannot transcend his arrogance Hindustani imperialism or, Anglo-Saxon lumpenisation, or, caste-class mindset, which he justifies with his dishonest, mechanical argumentation and rhetoric.

The *bhadralok Narodniks* openly and shamelessly misinterpret human history and even the universally approved 'Right of the People to Self-Determination' within the captive cliche of state - autonomy and chauvinistic jingoism — the exotic mask of hidden neo-colonialism and post-industrial imperialism. The aforementioned collective right is not a password for fragmenting age-old countries and historical states, but it has legacy in the historical prerogative, rationale and certain set of positive parameters, which a nation or people is legitimately entitled to.

The instruments of the United Nations and inter-governmental treaties have fairly established the standard and universal construction of the self-determination principle, from which misconstructions and perverted neo-colonial exhortations may not earn respectability, validity and credibility. Should any original constituent unit of the original *Bharat* urge upon secession from the original state, its legitimacy and justification would be subject to a critical political discourse. Even today, no original constituent unit of *Bharat* has ever fought a war of national liberation through a military medium or, otherwise with the *Bharatiya* union government. The instance is not at all comparable to the reversion-process, strongly advocated by either an annexed state or, occupied territory or, an alien-dominated race or, by an alien-nation and people, who can no longer be equated with the metropolitan populace. The latter process is demonstrated by North-eastern states and Kashmir.

The universal validity of the right of the people to self-determination has been empirically proved by one hundred and thirty-five newly established countries during the period of half a century of the installation of the UN. During the last decade, at least twenty independent countries emerged out of three east European countries in the exercise of their right to self-determination. No bloodshed was witnessed except in the case of Bosnian civil war, which like the racial arrogance in India gives a clear evidence of simulated Serbian racial arrogance and chauvinism. Puerto Rico remains an associate state of USA by the choice of Puerto Ricans, who in plebiscite have opted so. By a 50:49 lead in a referendum, held on 30 October, 1995, Quebec continues to remain in Canada. Unlike the 50 year-old national liberation movements in Manipur , Nagaland and NES and similar imbroglio in Kashmir, Sien-Fienn-IRA militancy is three decades old in Northern Ireland. The thick-skinned arrogant British rulers thought it too long to ignore the Irish right for long 30 years and hence, in December 1994, British Prime Minister signed an agreement called 'Downing Street Declaration', which formally recognises the IRA's claim to Self-Determination. They reached at an agreement in April, 1998 for ending the conflict and Northern Ireland executive to start functioning in March, 1999.

While de-colonisation process is widely traced to the installation of the United Nations in 1945 and its de-colonisation movements since 1960, the American Declaration of Independence on 4 July, 1776—two centuries ago- remains the watershed in de-colonisation.

The 20th century leaders have been immensely benefited by the American experience, based on the 1776 Declaration viz., equality and liberty of men, derivation of power of government from the consent of the governed, popular sovereignty and peoples, right to abolish or, institute new government. Thomas Jefferson's draft and ideology, followed by his constitutional revolution in 1800 Pain's pamphat 'Commonsense', Thomas and George Washington's refusal to accept crown as well as the third term in a key-position had demonstrated rebel thought more than two centuries ago. In some regimented Asian society, *Bhakti* may be accorded to only a deified bourgeois leader as father of the nation, but

Americans recognize Samuel Adams as father of war of independence, Thomas Paine as father of enlightenment, George Washington as a father No. 1, and Thomas Jefferson as father of Constitution etc. No body has been selectively deified. Human progress is the first casualty of deification.

Anti-colonial Attlee's government resolved and acceded to long outstanding Congress demand, of right of self-determination as endorsed in 1918, for the British Indians. Quarter of a century (not half a century as in the case of Manipur, Nagaland, Kashmir and NES) is too long for a metropolitan continental power to ignore and suppress legitimate national questions, which have been reinforced by historical prerogative and legitimacy. Some neo-Nazis could not even tolerate the Indian premier's casual offer of 'Short of Azadi Status' to Kashmir in the wake of Chrar-e-Sherif fiasco 1995.

Neo-Nazi approaches reflect the indelible spiritual roots as religiously ingrained in Manu's cannibalistic prerogative against women, weaker sections and the autochthon, depressed classes and also in Bishnu Gupta's Arthasasthra (Kautilya), which dwarfs Machiavelli and Clauzewitz in the art of gobbling up small states, weak neighbours through the imperialistic Mandala quicksand. The horrendous legacy is literally practised and followed by the ruling imperial class against the annexed peripheral states. The neo-Nazi Manuvians and Kautilyans, occasionally disguised as leftists also openly endorse the costliest and counterproductive national oppression and subjugation of legitimate national questions through military means and mischievous misinterpretation of the universal right to self-determination. The pseudo-revolutionaries (lumpen bourgeoisie), who project themselves as radical reformists and state autonomists *a La* one time social democrat and narodniks defend the *status quo* by way of mild verbal chastisement, which preempts the premises of the revolutionary contradictions. Regimentation, as justified by the defenders of Bastlle in this age and epoch postpones the long overdue *perestroika* of the Indian colonial structures, safety valves and the unbearable *liet motifs*, before it happens. *Perestroika* may be delayed, but it cannot be shelved by colonial logic and immoral authority.

Hegemonic constitution

There are three broad schools of thought as regards the contemporary, post-1947 Indian constitutionalism, which best serves the feudal and imperial ruling-classes.

Firstly, the orthodoxy and conservatism, which fossilizes the misplaced internalised deification of the bourgeoisie arbitrarily gave to themselves a constitutional instrument, which would perpetually resurrect their class-caste, feudal and hegemonic interest. The reformists and *status quoists* vehemently articulate in their vocabulary, their deep-rooted interest — be it presidential or, cabinet form of government and unions' charitable devolution of a fragment of it's iniquitous authority to mild state autonomy or, otherwise to the abolition of article 370 or reviving the pre-1953 format of article 370 of the Constitution within the deified *Bania* constitutional framework. This approach has been a direct negation of the 'Quit India' spirit and the idea behind the creation of a republic India from out of several building blocks, some of which had never been conceived within the established boundary of *Bharat*, as it existed. That is why M.K. Gandhi in 1946, J.P. Narayan and Mohammed Ali Jinnah repudiated the non-sovereign Constituent Assembly, which drafted the present Constitution. The hegemony, internal-colonialism and neo-imperialism would continue with the existing structure and faith, which had contradicted 'Quit India' spirit and the Cabinet mission plan, from its inception.

Secondly, the theory of the post 1973 basic structuralists, who, being interspersed in various camps, stretch the limits of constitutional amendments to the last borders of reform, without reaching out to the interpolated basic constitutional structures like — federalism, rule of law, fundamental rights and judicial review. Coincidentally, the standards are the widely accepted super-eminent principles of a modern constitutional government. A newly framed constitutional instrument inspite of its re-structuration, should invariably reincorporate these constitutional standards in the text of a new draft. Some middle-of-the-left power-elites may privately subscribe to this level of re-structuration, but they hesitate to go beyond and initiate political action at their own level. The false arguments interpolated by the pseudo and official Marxists — the new power-sharing opportunistic section or, Milovan Djila's 'New class' or, what Mao Dze Dong called 'Capitalist Roaders', propagate a false alarm that the feudal casteist class Constitution may be substituted by a fresh MNC Constitution, inspite of their taking the MNC bull by the horns.

Jargon-making system analysts — the brainchild of Hindustani monopoly press — also subscribe to this feudal philosophy since their hegemony and manoeuvering possibilities are best guaranteed by the false pro-change mindset, conveyed by media projections. They are ready to bless any constitutional upgradation of chapter IV principle of cow-slaughter prevention to chapter III rights as new revolutionism, whose last frontier culminates here itself and not beyond. At most, they may add 'Uniform Civil Code' in their false cosmetic revolutionary agenda. Yet casteist endogamy would continue.

Hindustani Bhadralok communist parties — Antonio Gramski's foreshaken orphans — also share the same hegemonic philosophy, because the falsehood of their reconstituted ideology entitles them to bourgeois power, for which they remained hungry for too long. A typical leftist urchin, who joins in what CEC T.N.Seshan calls 'election of the criminal carnivals' is sometimes worse and more degraded than the post 1942 lathi-wielding Gandhian dadas and violent knife-wielders. The system serves them all best with casual mercy being showered on the peasantry and lower middle class. Every epoch turns out turncoat opportunists, who are fond of cosmetics, French perfumes and Hyde park rhetorics, but the reality is different when re-structuration is long overdue. Mask is not removed.

Thirdly, the pleas of the re-structuralists and advocates for a complete re-drafting of the post 1950 feudal, hegemonic Constitution raises the need for convening a democratic Constituent Assembly, to be equally represented by the states. The strongest contradictions against this plea hail from the fanatical Kautilayan - Manuvadis, their cohort power-elite *nouveau riche* and also from middle class perceptions, which do not accept, 'Equality of states' in a federal setup. A typical Hindustani, who had never experienced a Bastille, an October revolution or Peasant revolution has no alternative than accepting a deified paperwork because of the *Bhakti* culture, which emasculated his basic manhood and disempowered his basic rights.

However, the need of the hour, as indicated by the ongoing widespread political turmoil that covered the period from 1949 till today strongly reinforces the legitimacy of political expediency to restructure the union and adopt a new Constitution. It is time to de-construct and dismantle structural and feudal hegemony, notwithstanding the contrived hindrances, as preferred by the obsolescent feudal power-elite, who cling to their vested class-obscurantist-feudal interest, that is best served by an instrument of their own making in 1949-50. There is a rationale when A.B. Vajpayee government proposed a review of the Constitution in 1998.

First principles of constitutionalism

That a modern constitution is a political instrument, not an incantation of the self-proclaimed holy priests, ecclesiastics and moulavis and imams should be clearly understood. This is an exclusive human domain, wherein the basic civilised principles of man and the nation are continuously reflected or, people-specific culture that has hitherto been attained. The human political representatives prepare the draft for approval by the individual citizens through a referendum, participated by one and all. However, the power-elites vicariously assume the responsibility of the entire mass and their class-will is thrust upon the mass by abusing the basic constitutionalism. India's spirit of Constitution is an example of this significant aberration.

Placing a draft constitution to a popular referendum is not an unprecedented event in the twentieth century. However, class constitutions of the bourgeoisie had, as a rule, never been put to a referendum, because the deeply entrenched class causes would be overturned by the overwhelming mass. The same fear-psychosis for the multi-racial and plural Indian populace had prevented the bourgeois, zamindar-brahmin-dominated Constituent Assembly from seeking a popular mandate over their own class-hegemonistic copy of the constitution. It is nothing but a class will legitimized. The constitutional fraud is printed in the first line of the class draft in these words — 'We, the people '(sic. We — a handful of Zamindars, 90% Brahmins and brown racial chauvinists). The 400 million — 'We, the People' have never been given an opportunity to give a single opinion on the draft. University dons and ex-judicial servicemen, who served the bourgeoisie justify this fraud by their queer nihilist logic and perfidy, handed down to the helpless common men. But we dare state that this is a fraud like a white-lie and that time has come to rectify this open fraud. It needs courage. The class will ought to be substituted by popular will.

Nearly all the post 1948 Universal Declaration of Human Rights political constitutions have domestically endorsed the basic economic, civil, social and political rights of man to a considerable extent.

This is a global prerogative, from which derogation is not possible and any derogation would be ridiculous in the comity of nations.

Following the post 1960 global de-colonisation movement, as mandated by the UN, the 1978 Soviet constitution formally incorporates entrenched provisions like the indispensable Right of the People to Self-Determination, right of the constituent states to secede and also the Soviet constitutional obligation to support legitimate national liberation movements worldwide. The making of Soviet Union and creation of Indian Republic followed the same historical process, considering the analogous pluralism and multiple legacy (see Ch.II *infra.*)

CIS like European Union provides a commonwealth of all the one time Soviet states following the post 1991 events. A non-feudal, anti-colonial constitution of India should, in contrast to the existing hegemonic instrument, thrust upon by the charismatic bourgeoisie, invariably incorporate the global standard on self-determination and state rights, without following and emulating pro-imperialistic political constitutions of some of the super-powers. The very fact that the Indian ruling class had endorsed all the UN Charter and treaty obligations reaffirms the expediency of this prerogative. What has been left out is the ordinary incorporation of the global obligations in the domestic constitutional provisions. Racism, jingoism, obscurantism and class-caste prejudices obviously obstruct any healthy effort, made so as to formalize these obligations in the constitutional text.

Nationality questions, as found in the context of multinational arrangements substantially differ from ethnic tensions that crop up in mono and uni-national states. Like the former Soviet Union, the republic of India is a conglomerate of multiple nationalities and nations. This fact cannot be historically repudiated at all. Even a school map illustrates the fact succinctly for everyone. Some Hindi heartland or, core Aryabrata states may argue in defence, the false proclamation that India is a single united nation, but the peripheral, specially — the annexed and occupied states — would not at all subscribe to this imposed falsehood except on the condition of suppression and military regimentation, which is unacceptable in this age of de-colonisation and humanisation of political structures. The constitution has been rather imposed by arranging forced consent on paralyzed people.

It is also true that each and every tribe does not constitute a nationality, since a tribe is an enlargement of a family and tribal stage is ordinarily a passing stage towards nationhood. Legitimate national questions should have been respected by a fair democratic constitution. Constituent states are equally entitled to adopt state the constitutions, since state entities cannot be treated like administrative units of quasi-unitary constitution.

States and the federation of states share more or less the same economic space. A new constitution should also address itself to the nature of political economy to be pursued. Today's post-Soviet order (or disorder) has witnessed the pervasive western dominance in the global economy and the increasing economic inequity. Somalia and Germany are not economically equal in the new order. In this context, economic integration also increases; however, the ideal economic interdependence as the world desires is evasive because of western predominance and stark poverty of the rest of the world. We also have witnessed the consequential fall out after the adoption of socialist market economy in the communist countries of today. The economic rights of states and individuals have to be radically endorsed in the proposed constitution, which would predictably be opposed tooth and nail by native as well as foreign MNCs, since it would be more convenient for them to pressurize and win over the leadership of a unitary nation state rather than negotiating with several empowered states of the confederation or federation, some of whom may even not dance to the tune of the MNC's. TNCs and MNCs require macro states for the deal. This advantage is broadly comparable to the negotiating advantage, as provided by the post-GATT WTO, wherein the disunited weak and meek would not be able to budge the heavyweights. The weak cannot bargain in the market of the strong, who dictates terms — take it or, leave it.

The proposal for recasting the asymmetrical, hierarchical hegemonic Bharatiya Constitution will remain merely academic, unless the opinion-leaders, power-elites are elaborately stimulated and provoked, since *status quoist* mindset has already blunted the political wisdom of the power-elite and their military tools. In the past half a century, military actions, thrust upon the peripheral states in lieu of the much awaited political resolution by the metropolitan or, administrative union-authority have been found to be counterproductive.

No statesman would recommend ruthless state terrorism against legitimate nationality questions and people's Right to Self-Determination. However, the ruling class may buy time and postpone the solution in the same way as the British did since 1918 to 1947; besides, it would be a sadistic pleasure on the coterie's part to witness a repeat of Nazi scenario off and on and anticipate the 'prince' of Machiavelli to subdue and rule the subject people. The casteists, feudalists, racists and obscurantists also throw their entire weight behind the 'Prince'. The spokesmen of the bourgeoisie, pretentious *avant garde*, who embellish the darbar cannot make an issue out of this malaise, save pouring out some old rhetorics and new polemic.

Concepts need historical clarity, objectivity and openness in assessment. Where is the expanse of *'Akhand Bharat'* whose original outer limits are fixed at Vindhya hills and alluvial soil of Hastinapur and its surrounding Gangetic plain ? Nobody can understand Jharkhandi national question or, for that matter — the strongly articulated national questions arising from Manipur, Kashmir, Nagaland since 1947 and later on in Assam, unless the pandits accept the truth that Assam (Kamrupa) came to British - India fold in 1826 by virtue of the Yandaboo treaty, to which Assam was not a party and the sovereign state of Manipur had been treacherously annexed by military means in 1949 to the 'Dominion of India', in the same way as three Baltic states have been annexed to Soviet Union in 1936 by adopting a secret Soviet-Germany treaty, which has been revoked in 1991, by undoing the disputed annexation. The politically literate red army did not intervene for the retention of Soviet empire in 1991.

The political malaise is also characterized by economic colonisation, socio-cultural colonisation, and the quality of life in these areas are relatively pitiable, because of the exploitation by the Hindustani bourgeoisie, who own the sword, state-purse and control the flow of capital within their own clan-circuit. The ongoing global de-colonisation movement is insularised in these colonised areas, yet the contradictions have been judged to be antagonistic and belligerent by the national liberation movements. Lumpen jingoist pandits project these contradictions as ordinary law and order problemsand developmental issue as their farcical cosmetic solutions are merely meant for a face-lift and renovation of imperialism in an age, when imperialism is the pariah, an outcast and taboo.

2

Constitution and Multi-National Questions

A constitutional review commission, as proposed in 1998 by the ruling party could open-endedly review the Constitution of India, which ordinarily serves as the political vocabulary of the official nationalism. The perceptions differ on the subject. The stereotypists would concede as many amendments as they are required. The optimists would project a constitution as a living, organic, political contrivance, intended to represent the aspirations of succeeding generations. There may be power-elites, who may impute divine sacrosanctity to such a human political mechanism, which can only break on the pressure of history, if it lacks elasticity. A minuscule, conservative faction takes the entire country into siege by withholding human progress in India.

The paradox of Indian official - nationalism, symbolised by the present Constitution is found in its incompatibility to effectively represent the legitimate ethnic (read ethnos as national in Greek) aspirations of the multinational mega-state. The language of misconceived economic nationalism cannot supersede the primordialism of 'cultural and linguistic nationalism. In this age of enlightenment, informed by ongoing de-colonisation, post-industrialism and nation-states (some of the nations are poly-ethnic) are on the rise. It would be rather untenable to make veiled attempts to reverse this post -war worldwide devolution trend. As many as one hundred forty additional nation-states have emanated in the brief fifty-year-postwar period since 1945. The UN which enlisted a meagre fifty independent countries in 1945 has 185 members by now.

The national aspirations of more than 10 UN Trust territories, not less than 48 members of the UNPO (Unrepresented People's Organisation) and a couple of historically transposed nations remain legitimate. The next century may unfold the UN roster to as many as two hundred to two hundred fifty independent countries, it could be a fivefold of what exists immediately after the end of the last war. The inevitable political devolution that we envisage would however, be complemented by increasing regional and global economic interdependence and the rise of continental conglomerates like the CIS (of the republics of the former Soviet Union), European Union, so and so forth, which would fill in the common economic, military and political space. New structural arrangements could also be conceived.

India may downsize its HDI and human development further and further in the process of its counter-productive romance with its uncalled for official nationalism and in her pursuit of the nostalgic *de ja vu* with Churchillian imperial passions and glorification of militarisation in the North-East civil society. The primordial, cultural, linguistic and historical nationalism in the North-East, however, remains incompatible with the official nationalism, militarily enforced top-down and the engineered forced consent. The Constitution, as it operates today, is the legacy of Indian imperial will — the successor of the British imperial will — can no longer be defended in terms of post-colonialism, at a time when de-colonisation of neo-colonial systems has not come to the ultimate end. The uncompleted agenda of old forms of colonialism and emerging new patterns of neo-colonialism render the use of the post-colonial idiom not only absurd but also intriguing. 'Transposed nations' address themselves as Xeno-nationalism within the contours of the official nationalism. Here, we de-ideologise nation as an historical stable community with its inherent demographic-territorial-cultural-economic and psychic paradigm. Political constitutions, which keep the national icebergs wisely submerged through incompatible instrumentalities, ostensibly glorified as official nationalism, lack the legitimacy to endure. So did the fifty constitutions of the 1945 vintage. The next century would take the pride in witnessing a plethora of more than two hundred constitutions. It is at this crossroads that Indian official nationalism is stuck up with a constitution, that downsize the paradigm of national coalition, which is a social reality. Indian ruling class struck out of legitimate national questions from their agenda in order to maintain hegemony.

Every birth — either of a child or a nation — is accompanied by birth pangs. The historical reality of birth pangs did not at all foreclose the birth. However, the wiser statesman of this age could make the birth pang anaesthetic as it happened in the case of the 15 states in Soviet Union in 1991, two states in Czechoslovakia and 5 states in the case of Yugoslavia. Bosnian 'ethnic-cleansing' is a Nazi remnant of the Croatians, who stood with Hitler, chauvinism of the entrenched Muslims and arrogant Serbs, who are closely comparable to the Indian heartland chauvinists. In this age of political enlightenment, there is no alternative to voluntary union of states and the legitimate exercise of the right of the people to self-determination. This universal standard is equally applicable to the historical, stable, 'indigenous people' of the North Eastern States. Some quarters have mistaken history for ideology. For those who mistake history as ideology, it may be recalled that the nonviolent approach of Congress leadership enjoined the holocaust in two world wars, 10,000 lives lost in Quit India movement, 10 lakh lives lost in Bengal famine in 1943, 20 lakhs in partition, thousands killed in Hindu-Muslim riots, 30 lakh lives lost in Pakistan vivisection-war of 1971 and several thousands of lives decimated in the militant armed struggles. Contemporary statesmen, therefore, make efforts to undo historical mistakes by keeping aside the military machine, in resolving national questions, national dependency, alien rules and new forms of inscrutable neo-colonialism. We have cited the example of the emergence of 22 independent states in just one year or two in 1991-1992 in eastern

Europe and Euro-Asia. Had the present constitution of India, fully reflected the legitimate national aspirations of the indigenous people of the North-East, this region should have not at all been militarised to the teeth and regimented for half a century. It is common man's knowledge that a civil society that suffers from prolonged militarisation would naturally react differently and whatever may be the erudite advocacy of military governors in the region, human rights remain at the receiving end. The rest is polemical discourse designed to entertain the romance of debate, which the suffering humanity may take with a pinch of salt. Compradors would have to address national questions from their postulation, dogmas and embedded interest.

Analogy and demonstration are also helpful in resolution of questions on economic, national and blended issues. Since the Marxist-Leninist approach to the resolution of national questions directly strike at the root of the imperial structures, and their praxis dismantled colonial structures in this century, we do not impute class components into national questions; and the proletarian internationalism, did not in the past contradict national questions. Nation states would, however, remain united against imperialism and colonialism. Right of the people to self-determination in the context of global capitalism, which differs from the economic commitments of the emerging state in the socialist canvas, is by now a universal standard. The right as such, is devoid of ideological trappings. The Soviet constitution of 7 October, 1977 that revised the earlier two constitutions was explicit in conceding these rights within the constitutional framework.

The former Soviet society bears the closest resemblance to the Indian society in terms of multi-cultural , multi-linguistic, multi-racial, multi-linguistic diversities and also to the super-nation building process. The constitutional expression of the national aspirations should also be in the same track. The annexation of three Baltic states in 1939 by the Soviet leadership bears close resemblance to the annexation of the three North Eastern states of Assam, Tripura and Manipur in 1826 and 1949 by the erstwhile ruling clique. When the three Baltic states felt the slightest discomfort in remaining within the Soviet Union in 1990, they have been allowed to exercise their free will in 1991. Nations continue to retain rights, because of the weight of their history.

The 1977 Soviet Constitution[1] was an improvement on the 1918, 1924 and 1936 versions. Articles 28,70,72,78,120,110,115 have provided respectively for Soviet constitutional support to national liberation movements in the world, for a federation of nations and nationalities, 'right of the republic (read state) to secede', retention of state boundaries in tact, representation of a vice-chairman in the top presidium from each state, equal representation of each republic (state) by 32 deputies in the soviet of nationalities (like Rajya Sabha) and constitution of conciliation commission or, referendum respectively. Justice Krishna Iyer appreciated the constitution for : "This is a unique instance of the entire people taking active part in the process of constitution making". (His speech in the House of Soviet Culture, Delhi, 1977). Veteran parliamentarian Hiren Mukherjee and many progressive scholars applauded the 1977 Soviet Constitution, while Indian imperial scholars considered it as blasphemy and a challenge to their hegemonistic, imperial priesthood.

Constitutional resolution of national question in West & East

How the western and the eastern systems respond to similar situations of constitutional crisis calls for profound attention of one and all. We cite a few cases.

The United States of America has brought Puerto Rico on 25 July, 1952 to the fold of the USA. Plebiscites have been conducted in Puerto Rico in 1951 and 1967. In 1981 the Puerto Ricans have been given the choice either to remain in commonwealth with the USA or, to be independent or to continue to remain as the 51st state of the USA. They opted for commonwealth — the confederal status. The position does not change, since only by 5% of her population voted for complete independence, following the referendum in November 1993. On the initiative of US President Mr. Jimmy Carter's support to Puerto Rican self-determination, American joint Congress fully espoused in 1979 the self-determination of Puerto Rico. Till a subsequent referendum supersedes the 1993 referendum result, it remains in commonwealth with the U.S.A. The UN de-colonisation committee has approved on 11August, 1998, Puerto Rico's right to self-determination[2].

The United Kingdom has conceded independence to several countries numbering about 50 which are now in the British commonwealth of states. When Indian Congress demanded self-determination by a resolution in 1918, the Labour party nearly conceded it in 1929 eleven years after the demand, passed resolution in October 1935 towards conceding Indian demand. It sent Cabinet mission in 1946 in order to retain Indian confederation without inviting partition and conceded independence one year ahead in 1947, before it was due in July 1948. UK conceded Irish independence in 1922, but partitioned Ireland. In several cases, the British conceded independence to nations very smoothly.

Tony Blair's Labour government which by commanding more than two third majority in the house has the necessary political capacity to deal with and make effective negotiation with the militancy in Northern Ireland and hammered out a political deal on April 10, 1998. The 69 pages agreement deal provides for a 108 member Northern Ireland Assembly, Cross Border (North-South) Council — an all Irish affair and Council of the Isle, which would represent British, Irish, Scots and Wales. The agreement was put into referendum in both the South and Northern Ireland on 22 May, 1998. Britain would gradually leave the Northern Ireland governance to the Catholics and Protestants of Northern Ireland with a population of 1.5 million. The Conservative party of John Major which survived with the support of Protestant MPs of Northern Ireland lacked the two-third majority in the parliament that would have enabled him to make an effective deal in the Irish militancy issue. As it is lacked that much political strength required enough to match with the authoritative deal, it could not advance beyond making the Downing Street Declaration[3] on 15 December 1994. Brighton conference of Labour party in 1995 even considered Kashmir issue as British imperial burden. The long term implication of the 10th April Belfast Agreement is obvious, the Brits would end their sway over Northern Ireland and the majority people of N. Ireland would self-determine political future on their own in the next generation. By February 1999, the Northern Ireland Assembly could function, as the result of May 22 referenda in North and South are found conducive to the agreement. The details of the agreement are not examined for want of space. Weapon de-commissioning is also a part of the agreement.

Scottish referendum started with 1956 referendum. In 1979 also, Scotland had another referendum about her future status. In 1997 also, it had one more referendum, on the basis of which the Scottish parliament would come to exist in 2000 A.D. At the moment, Scots have not opted out of the United Kingdom. The Scots normally occupy more than fifty per cent of the UK cabinet and other decision-making bodies leaving the rest to the Brits and other nationalities. This enormous political clout and economic power they enjoy desist the majority of Scots to opt out of the political arrangement with the Brits in UK.

Quebec in Canada has conducted series of referenda since 1980 to 1995. The last and third Quebec referendum was held on October 30, 1995. 50.6% voters opted for Canada and 49.2% wanted to leave Canada. Constitutional determination of the future of Quebec is, therefore, postponed till the next referendum. India follows western constitutionalism, constitutional practices and traditions after her adoption of liberal democracy. The leadership, however, desists themselves from looking at the constitutional methods, invariably adopted in more or less similar situations, in the West.

The East has faced similar crisis-situations arising out of national questions. The Soviet Union has deliberately abstained from using her invincible mighty Red Army against any of the 15 republics (read states) which would like to remain independent. The powerful Red Army strength is double the population of Estonia with a meagre 1.5 million (15 lakhs) population and KGB in that time was equally strong. But the Soviet leadership — both civil and military - kept their article of faith in desisting themselves from letting the Estonian blood shed for the romance of retaining Soviet imperial-instinct.

Yugoslavia and Czechoslovakia too followed suit. No Pol Pot of either the brown or yellow hue has been given the opportunity to seize the historical opportunity to deny legitimate national questions. Bosnian case is different, in that ethnic-cleansing was practised even by the ruling regime. International criminal jurisdiction has been set up for Yugoslavia and Rwanda in 1993 and 1994 respectively. Kosovo in 1999 is a unique case.

The constitutionalism of colonial or annexing country has to be put to a test by considering the rules of the game played by the comity of nations. I take up two pertinent issues on this score in the present day context. The issue of annexation and the issue of the right of the people to self-determination. There are some other complex formations as well.

A glaring example is annexation of Kuwait[4] by Iraq in '90. This case would demonstrate as to how far annexation is acceptable to the civilised world. The UN Security Council passed the resolution on 9 August, 1990. The excerpt :

The Security Council....

> " I. Decides that annexation of Kuwait by Iraq under any form and whatever pretext has no legal validity, and is considered null and void."

The Constitution of Iraq had considered and incorporated Kuwait as her 9th province and Iraq ruling-class was categorical in keeping Kuwait within her territorial integrity. Iraqi constitution however, fails the universal test that a country should not be annexed. The rest is history.

The world taught Iraq a lesson, which the rest of the world and Iraq would not easily forget. It is also true that every occupied and annexed people and territory could not be considered as fortunate as Kuwait(It has oil and gets justice). Article 2(4) of the 1945 UN Charter forbids use of force for violating territorial integrity and political independence of a country. East Timor[5] would exercise the self-determination rights in August, 1999.

The second issue is about the right of the people to self-determination. Article 1 of the International Covenant on Civil and Political Rights, 1966 renders the Universal standard as follows:

> "I. All peoples have the right of self-determination. By virtue of that right they freely determine their political status and freely pursue their economic, social and cultural development."

Article 1 of the UN charter clearly provides for this right of the people.

Several governments including the government of India have signed and ratified the treaty. The government is under international and constitutional responsibility to concede the right to legitimate people. The government of India expressed reservation to this article by qualifying this right to people of alien race, people under foreign domination and rule. The UN Human Rights Committee in July 1997 has recommended that government of India has to "review these reservations and declarations with view to withdrawing them," (CCPR/C/60/IND/3, UN HRC, 14 July - 1 August, 1997).

The Constitution of India should reflect in both letter and spirit, the universal and inalienable right of the people, as agreed upon. The people of the Soviet Union and the constitution-makers reflected these rights of the people in their 1977 constitution. The comprador intellectual powerhouse and ruling-clique of India may misconceive the universal rights of the people (nation), which they have accepted obligatory as a cutting edge to their hegemony and birthright of conquest. Jawaharlal Nehru has stood for conceding the 'right to secede' to legitimate state and people after ten years of adopting the constitution (page 534) in his 'Discovery Of India' .. All the leftists concurred with that principle of governance and right as such in that period.

Nationalism is a very strong force in this century and the map of the comity of nations has been drastically altered by this force. It's justification lies in the absurdity of imperialism, fascism, colonialism and the 'new forms of neo-colonialism' in post-colonial states. Federations, confederations, regional unions are newly invented political arrangements, which fill in the political space, left nearly untouched by the presence of nationalism. Poly-ethnic nation-states also occupy the said political space, but tiny ethnoses which number about 2,000 in this world are not viable enough to emerge as nation states. Several factors and paradigms inhibit their emergence outside the poly-ethnic states. Assimilation, integration and autonomy are the mechanisms that retain them within the poly-ethnic states. 'Right of Indigenous People' reinforces these norms.

In the case of continent called India, it may be said that there are ninety nation states in the world comparable in size and population figure to the north eastern states. The present territory of Assam, as for instance, much reduced several times in the past, is three times the size of Israel or, bigger than four times Kuwait. It is still bigger than Ireland, Georgia, Lithuania, Panama and several others. Manipur is still bigger than Israel, which will now part with a segment of the territory to Palestinian authority, that would emerge as an independent state in the early 21st century.

Constitutions of the world are explicit language of the stable or imagined political communities, nations or peoples. Constitution of India happens to be a species of the larger genus. Constitutions which fail to provide legitimate, historical rights of the people (nation) have been found to be incompatible and transient. The new world order in the next century will still uphold these inalienable, universal rights of the people and those contrivances, instrumentalities which are outrageous to the legitimate instrumentalities and structures. 'Unjust political arrangements' values should give way to more compatible and legitimate constitutions whose practices logically result to inevitable national oppression and new forms of inscrutable neo-colonialism bear the seeds of internal dissensions, and hence, overburdened by their own inner contradictions, they are destined to break down.

References

1. Boris Topornin, The New Constitution of the USSR, 1980.
2. 1497th, 1498th meetings, 10 and 11 August, 1998 of UN Decolonization committee in UN, G.A.A/53/23(Part I), 24 September, 1998.
3. N. Sanajaoba, Right of Oppressed Nations (and Peoples), Omsons, ND, 1996 p. 84.
4. Security Council Resolutions, Ibid. p. 115-119.
5. See UN, G.A. A/AC. 109/2111, 1 June, 1998 — East Timor, working paper prepared by the Secretariat cf. James Dunn, International Law and the Question of East Timur, C11R/IPJET, 1995.
   On Self-determination of Western Sahara, *See* OAU Reso. 104(XIX) of June, 1983, UN G.A Res 40/50 of 1985 Dec. 2, Security Council Res 658 of 27 June, 1990, Res. 690 of 29 April, 1991 etc.

3

Judicial Activism

Substance and Polemic

Governance by Mandamus

The discourse on Judicial Activism in the late 1990s has been prompted by three camps: firstly, the camp that swears by judicial restraint; secondly, the camp that envisages judicial activism as a *sine qua non* of the independence of the judiciary; and thirdly, the moderates who desire that judicial activism should be limited to selective class of actions and solely to the jurisdiction of the disadvantaged groups. Within the province of the polemic, questions are being raised if governance could not be done effectively without a judicial fiat or, mandamus.

Independence of the judiciary is a universally accepted value in the justice system; judicial activism is not. Aggressive judicial activism, like judicial despotism is a rather disputed proposition among the jurists and scholars. The federal jurisprudence has fairly established judicial review as a basic structure of the Constitution, which has been made equally compatible with other basic structures like democracy, separation of powers, rule of law, secularism and federalism. No controversy arises, as long as these mutually compatible constitutional values do not disturb the constitutional symmetry and balance of powers. Issues arise at a time, when governance is apparently done by 'Mandamus' and subsequent contempt of court, by default. Judicial activism would not have provoked any sensible mind. Save the delicate institutional relationship among the three creatures of the Constitution that has been eventually disturbed. It has been observed that judicial power or activism is inversely proportional to the political process in the last few decades. The weaker the political process, stronger is the judicial power and the reverse is partly true.

The free market Supreme Court judges, who swear by the post 1991 economic liberalisation and vindicate the primacy of the Chief Justice in the appointment of appellate court judges over the executive in the process of consultation now, construed as 'concurrence' took over the governance by default, because the political process has been found deficient due to the rule at the centre by water-thin-minority government that manages a majority by questionable means or, by the coalition government that survives by outside support.

Post 1977 emergency judiciary compensated the citizens with liberal dose of human rights and vulnerable-groups jurisprudence, and post-liberalisation judiciary did reenact the drama by delivering with revolutionary decrees reminiscent of the early Bolshevik political decrees like - orders to shift away 9,000 industries urgently or, pay pensions to several lakh of pensioners; several thousands of workers articulate the danger posed by their uncertain life. Article 141 of the Constitution rendered every order of the Supreme Court to reach out to every inch of the Indian landscape. The executive is in disarray and has found their constitutional obligation nearly abdicated. The constitutionalism has been stretched out to the last limit to the delight of the millions of observers, who herald the new messiah albeit in a wrong shoe.

Unlike benevolent dictatorship or military administration, democracy is relatively slow moving and every democratic process takes time. But democracy has been accepted, because the ship of democracy hardly sinks unlike the governance by Mandamus, which gives the quickest result because of the PIL (Public Interest Litigation) technology. It indicates a demonstration of *ad hocism* due to the deficiency of the institutions. There are defenders and opponents of judicial activism. We, however, keep the focus on the institutional relationship of the constitutional creatures inspite of enjoining the judicial revolution from the bench or ivory tower, which would not endure the heat and dust of political revolution. Is it a means to pre-empt a large scale popular upsurge in the wait or sheer regal benevolence? Activism is in the dock and time has come to judge the judges. The judicial power should not remain unbridled without explicit accountability — both external and internal.

Former Chief Justice of India, A.M.Ahmadi, who led the judicial crusade against executive dysfunction admits in his Zakir Hussain Lecture that the 'aggressive judicial activism' which he had espoused, is a temporary phenomenon. We can read many things in his admission of the aggressive approach and transient enterprise. This unusual approach has invited PIL bill from Law minister Mr. Khalap, now shelved. The note, sent by the law ministry meanwhile furnished the governmental response to Ahmadi's stance:

> "The judiciary has digressed from its traditional duties and functions as an interpreter of the Constitution and the laws, and has entered into a field in which it has no competence. Safeguards for judicial action, and barriers of self-restraint and detachment are becoming thin day by day, and the judiciary has failed to recognize that it can not be a substitute for the failure or the irresponsibility of other branches of the government and start delivering increasingly legislative or administrative judgements".

The shelved PIL bill had a number of faultiness and weakness including the conditions for deposit of amounts, punitive fines and definition of the poor man; however, the institutional argument, it throws open contains substance worthy of insight. The judicial ideology is answerable to the basic premise of the aforesaid note. The executive and the legislature should not be induced to perceive that they have been made vulnerable to an intra-institutional assault in cold blood. Beyond the glaze of the multimedia floodlight, institutions have to function and do operate peacefully and when institutions do partake of early signal of permanent decay, we think of re-engineering the old institutions or, reinventing a new one.

Judicial activism does not match with the re-engineering or re-inventing paradigm. The concern is rather for making the institutions work within their own respective domains. The intra-institutional relationship that is in need of continuous reinforcement, may be relegated to the receiving end, in the event of a silent struggle for supremacy between the coordinate and collateral wings of a constitutional government. We perceive this mindset in the post-emergency (1975-1977) and post-liberalization (1991-) federal jurisprudence. Among the jurists, who zealously espouse judicial activism, the names of former chief justice P.N.Bhagwati, justice Krishna Iyer, Desai, Chennappa Reddy and Soli Sorabjee, professor Upendra Baxi strike the juristic imagination and memory. P.N.Bhagwati had upheld the Constitution as the supreme lex — that is the constitutional supremacy and the judiciary as ultimate interpreter of the Constitution[3]. In another sense, root for judicial supremacy had been already instituted without contextually defining the popular sovereignty, that an elected parliament represents. Capilleti's 'Access to Justice' (1979) had pleaded for massification and diffuse-rights, which had given a dent to the would-be-activist judges; besides affirmative actions, *pro bono* public stream of 1960s, 1970s, US Supreme Court judgements had impressed them. So far so good.

The birth place of judicial review, however, had painstakingly evolved the checks and counter-checks along with the judicial review mechanism. American Supreme Court judges are nominated by the executive President and the nominations are subject to laborious senate hearings before senate approval is given to any executive appointment of the would-be-judges. The un-elected judiciary, which is not accountable to popular sovereignty, has to pass minimally through a transparent, open-government public scrutiny via the elected Senate[4]. Even after appointment, American judges are assessed by '*performance commission*'. The limits of the Indian judiciary had therefore, been enunciated, at its inception. It is a limited judiciary. No limited government of this century can ever afford to nurture and inflate an unlimited judiciary. Communist judges are elected and accountable to the people. But we do not have a communist state and communist judiciary.

Courts of P.N.Bhagwati, Ahmadi and possibly J.S. Verma are invariably activist-courts on their own admission. Chandrachud , Venkatachaliah and other pre-emergency courts had been found to be maintaining judicial restraint, although A.N.Roy court acted as a committed judiciary espousing the Kumarmangalam thesis. R.S.Pathak court and R.N.Mishra court, which rendered the maximum numbers of environmental verdicts may be assessed to be level headed and judicious courts by their upholding PIL cases within certain justifiable parameters. J.S.Verma court in 1997 could be characterised by its cool and cautious judicial activism bordering around judicial restraint. PIL which is not yet institutionalised in the body polity of the judiciary through legislative intervention has been used as the powerful Genie of the Arabian nights. PIL should not be left to the absolute discretion of judiciary. It should be first institutionalised in the constitutional text.

In 1982, the Law Commission of India circulated a questionnaire relating to the role and temptation of the judiciary to operate as the third legislative chamber. Justice Tulzarpurkar solicited the juristic responses to the third-chamber-syndrome. The architect of the 'Basic Structure' constitutionalism — Justice H.R.Khanna has expressed that Indian judiciary has been working as investigating agencies against corrupt politicians, but the judges should not take over country's governance He said, "This can disrupt the constitutional balance and end in a disaster". The basic structuralists have to appreciate the delicate structural balance, that the contemporary constitutionalism has espoused. The apex judiciary should appreciate that India's parliament has not chosen the British path of parliamentary sovereignty inspite of overwhelming British influences, and the apex judiciary could reciprocate this gesture by withholding urges for grafting judicial supremacy.

The activist judiciary would have been tempted to play a Mother Teresa whereas it should not, despite all the shortcomings and impotence of the elected parliament. However, the PIL achievements, strictly confined to the basic justice-needs of the marginalised, vulnerable groups and exploited classes even while diluting the *locus* requirements as stipulated in articles 32 and 226 of the Constitution, have earned broad juristic acceptance. Human rights jurisprudence, environmental jurisprudence and vulnerable-group jurisprudence are a class by themselves unlike the PIL cases, characterised by deep political clouts. The Indian private-law-litigation has yielded nearly the largest ground, it can ever concede to the emerging post-emergency public-law-litigation. By playing to the gallery, the millions would be rather happy, if the corrupt politicians and the organised mafia are hanged to the nearest lamp-post; but the common law jurisprudence unlike the Bolshevik jurisprudence has absolutely shorn off the catharsis in Hamlet's Denmark. The democratic state moves slowly, but it is safe and secure in the turbulent high seas, which are unpredictable.

The judiciary upholds the executive accountability and there is substance in this philosophy. Similarly, the concept of popular sovereignty asks a pound of flesh from the judiciary in terms of judicial accountability. Impeachment procedure under article 124(4) of the Constitution sets the Supreme Court Judge V.Ramaswamy scot free; he had been found guilty on 11 out of 14 charges as per the report, submitted by Speaker Rabi Ray on 20 July, 1992. The loopholes of the system allowed the criminalised Supreme Court judge to go scot free. What a pity? In their *obiter dicta*, sensible jurists awaited, the mention of the failure of the justice on this count so that the legislature may take note of this justice-failure due to the faulty mechanism, known as impeachment on 'misdemeanour' and 'incapacity'. Surprisingly, no activist judge had taken a serious note of the immunity of Supreme Court Justice V. Ramaswamy. Resignation of Bombay High Court chief justice Mr. Bhattacharya had not wiped out the financial offence, he had committed against the state of India. Many of judicial offences are kept under the carpet. J.S.Verma's proposed code of conduct for judges should not have been shelved. Prevention of Corruption Act 1947 could have covered the judges and the definition of corruption calls for enlargement so as to include favouritism, nepotism and other white collar crimes committed on *qui-pro-quo* basis which escape statutory notice. Structuralists would not discriminate in articulating the need for the accountability of the three departments viz., the legislature, the executive and the judiciary. The Supreme Court verdicts have taken the least notice of the accountability-structure in its totality. The judiciary has recently decreed that MPs are public servants for the purpose of Prevention of Corruption Act 1947, whereas the judges are not. The judgement is obviously deficient. The commodification of justice has characterised Indian system of justice with organised impunity.

The governance of the country by Mandamus is found to be rather an aberration than an honest effort, aimed at re-engineering the constitutionalism and its institutional structure. Should the popular sovereignty opt for shifting the democratic paradigm to another alternative form for achieving quick results, the activist judiciary cannot and should not decide by acting as the surrogate of popular sovereignty. That is why even Jefferson and Abraham Lincoln in their epochs had found judicial review to be skeptical on occasions, although judicial review had come to stay in the management of written federal jurisprudence, because of its intrinsic constitutional need. The judiciary ought not to be harnessed knowingly or unknowingly into the politician's gameplan of the most injudicious kind, we have witnessed in the post-Lal Bahadur Shastri epoch. If it also plays often into the gallery, no worthwhile institution would have remained outside the gallery-drama.

Third chamber syndrome

The provision of safeguarding the life and liberty as per article 21 of the Constitution has been fairly enlarged by judicial construction and a wholesome code of human rights jurisprudence has been evolved out of the judicial construction. Mohini Jain (1992) and Unnikrishnan (1993) judgements have elevated the *right to education* from the directive principles to a fundamental right. Had the Supreme Court similarly legitimised the *right to work* in the directive principles as a justifiable fundamental right, India should have witnessed Bolshevik II, without having the necessary popular preparation and adequate resources to fulfil the aspiration. The union government has assured to the people that *right to education* should be a fundamental right. The apex court is reticent on *right to work*, notwithstanding the fact that it admits newspaper clippings for the purpose of Article 32 and admission of PIL.

The Constitution in its Articles 32, 226,227,21,142 and 141, among others, has authorised the judicial intervention whenever citizen's fundamental right is in danger for one reason or another. The Supreme Court has not failed in its obligation. The apex Court, however, is in its slumber, on Manipur petition in 1980 and Nagaland petition in 1982 questioning the validity of the Armed Forces, Special Powers Act 1958, which has carried a censure and stricture from the UN Human Rights Committee since 1991 and all the conscientious world bodies. In August, 1997 the apex court heard the petition after seventeen years of admission and has reserved its verdict on 23rd August, 1997. It gave its verdict on 27th November, 1997. Considering the speed (otherwise supersonic) of admitting public injury cases and disposal-velocity, the slumber of the Supreme Court like Rip Van Winkle over a statute, which has been considered draconian by millions in seven states of the country, the silence of the apex court on this count smacks of sheer lack of accountability. "Justice delayed is justice denied" — is the forgotten mandate for the apex court. In its 17 year long slumber humanity has been lost irretrievably in a part of the world.

When we address to the separation of powers, we once again assess that the enlargement of the apex court jurisdiction could be done exclusively by the parliament under articles 138,139 and 140 of the Constitution. The Supreme Court cannot enlarge its jurisdiction on its own, by rendering these articles as redundant. The executive appoints the judges as per article 124(2) of the Constitution. In 1993, nine- members bench of the Court [6] decided for the primacy of the Chief Justice over the executive and constructed *'consultation'* as *'concurrence'*. The check and balance which has been found in the US Senate hearing and approval - procedure in confirming executive appointments should have been cited by the learned judges so that the executive and the judiciary could be made co-accountable. The parliament's unlimited constituent power, as provided in Article 368(5) could be used if necessary to set up a constitutional court, which was the intention of the Constitution makers at the beginning or, to totally restructure Indian judiciary *a la droit administratif*. The step could, however, divorce the system from the Common law tradition and paradigm of parliamentary supremacy.

Articles 121 and 122 provide for safety valves to both the judges and the members of the parliament and the two wings could maintain the respective sanctity and privilege on reciprocal terms. The judiciary has struck down the exclusion of judicial review provision in article 7 of the tenth schedule of the Constitution as void[7]. In utter disregard of Indian Speakers' conference resolutions which provided for the non-personal appearance of the Indian Speakers before the judiciary, the apex court made a point that Speaker Borobabu Singh of Manipur be picked up by a security force aircraft just to make him appear for a moment before the apex court. The gesture for confrontation and head-on-collision has not satisfied the inter-institutional prestige. It may not be activism case, but unbridled arrogance at best. It has further enlarged the province of judicial review in its historic judgement on 11th March, 1994. Watershed judgements are also found. The court has made article 356 judicially reviewable, which otherwise have been barred by article 74(2) and the Prime Minister's advice to the President could be materially tested for *mala fide*. Inspite of the approval of the President's rule by the two houses of the parliament, *status quo ante* had been restored.

T.M. Pai Foundation v. Karnataka[8] **Taz Trapazium**[9] decisions, **Indira Sawhney v. Union of India**,[10] **S.R. Bommai v. Union of India**[11] and several other human rights, environmental judgements have unambiguously fallen within the enlarged jurisdiction of the apex court.

K.K. Vasant v. State of Karnataka[12] had a ruling that the court should not intervene in the routine state administration. Similarly, **Rural Litigation v. UP**,[13] **Shimla Medical College Case** and **Sachidananda Pande v. West Bengal**[14] among others, upheld that there should be limited judicial intervention in the governance. PIL doesn't empower the judiciary to encroach upon the constitutional obligations of the administration. In the **Bandhua Mukti Morcha**, 1984, Chief Justice R.S.Pathak upheld the PIL intervention as being entrenched in certain trappings and qualifications. PIL has not so far been statutorily institutionalised or streamlined either. Like the chancellor's foot in the days of medieval equity courts, its range varies in the shoes of the activist judiciary and rhetoric of populist judges.

Several judgements carry the stigma of having political clout and the verdicts are not totally devoid of political ramifications. **Ayodhya judgement**[15] rendered the presidential reference superfluous; however, 2(out of 5) judges — A.M.Ahmadi and S.P. Barucha stated that the impugned Act slanted in favour of one religious community against another. December 11, 1995 SC judgement on the endorsement of Hindutva as Indianisation, August 22, 1966 SC order on the transfer of Narasimha Rao case from one magistrate to another, Manohar Joshi v. Bahurao Patil, Bal Thackeray, V. Prabhakar, K. Kunte, Kuldip Singh judgement on Sarala Mudgal v. Union of India on Uniform Civil Code,[16] judgement on the offering of citizenship to 65,000 Chakma refugees from Bangladesh, SC's steps on 14-15 February, 1989 on the Bhopal Gas leakage case for a settlement for 470 million dollars against the original claim for 3 billion dollars, SC order in 1996 by granting immunity to 6 UCC officials[17] and several others, carry with them, deep-structured political clout. The province of judicial review and other judicial powers had been so much stretched so that the exercise could be suspected to be judicial subversion or imperialism. As early as 1982, Justice Tulzarpurkar evaluated that these disturbing trends were created due to the arrogation by the judiciary of the role of administration. PIL should be confined meticulously to the grievances of marginalised and vulnerable social classes. It can not be used as an extension of the tumultuous Indian political equations. What is forbidden at the front door need not be solicited through the back door. Whereas socio-economic revolutions have to be carried out by the executive and the legislature, the power to overhaul the system lies with the people. The existing judicial system could also be cleared out only to be substituted by another with popular sovereignty.

The experience of the federal jurisprudence in the USA, which has profoundly influenced the psyche of India's nascent judiciary might have been received on an incomplete note. Michael Kirby — one of the seven judges of High Court of Australia[18] cautioned that big leaps are for the parliament and not for the judiciary.[19] The grafting of judicial review in the civil polity of Anglo-American framework took at least two centuries starting from Justice Coke's statement in Doctor Bonham's case in 1610 to Marshal's dictum in Marbury v. Madison, 1803. From 1803, Judicial Review has a history till 1997.

The judicial activism in the USA had benefited the business community during 1890-1930s and the economic management in the period 1930s to 1969. Till 1969, the socially disadvantaged groups had been benefited. In the 1970s, the discrimination against women was the focal theme. Since 1980s to 1990s, the civil liberty cases declined at a time, when these cases have become the concern of PIL and judicial activism in India. We may call it reversal of roles in the two Supreme Courts. Activism arose during the administration of Labour government of Wilson in the UK. In 1951, the House of Lords stipulated that judges can not fill in the gap, left by the legislature much to the chagrin of Lord Denning. By now, judicial activism is on the plateau in UK and USA and Indian judiciary is in search for stability by transcending the juridical entropy.

The third-chamber-syndrome, as clearly found in some of the Supreme Court judgements, better known as *'aggressive judicial activism'* in the words of chief justice A.M. Ahmadi calls for discrimination from those PIL verdicts, which are strictly meant for the vulnerable groups, who have the least access to the one time five-star-style jurisdiction of the apex court. But the judicial domain could not be further and further stretched out till the legislature and the executive are undermined institutionally and in terms of people's credibility. Parliament may have and do have criminals and mafia as members[20]. These members are dishonourable and corrupt, but the parliament as a democratic institution should not be seen as dishonourable and unworthy of the trust, derived from suffrage and franchise. Herein comes the accountability of the judiciary to see that constitutionalism thrives on the three pillars, which are co-ordinate. Above all, in democracy, the parliament represents popular sovereignty unlike the appointed offices like the judiciary, which is not accountable to the executive either. Chief Justice A.S. Anand [21] cautioned that judicial activism without restraint may lead to judicial adventurism.

Judicial accountability

Open government, democracy, rule of law transparency and accountability are some of the significant basic values that inform the democratic institutions of the contemporary polity. In the open-government era, citizens are not accorded with the basic rights like the right to information and machineries like the ombudsman, which could be set up on all the sectors of governance; but the Lokpal bill does not take off. It has many a loophole as well. The apex court could have directed the legislature on this subject before two decades, but that did not materialise for a long time. Former chief justice S.S.Verma stated in August 1998 that appellate judges should be brought under the Prevention of Corruption Act .

Judicial independence has been accepted as a basic structure on equal terms with separation of powers, democracy and rule of law. These structural elements are equally important and no primacy has been given to any one of them over the other by the basic structuralists on one count or another.

Whenever the political process is at fault or deficient, one wing of the government makes attempt to compensate the other in order to maintain the constitutional symmetry, so far so good with bona fide intentions. The accountability of the coordinate institution can not and should not be merely confined to the executive and the legislature. It should also be a deep structured concern of the judiciary as well. The need to evolve '*judicial accountability*' should be considered along with the proposal for National Judicial Commission and idea of 'Performance Commission' of the USA. Independence of the judiciary has very few opponents unlike the committed or ideological judiciary. The problem lies in the exercise of the independence, which should not erode, undermine or underestimate the coordinate institutions like parliament and the executive. The achievements of the appellate judiciary in rectifying the grievance that the vulnerable social sections had suffered from, had been given full marks by all conscientious jurists and scholars alike. The problem comes in when judicial independence is seen to have been self-indulgent towards judicial despotism, imperialism or, aggressive judicial activism. The third-chamber-syndrome could also be removed by the weakest of the three constitutional institutions, which has neither the sword nor the purse. Its strength lies in credibility and popular trust only.

The problem that India faces in the form of stark poverty and massification of suffering is an inherited political legacy, which should be the burden of the politics and not of the justice machinery. Part of the burden, the judiciary can carry with, but it has a jurisdiction, allocated by the constitutional text and also by the unwritten constitutional text of the popular sovereignty. The judiciary would find it too cumbersome to interpret the unwritten text, while the interpretation of the written text is convenient for the articulation and materialisation of the spirit within. Massive justice calls for the mandate of massive constituency.

References

1. See Advocates on Record, S.C.1993.
2. JMM case 1997.
3. Rajasthan v. Union of India, SC,1977; Gupta v. Union of India,SC, 1982.
4. Indian counterpart of Council of States.
5. Times of India, 13th Jan., 1997.
6. S.C. Advocates Records Assn.v. Union of India, 1993 October.
7. Borobabu case, 1991 and other cases.
8. 5th August,1995.
9. S.C.,30th Dec.,1996.
10. S.C.,1992.
11. S.C., 1994.
12. AIR, 1992 Karnt, 256.
13. AIR, 1988 SC 2187.
14. AIR,1987 SC 1109.
15. S.C., 24th October 1994.
16. S.C. 1996.
17. *Contra* Oleum Gas Leakage Case, S.C. 1987 M.C. Mehta v. Union of India [on absolutely strict liability doctrine.]
18. Comparable to Supreme Court but for the name.
19. Times of India, 7th Dec.,1996.
20. Vohra Report.
21. His speech in Rajasthan High Court on 29.8.1999 in the Hindu, 31August, 1999. He states,"The danger of judiciary creating a multiplicity of rights without the possibility of adequate enforcement is a real ore. It must be guarded against." — C.J. A.S. Anand.

4

Open Government and C.A.G.

Public accountability of financial transactions as provided under articles 148-151 of the Constitution and as undertaken by the executive governments has been apparently reduced. All the limbs and organs of the polity, society and the Constitution are fuelled by the precious life - giving oxygen, the public money. The Comptroller and Auditor General of India (CAG) is a watchdog[1] who sees that this precious life-giving oxygen has not been squandered away nor subverted from within. We can cite a few cases. It has pulled up Indian Navy for defective budgetary procedure and inadequate monitoring of projects[1a]. The CAG did not mince no words in touching upon popular small screen hearthrob 'Chandrakanta' by objecting to its extension from 52 serials by Doordarshan[2] in a manner affecting the spot booking rate. As reported by UNI on 27th March 96, the CAG criticised Government of Tripura for underutilising 82-95% of funds, meant for state Pollution Control Board. These are a few instances which highlight the CAG Report. This is a test case of the widespread malaise in the states. The CAG's *post mortem* of the propriety of financial administration leads to the accountability of the executive to the legislature through its mechanisms like the Public Accounts Committee and on occasions, the Joint Parliamentary Committee.

The CAG like the CEC, remains a silent constitutional creature equipped with enormous constitutional responsibilities without coming up at the centre stage of high visibility till it passes expert comments on the historic mystery called BOFORS[3] ,which still defies description in this age of

Hawala democracy and scam morality. Other countries entertain public debates about financial impropriety, committed by the people at the corridors of power. The only difference between India and other countries in similarly placed situations lies in the simple common sense morality that Italian premiers, Japanese prime ministers or, South Korean presidents would not hesitate to resign at the very moment they lose public credibility. In BOFORS or other subsequent scams and Hawala events, the traditional Indian mysticism prevails upon the credibility issue.

Public memory is short, but what the legislator N.K.P.Salve remarked about CAG is on records. India's CAG raised issues with BOFORS in his report in 1989 and honourable Mr. N.K.P.Salve called the CAG in public as *"that Charlie"* who 'needed a kick in the bottom'[4]. The CAG, unlike the Supreme Court judges, remains unprotected in his assault on the squandering of public money. T.N.Chaturvedi[5], the former CAG of BOFORS fame withstood unwarranted diatribes, let loose by BOFORS lobby by stating that 'the office of the CAG is the one office in the Constitution which has no power and authority... What I mean to suggest is that CAG is a very lonely, and a very helpless office at times because it has no protection of any kind and no authority to enforce its decision'. The BOFORS mystery is more enigmatic than the Bermuda triangle, although every one knows that the ship's treasure sinks herein. Buying of defence guns like 155 mm FH 77B howitzer involves multilayered kickbacks. Lt. General Hridaya Kaul answers to India Today interview[6] that in favour of a recommendation, company offered 2.5 crore in any currency. Narasimhan Committee, among others, takes note of the frauds, malpractices, scams etc.[6a] The secretive clauses have strengthened these frauds. The CAG Mr. T.N. Chaturvedi was assailed for performing his constitutional obligations in 1989. Arun Singh answered to the interview[7] that the CAG Chaturvedi has done "what he had to do, and I have no reservations about the CAG's role". He said, "I think he is perfectly justified in commenting on the systems".

The constitutional duty of accounting and auditing by a centralised constitutional institution known as CAG is the lowest-profile job ever performed by collateral institutions. The other institutions like the parliament, the executive and the judiciary and even the CEC operates in the high visibility zone; but CAG's constitutional importance is in no way inferior to that of its collateral institutions. Its relative importance had been enunciated by no less a constitutionalist than Dr. B.R.Ambedkar[8] in these words:

> Personally, speaking for myself, I am of the opinion that this dignitary (*sic*.CAG) or officer is probably the most important officer in the Constitution of India. He is the one man who is going to see that the expenses voted by Parliament are not exceeded, or varied from what has been laid down by Parliament in what is called the Appropriation Act. If this functionary is to carry out the duties — and his duties, I submit, are far more important than the duties even of the judiciary — he should have been certainly as independent as the Judiciary.

Independence of the CAG

The office of CAG should be independent of the executive, and the Constitution has provided a framework of its independence in chapter V, part V of the Constitution. Articles 148,149,150,151 provide for its appointment, service conditions, duties and powers, form of accounts and submission of audit report to the President or the governor.

It has the status of a judge of the Supreme Court, although its salary had been proposed at a stage at Rs. 60,000 per annum against Rs. 5,500/- per mensal of the President of the Union[9]. It had been, however, slashed down later. The Auditor-General of India at the commencement of the Constitution continued to be the CAG after the promulgation of Constitution.[10] The independence of the Auditor-General (now CAG) was maintained by the Government of India Act 1935.[11]

The Comptroller and Auditor General's (Duties, Powers and Conditions of Service) Act 1972 has narrowed down the independence of the CAG, who should be treated on par with the chief justice of India in order to maintain his autonomy and independence. There is a suggestion that the administrative expenses of the whole setup of the Indian Audit and Accounts department must be charged on the non-votable head — the Consolidated Fund of India. The opposition parties may also be *'effectively consulted'* in the process of appointment of the CAG inspite of considering his appointment as a ruling party's exclusive business. The Constitution may be amended with a view to according greater independence to the CAG in all the stages of his appointment and service conditions.

Dr. B.R.Ambedkar felt that the CAG was made to be less independent than his counterpart. He spoke in the Constituent Assembly[12] :

> But, comparing the articles about the Supreme Court and the articles relating to the Auditor-General, I cannot help saying that we have not given him the same independence which we have given to the Judiciary, although I personally feel that he ought to have far greater independence than the Judiciary itself.
>
> I moved an amendment to the original article 122 vesting in the Supreme Court the appointment of officers and servants of the Supreme Court. I see both from the original draft as well as from the amendments that are moved that the Auditor-General is not to have any such power. The absence of such power means that the staff of the Auditor-General shall be appointed by the Executive. Being appointed by the Executive, the staff shall be subject to the executive for disciplinary action.

The independence of the CAG could be constitutionally protected on the line of the independence enjoyed by apex court, by making suitable amendment of the Constitution so that the CAG may not ride on an unruly horse whose bridles are at the hands of the executive. The CAG should not be taken for a ride by the executive. The *'Charlie'* image, imputed to CAG by national leaders whenever scams come to surface should be erased out by providing inbuilt safety valves, which are yet to be designed

Irresponsible statements made in the parliament or legislature by irresponsible people whose deals have been pointed out by justice Dhingra of Delhi High Court in 1996 at a time, when Hawala spared almost nobody including the holy cows, against the CAG could be checked by extending the spirit of article 121 of the Constitution[13] to the CAG. The proposed extension of article 121 to the CAG may be couched in these words:

> No discussion shall take place in the Parliament with respect to the conduct of the CAG in the discharge of his duties except upon a motion for presenting an address to the President praying for the removal of the CAG.

Smart Watchdogs

At present, the duties and powers of the CAG are regulated restrictively by the Parliament. The watchdog watches merely at the emerging parallel, regime of black-money-monster and also at the reckless squandering of public money by public servants. So, tighter is the noose around the independent watchdog, the more licentious is the intimacy of the black-money-monster with the hard earned public money. White collar crimes are found to be smarter now-a-days than in the colonial period. Hawalas, scams and Bofors are simply the detected tip of the iceberg, whose subterranean empire is unfathomable.

In the same way as judicial activism develops for reasons of justice, audit activism also gains new heights in the new audit enterprise. T.N. Chaturvedi[14] has rightly visualised the emerging audit evolution in his words, " The audit has also to cope with various areas of administration, so the audit also develops. It evolves, it is not rigid, it is not stultified. You have got this new thing for accountability and for performance". The CAG has to audit 'the social development programmes, science and technology and defence and so on'.

Although the CAG is entrusted with post-mortem and morgue management as it is widely believed, the

'Comptroller' is an institution who controls issue of public money. In the constituent Assembly, members noted the duties of the CAG, which transcend the accounting *per se*. T.T. Krishnamachari observed that CAG has a number of duties[15] ; R.K. Sidhva felt that the CAG has all the powers as far as audits are concerned and asked why certain of his powers should be transferred to the Parliament.[16] Sri Biswanath Das lamented that he was 'absolutely left to the mercy of the legislature.'.[17]

The rule making power of the Supreme Court [18] for regulating the practice and procedure of the court could also be made available with the CAG, since consultation with the President on this count is more than formal and consultation connotes, now-a-days, effective consultation. Under all circumstances, the rule making power of the CAG need not be narrowed down. The *'doctrine of pleasure'* of the President should be construed so as to accord full and effective rule making authority to the CAG.

As regards, the separation of accounting and auditing, there are two compatible viewpoints so far. The first projection is that both the functions should be combined; but the problem about the saving central accounts from judicial review by way of inclusion in the Schedule IX is in need of review. The ARC Report [para 3.8][19] found favour with the prevailing pattern of 'combined audit and accounts'. However, the second approach envisages the continuity of British colonial legacy, based upon expediency and economy, through this combined function. Constitutional experts[20] project that accounts belong to the executive function, while audit belongs to quasi-judicial function and hence, these two functions should be dissociated.

India can transcend the post mortem function of the CAG in order to enable the CAG to put a brake on the system before the impropriety would be committed. In the UK, the Comptroller controls issue of money without parliamentary authority, prevents issue of money for unauthorised purpose and excesses over the grants made by the parliament.[21] Considering the widespread epidemic of the financial mal-administration in India, the preventive strike of the CAG before the inchoate offence has been completed, should be brought to the enlarged jurisdiction of the CAG. This is inevitably the Hobson's choice in a system, run by the Hawala morality.

Transparency

Open government remains a misnomer to the preachers of open government in India. The presence of the colonial Official Secrets Act, absence of *'Right to Information'* in the Constitution, the inbuilt opaque mechanisms of pro-colonial Indian bureaucracy and its hegemonic style, reinforced by widespread 'Secrecy clauses'22 provides a regimented and authoritarian form of government in the guise of democracy. Clean, compassionate and open government had never struck the imagination of either the executive or the bureaucracy.

Notwithstanding certain moves by the Supreme Court of India in order to initiate open government at the level of judiciary, it has made the least dent to the other wings of the government. However, a common law country like the United Kingdom, which had already set out for open government enlarged the scope of its existing open government in 1994. In Britain in the year 1994, Government's Code of Practice On Access to Government Information [23] has enforced the administrative practice in all the departments — (i) to publish facts and fasts found relevant in making policies, (ii) to provide explanatory materials on department's dealing with public, (iii) to give reasons for administrative decisions, (iv) to publish full information and (v) to release information on policies and answer specific requests. The essential open government philosophy of the administration including the financial administration is yet to be accepted by the authoritarian North and South Blocks in New Delhi and the pro-colonial minded bureaucracy that considers governance as a secret mission elsewhere in India. It calls for a radical *glasnost* from the corridors of power. The CAG should no longer be made a hostage to the secretive clauses of laws, rules and norms.

Open Government

Accountability like transparency and credibility appears to be administrative jargon of contemporary political linguistics, which even Noam Chomsky would find difficult with and which has probably been erased out of Indian administrative lexicon. CAG reports are, therefore, not received in the right spirit they ought to have been received. N.K. Salve's doctrine labels CAG report with utmost disgust and phobia. B.R.Ambedkar would regard CAG as the most important constitutional functionary, supposedly more important than even the Supreme Court in certain aspects, but N.K. Salve's followers call CAG as a *Charlie* to be kicked at his buttock. His political linguistics itself gives testimony to his mind-set and culture. In this context, PAC and JPC continue to be the available platform through which accountability to the legislature is maintained. The parliamentary discussion of CAG report [24] has been conceived from the strategies of ruling and opposition parties. A fair demarcation line is yet to be drawn between fair discussion, based on convention and aggressive parliamentary practices. However, CAG is an institution that calls for parliamentary protection.

As discussed above very briefly, we may fairly conclude that notwithstanding the degeneration, suffered by the CAG and its network and institutional rivalry as witnessed time and again, the importance of the CAG and its constitutional significance calls for radical re-enforcement. Unlocking the public exchequer can be made transparent and fully accountable.

The Constitutional provisions which prevent the full independence of the CAG, block the heralding of transparency, open government and public accountability have to be reviewed and suitably amended, if necessary. The crying need is obviously felt. Constitutionalists would ungrudgingly endorse what Dr. B.R.Ambedkar spoke about the CAG as the most important constitutional functionary, albeit the fact that the institution of CAG is as important as the Supreme Court, the Parliament and the union executive and any of these collateral institutions should refrain itself from kidding the other in order to maintain intra-institutional harmony.

References

1. Tarak Chandra Goswami, ' Degrading Trend in the system of Public Accountability in India, 'Convention on 'Save IA & AD', Guwahati, 30th March 1996.
1. UNI, CAG Report in Times of India, March 12, 1996, p2.
2. Prakash Nanda, CAG finds fault, in Times of India, 14 March, 1996.
3. Thomas Abraham, Ripping the Masks, Bofors, Frontline, August 13, 1993 p.4 and also Frontline July 9-22 1988.
4. Interview, Surya India, September 1989, p.17.
5. ibid. p.12.
6. India Today, 15 September, 1989, p.26.
6a. Workpaper *infra* f.n. 19.
7. ibid. p.31.
8. CAD(Constituent Assembly Debates), Volume VIII, p.407.
9. B.Shiva Rao, The Framing of India's Constitution, Vol. IV, p.407.
10. Article 377 of Constitution of India.
11. B.Shiva Rao, The Framing of India's Constitution, Vol.V, p.413.
12. op. cit.,f.n. 8, p.408.
13. Article 121 of the Constitution of India.
14. Supra f.n. 4 p.13.
15. CAD, Vol. VIII, p.410.
16. ibid. p.412.
17. ibid.p.407.
18. Article 145 of Constitution of India.
19. Workpaper, Convention on Save Indian Audit and Accounts Department to protect people's interest, Mimeo, 30 March 1996 as circulated.
20. M.P. Jain, Indian Constitutional Law, Rep. 1994, p.49.
21. ibid. p. 49.
22. Supra f.n. 19, p.3.
23. Journal of Public Administration, IIPA, 1995.
24. P.S. Reddy, The Comptroller and Auditor General of India:, in N.Sanajaoba. ed, Gauhati University Law Journal, volume IV, December 1990, p.100.

5

Constitutionalism of Princely State

Constitution of the erstwhile princely state is rarely heard of Constitutional historiography of continental India incorporates the constitutionalism of British India on the one hand and the amorphous counterparts in a few of the leading princely states. The former is fairly known, but the latter has escaped academic notice and attention.

The political constitution of the princely state that functioned before states had been incorporated into the Indian Dominion not only bears historical significance, but also demonstrates the ambit of the constitutional culture. We take up the Manipur Constitution of 1947 as a harbinger of constitutionalism. Interestingly, values have been found deeply embedded into the instrument.

A.V. Dicey's 1885 treatise -'An Introduction to the Study of the Law of the Constitution' is the Western constitutional classic which moulded the present scheme of constitutionalism and the 'Rule of Law'. The standard of political achievement and constitutional administration of laws in the Western context is measured even today by Diceyan yardstick. Manipuri constitutional culture and 'Rule of Law' is also evaluated by the above yardstick. The process of evaluation of an oriental system by another system - index may not be the best imaginable scheme of things, yet certain analogy prevails somewhere in the systems. Manipur had entered into Anglo-Manipuri mutual defence treaty[1] on the 14 September, 1762 that this arrangement had brought the Manipuri polity closer to that of the British. The system - variance had been narrowed down in the next couple of centuries due to reasons of history. Some of the other princely states entered into similar arrangements.

Early Manipur state, better known as 'Kangleipak' had nurtured elements of democracy[2] in its monarchical polity. The *puya-'Khunthong Nipan Lamyenba'* records that early Manipur had been divided into 32 administrative divisions, each division being led by a popular man selected by the king and the king could not act in arbitrary fashion.[3] A profound sense of independence had also been deeply embedded in the popular psyche, which had been reinforced by several socio-political and economic institutions.[4] The institutions that provided the Manipuri constitutional framework and social institutions[5] existed before the British intervention in Manipur affairs. Scholars have discussed the Manipur Constitution [6] in details. Before we discuss princely state constitutionalism and 'Rule of Law', we present the classic Diceyan enunciation of 'Rule of Law' in the broader common law canvas to start with. The princely state constitution does not lose the significance, as the instrument contains constitutional values of historical ramifications.

Dicey's rule of law

A.V.Dicey assumed the omnipotence of the central government in the country and the supremacy of the law with respect to the rights of the individual. As opposed to rule by man, rule of law is impersonal and transcends the brutality of arbitrary regimes and administrative discretions that more often than not are susceptible to excessive and widespread abuses. He had crystallised the three components of Rule of Law[8] as follows :

> It means, in the first place, the absolute supremacy of predominance of regular law as opposed to the influence of arbitrary power, and excludes the existence of arbitrariness, of prerogative, or even of wide discretionary authority on the part of the government.

> It means, again, equality before the law, or the equal subjection of all classes to the ordinary law of the land administered by the ordinary law courts; the "rule of law" in this sense excludes the idea of any exemption of officials or others from the duty of obedience to the law which governs other citizens or from the jurisdiction of the ordinary tribunals.
>
> The "rule of law", lastly, may be used as a formula for expressing the fact that with us the law of the constitution, the rules which in foreign countries naturally form part of a constitutional codes, are not the source but the consequence of the individuals, as defined and enforced by the courts; — thus the constitution is the result of the ordinary law of the land.

In his introduction to Dicey's classic work, E.C.S. Wade extrapolates the rule of law by taking into account the gradual constitutional evolution in the common law. In his words,[9] Wade wrote: "The rule of law presupposes the absence of arbitrary power and so gives the assurance that the individual can ascertain with reasonable certainty what legal powers are available to government if there is a proposal to affect his private rights. "The independence of the judiciary remains the central core of the crystallised rule of law. Wade wrote[10] : " There are, of course, two aspects of judicial independence — freedom from dictation by the Administration and freedom from control by Parliament." The Rule of Law conception has transcended common law jurisdictions since the last world war second,[11] and in its universal import, it connotes the political and civil rights of the individual. The Supreme Court of India, on its part has enlarged its respectability and bindingness by way of accepting and recognising the 'Rule of Law' as a basic feature of the Constitution of India.[12] Subsequently after the upgradation of the 'Rule of Law' to the primacy of the basic structure of the Constitution of India, the judiciary and its judicial independence indispensably remains the bedrock and corners tone of administration of justice under all circumstances. By now, the Rule of Law carries the human rights import.

Constitutionalism

The ancient Asian state of Manipur, as it has been known as such since the proselytisation in the 18th century only, had passed through trials and errors, political upheavals of all kinds while keeping the centralised Manipur administration, economy and market in tact, before it could evolve its own constitutional culture and 'Rule of Law'. It took millennia to construct and re-construct the Manipur nationhood from out of primordial tribalism, blood feuds, clannish outlook and intra-ethnic skirmishes particularly among the seven predominant ethnic principalities that constituted the state.

The constitutional values so far evolved till the end of the monarchy incorporate democratic values against arbitrary use of power by one man or clique. The were : *'Ningthou Pongba Tara'*(=ten kings), *"Leibakna nama Ningthouna Nama"*(= the people at one side of the balance and the king at the other side of the balance) and 64 nobles acting in tune with popular aspirations. Whenever the balancing act of administering justice would be disturbed, insurrections and rebellions eventually. Manipur history gives ample evidence to the palace revolts and insurrections. However, monarchy had never been considered as an idiom of republican institutions and it could not survive as a substitute of democracy; so it lapsed into oblivion. Manipur's past was responsible in its evolution of the constitutionalism through the ages. We now turn to the pages of the bygone era.

The royal edict of Meetei king Naophangba[13] laid down the paradigm of criminal justice in the 5th century Manipur state. The year has been given as 429 A.D. An eminent scholar Oinam Bhogeswor cited this year. The written edict or political constitution reached its stable and widely acceptable state with the adoption of Loyumba Shinyen in the 12th century A.D. by Meetei king Loyumba. It took seven hundred years to evolve a rudimentary constitution on since the regime of Naophangba to reach the constitutional thought of Loyumba in the 12th century A.D. Comparative constitutionalists would appreciate the fact that constitutional evolution takes several centuries, unlike the making of a constitution on a positivist note.

Naophangba had been a reference point, but Manipuri polity passed through protohistory, centuries before his regime. In 14th century B.C. or even earlier, king Kangba realised the meaning of truth as the knowledge and realisation of Sanamahi; it was a stage of food gathering though.[14] He had been succeeded by Malia Phambalcha in 1397 B.C. The era is controversial among the scholars. The *Numit Kappa puya* had depicted the rebellion of Ekma Haodongla against the oppressive regime of two kings — Nongdamhan and Taohuireng. In the proto-historical period, Manipur had her own Spartacus to fight out oppression. The event had inducted a modest dose of individual revolt against state oppression in a very rudimentary and primitive style. Professor Gangmumei Kamei[16] states that Nongda Lairen Pakangba had laid down the 'foundation of the social and political structure, and cultural and religious pattern of the Meities in the first century A.D.' Pakhangba had been given the credit for making law reforms and laying of the conventions.

In 33 A.D., Pakhangba constituted the council of ministers, 64 officials and the state departments viz., *Laipham Shanglen* (court of Justice), *Kuchu Sanglen*, *Khanba Shanglen*, *Naharup Sanglen* and *Pacha Loisang* (court handling the women affairs, presided over by Pakhangba's queen Laisna).[17] The *Pacha Loisang* had no parallel in India. Institutionalised political and legal structures that Manipur had since 33 A.D. for at least two millennia, only to be interrupted by occasional Burmese intrasigence and other interventions from expansionists could be largely have been responsible in the evolution of semi-democratic constitutionalism and its more democratic *alter ego* in the 20th century. In the middle of the 20th century, article 49 of Manipur Constitution, 1947 has even matured so as to declare that political crimes committed in the soil of Manipur should not be punished with capital punishments at all. We are yet to find out any other similar constitutional provision in any other 20th century political constitution. This unique provision could be a harbinger in a wider canvas. Hence, Manipuri people by and large, could not *en masse* tolerate barbaric demonstration of strength of authority and militarism while dealing with purely political questions by the executives. In 1891, the chief commissioner of Assam and his top British officials had to suffer extreme form of penalty in Manipur because of their arrogance, authoritarianism and aggression.

The topmost British officials had been tried by Manipur Top Garod and awarded capital punishment for committing aggression. As A.V. Dicey stated in his monumental classic, Manipuri constitutional values could not coexist with arbitrary authoritarianism and the attitude might not be easily wiped out by a stroke of pen either.

Prince Koireng (alias Bir Tikendrajit Sing), had been penalised for assaulting an Angami Naga, who carried limb of beef and outraged the Manipuri prince by his act.[18] The powerful Manipuri prince Tikendrajit Bir Sing had been punished with banishment to the island of Thangga for one year, as he was found guilty of injuring two citizens by the Cheirap court.[19] The credit could not be given to British presence merely, as the Cheirap court was an institution of Manipur. The common people had, therefore, evolved their political attitude towards the evolution of Rule of Law by defining their own role and status within the political framework, that could not evolve without their active participation. Punishment of a prince for misbehaving with a common man is an evidence of the Rule of Law in practice in a princely state.

Rule of law & Dicey

Diceyan scale of evaluating 'Rule of Law' in a former princely state is used herein, by considering the monumental contribution of A.V. Dicey to this aspect of constitutionalism and also by looking into Diceyan impact in the emerging universalisation of the 'Rule of Law' in comparative systems.

The Manipur Constitution adopted in Loyumba regime in 1100 A.D. — the *'Loyumba Shinyen'*[20] had the invocation of God, defined professional obligations, provided for *Pana*-territorial classification, state duty of the Crown, royal decorum, costumes, rewards, administration of justice, and the conscience-keeping of the generic Manipuri nationhood. Influenced also by the Western common law in part, the Manipur State Constitution, 1947 had reduced the erstwhile monarchy entirely to a figurehead and even under the cover of titular monarchy, republican upsurge overwhelmed the monarchy and after two years hence, *de facto* republicanism took over the scene. The Manipur king himself admitted several times that the sovereignty lies with the people of Manipur, and no longer with his person. In the past, *Pongba Tara*, 64 nobles, judicial institutions and above all, *'Chatnla Luptin'* (Manipuri Constitutional Convention) operated as safety valve against the arbitrary authority of the monarchy.

The Manipur State Constitution, 1947 — the shortest ever document of its kind in the world, in its eleven chapters, contains 58 articles. Chapter III deals with the executive, chapter IV and V the legislature, and chapter IX, the judiciary. Chapter X and VIII provide for fundamental rights, duties and the services. The equally short Constitution of the USA bears the hallmark of utmost wisdom and precesion. The longest document is not necessarily the best.

In Diceyan rule of law, every one — from the lowest rung to the highest echelon is equal before law. The inbuilt contrivance which perpetuated social, political and economic inequalities in either the British society or other society had been prevented from taking roots in Manipur. Manipuri womenfolk had not been disempowered from playing her own independent role in deciding her personal status or producing wealth on her own. Women-market, agriculturalist women and women agitations give ample testimony to the decisive role of the women in Manipur. Within the common law framework of Britain, the Anglo-Saxons had five-tiered feudalism culminating to the last in the hierarchy — the peasants who could be sold along with the land to the knights, barons, etc. Zamindari existed in

India. These iniquitous institutions did not emerge at all in the Manipuri society. Equality had been, therefore, deeply embedded in the tissues and psyche of a Manipuri. In its degraded form, it had also degenerated to out right individualism and opportunism that needed checks and balance through the constitutional conventions called - *'Chatna Luptin'*. As stated above, even the prince had not been spared from punishment as meted out by the *Cheirap* court.

Manipur Constitution, 1947 in its chapter X provides that "All citizens shall be equal before the law. Titles and other privileges of birth shall not be recognised in the eyes of law"(article 44); "all penalties shall be as determined by law" (art. 48), so and so forth.[22] Manipur Constitution recognises no emergency nor draconian law nor any arbitrary barbarism, disguised in the garb of law. As stated above, political crimes like even the violent overthrow of governments could be immune from constitutional strictures. Reference of the decision, taken under the Constitution could also be referred to extra-territorial jurisdictions outside the state (art. 57)[23] and it obviously connotes international tribunal or, arbitration in the comity of nations. Manipuri rule of law could be subjected to International 'Rule of Law'. Charges also could be framed against the king or queen[24] (article 8(c). The value of equality had been grafted deep down the bosom of the people heart and it can not be undone even by a subsequent value shift.

Customary law

The British Constitution is the product of common customary law and the judiciary creates the common law, which protects the rights of the citizens. The British constitutional history need not necessarily coincide with that of its Manipuri counterpart. However, similar stages of evolution of the laws could also be taken note of in other princely states. A princely state Constitution is *sui generis*.

Tribal customary laws had evolved into institutions and mechanisms of law, although tribalism that Manipur passed through before 33 A.D. might have been older than its British counterpart. The local self-governments, and the centralised Manipur administration had judicial institutions which evolved the legal norms and the ultimate product had been the conventions — the 'CHATNA LUPTIN' of the Meeteis. At a later stage, tribal courts and Islamic courts had been set up, although the women's court had been as old as Pakhangba had in 33 A.D. In 1947, Manipur had enacted State Courts Act, 1947 by covering the entire territorial jurisdiction of the state. The common customary law of Manipur made it amply clear that no punishment, least of all capital punishment could or should be meted out to any citizen without undertaking the due process of law and proper judicial intervention. If the Convention had been violated by anybody, whosoever powerful he could have been, people responded either by taking recourse to revolt or armed resistance. It may be noted that constitutional conventions are taken seriously in the United Kingdom. Customary law is equally important.

However, the Manipuri common customary law could not be defended as faultless. Sometimes, capricious decisions had also been taken and the criminalisation of the punishment had been found barbaric like *'Sugnu'* form of punishment or, drowning of the victim packed inside sack in turbulent rivers. Other penal systems might have been more barbaric and cruel than what had been practised in Manipur. Barbarism starting from the milder form in Manipur to the *Narbali* in the Bharata or, Anglo-Saxon cruelties is after all barbarism which violates the first premise of contemporary human rights standard. They are obsolete.

At the fag-end of the twentieth century, the classic mould of Diceyan 'Rule of Law' has been enlarged enough to accommodate the universal standard of human rights and legal regimes. The concept has been found to be very dynamic. What is not going to change is the inevitable access of the citizen and people to the judicial intervention and the accepted value of promoting the independence of the judiciary. The moment judicial intervention is removed from the administration of justice in the state, thereby allowing persons to take over the role of law and rule of law, tyranny steps into justice and the state assumes its tyrannical spectre. 'Rule of Law' has its impact in both thick and thin in all the civilizations. The Constitution of the erstwhile princely state deserves revisiting in the search for constitutional values. Besides, it enhances the curiosity for constitutional historiography. Plural societies are the eloquent testimony of heterogeneity and partnership of *sui generis* systems.

References

1. N.Sanajaoba, ed., Manipur Past & Present, Volume I,1988, p.472.
2. Dr. Ningombam Ibobi, 'Thainagi Manipurda Ganatrantragee Machak',Khongthang periodical, ed.Sairem Nilabir, vol. 2/4, 1971, Imphal p. 35.
3. ibid. p. 37.
4. Dr. Ningombam Ibodi, 'Maniprishinggee Ningtamba', Khongthan 1/1, 1970, p.1(ULA—Universal Literary Association, Imphal). *See* Critical Political Theories about Manipur, published in Khongthang since 1970 till 1995.
5. Shairem Nilabir, '*Britishna Loushindringei Manipurda Mashagee Lam Leingak*' in Khongthang, Vol 6/17, ed, Sanajaoba Naoria, August 1975 p.31.
6. Dr. Ningombam Ibobi, 'Manipur State Constitution Act 1947', in Sanajaoba Naoria ed., Khongthang, ULA, March 1975, p.9.
7. A.V. Dicey, The Rule of Law in his book, An Introduction to the Study of the Law of the Constitution, 1885, p.184.
8. ibid. p. 202-203.
9. Introduction by E. C. S. Wade, in *op. cit*. Dicey, p. cx.
10. ibid Wade, p. ciii.
11. E.C.S. Wade and Godfrey Phillips, Constitutional Law, ELBS, 1971, pp.74.
12. Indira Nehru Gandhi vs. Raj Narain, AIR, 1975 SC; Keshavananda vs. State of Kerala, AIR 1973, SC and other basic structure rulings..
13. Nongmaithem Ibohal, in Manipur Past & Present, Vol.I, 1988, p. 313.
14. Gangmumei Kabui, History of Manipur Volume I, 1991, p.59.
15. ibid. p. 60.

16. ibid. p. 85.
17. id. p.86, Cf. Jhaljit, Jyortirmoy Roy, W.I. Singh etc..
18. James Johnstone, Manipur and Naga Hills, 1896, p. 113.
19. ibid. p. 205.
20. N. Sanajaoba ed, Manipur Past & Present Vol. I, 1988, pp 299; see Gangmumei Kabui, in p.307.
21. Manipur Treaties and Documents, Volume I, ed. Naorem Sanajaoba, 1993, p.370; see other documents in this volume for detail studies on Manipur Constitution.
22. MPP, op. cit. p.375.
23. ibid. p. 376.
24. id p. 369.

Part-II

Rights Discourse

6

Human Rights in the 21st Century

The world order in the twenty-first century may witness polycentrism, economic interdependence, impact of information age, new Biology, new Physics on the one hand and universal concern for individual and collective human rights on the other hand.

Human right is a universal constant, which is susceptible to the influence of variables including zeitgeist, shifting cultural values, level of scientific temper of a civilisation, and the attainment of the political economy. Post-world-war-second human thought centred around the massacre, amputation, disappearance of and wounds inflicted upon millions and millions of men by men themselves; that haunting spectre is the mother of the contemporary global concern over the human rights. When the framework is extended to the space time continuum, the human rights scenario may be perceived with a futurological perspective.

Futuristic studies that have been integrated in the planning process of science and technology as well as research and development including the ongoing globalisation programmes the world over, could be fruitfully applied in the field of structuration, standardisation, enforcement and perspectivisation of human rights theme. Futuristic studies were initiated with an essay written in 1943 by Professor Ossip Flechtheim and courses imparted by sociologist Alvin Toffler in the late 1960's in the United States. The Ministry of Science and Technology, government of India constituted futurology-panel in 1973 and by now, some of the Indian universities make efforts to modestly respond to the preponderance of futuristic studies. The West and Japan had already exercised this culture with a definite edge. The writer makes a modest effort to make an assessment of human rights in the totality from the futuristic perspective. Nobody at the moment has ever witnessed the future, but every one is a part of the present from which the future would be constructed. This linkage of space-time profile provides for the core-assumption of futurology.

Notwithstanding the polemic about human rights in the recent past, after considering the ideological confrontations that occurred during the cold war period, we may state that the post-cold war era, more particularly at the fag end of the twentieth century, has evolved a near consensus about the rights.

The ongoing events commencing from the adoption of the Universal Declaration of Human Rights in 1948 to Teheran Conference 1968 and the World Human Rights Conference in Vienna in 1993 have provided certain markers that indicate a watershed in the movement. Most of the legal and political systems have, in varying degrees, responded to the prerogatives of the first generation of human rights by way of internalising civil and political rights within their domestic jurisdiction, despite adverse reports of occasional infringements. The reference points and standards have, however, been set and countries are now judged by their degree of deviation from these standards. This is no mean achievement of the global order in this century.

Unlike the first generation of human rights which are prohibitive to the states, the second generation of human rights empowers the state towards achieving the basic socio-economic rights of its citizens. The states largely fail on this second front. How far the states can succeed in providing for the second generation of human rights in the twenty-first century depends on some other considerations, which are largely political and on the system of economic or trade order in the context of the World Trade Organisation — a progeny of the GATT. Connected herewith is the input of the new Physics, new Biology and other developmental sciences to the domain of knowledge, wealth and power of the nations.

The twenty-first century envisages the dominance of economic super powers like Japan, Germany and European Union, the United States and the emergence of Asia-Pacific rim, represented by China, five Asian tigers and India, some of which stake claim to the top economic power-bracket of the next century. Second generation of human rights is directly interlinked with the level of the economic order that is being speculated upon and sought for and with wealth-creating power of the new sciences, as mentioned. The first generation of human rights would not remain safe without making grounds for a healthy, viable, equitous and a just set of second generation of human rights. Rhetoric and formalism could not substitute the basic *sine qua non* of the human rights set.

The trend of human right perceptions has turned into another direction following the Rio Earth Summit 1992 and the Copenhagen World Summit on Social Development, held in 1995. Group or collective rights are drawing increasing attention of the world opinion-leaders and decision - makers. The third generation of human rights, inspite of contradicting the earlier two generations, has all the more strengthened the legitimacy of the two generations. In terms of chronology, the third generation has taken firm political and ideological roots in the 1960s, when decolonisation process has been initiated by the UN. The next century will be equally concerned with the third generation rights.

The methodology to be adopted for ascertaining the futurology of the human rights in the twenty-first century cannot be based upon Kelsenian-purist conceptualisation or, on the dogmatic adherence to the *Volkgeist* doctrine of communalisation of laws. An opportunity is given to the world citizens on their right choice of values, considering the fact that they are strolling in an unprecedented information super highway — a new terrain of cyberspace and using new intellectual tools which are made out to meet the demands of the next century. Human rights research and decisions constitute a vital component of the quantum jumps and adventures, the new world order has undertaken. The fear of dominance, hegemony and neo-colonialism is yet to be totally removed from the role models and structures, we create — be it regional or global.

The new world order

Post-1991 world order has its own political and economic space. In the cold war period, human rights remained a subject of the ideological dispute between the two ideologically polarised superpowers. The American foreign policy objectives and humanitarian aid have been based upon American value-system and its perception about human rights, which in themselves are anti-communist and anti-socialist in content. The socialist version of human rights placed the political and civil rights next to the economic freedom of man. Marxian ideology treats economic freedom as the precondition for the enjoyment of other set of liberties: [illegible]ercian practice of human rights denied a position of equality to the coloured Amercian — the Negro, promoted discrimination in actual life and created indeterminate lumpen-proletariat among the white Americans. Till the other day, American women had been denied adult suffrage and even today, freedom of the citizens to set up communist party is equated with treason. The Soviet experience had its quota of human rights violations like imprisonment of political dissidents and perpetuation of a regimented party life, wherein the party *apparatchik* behaved not much differently from what they called as bourgeoisie. The new world order is either unipolar or multi-polar and the American order enjoys the primacy by default till China and the West could emerge at the top.

In the new world order, the third world perception of human rights centres around the re-conceptualisation of the unfinished agenda about economic emancipation of the third world. The polemic of the cold-war period about the primacy question still continues, since the third world considers the physical survival and material self-sufficiency to be primary. In this context, the euphoria about globalisation of economy and trade by way of breaking down tariff barriers and promoting equal market access by all the members of the World Trade Organisation and alteration of national patent laws to suit American interest calls for deeper examination. Even economic giants like Japan is threatened, occasionally by the USA. Other countries like China, India, Brazil, among others, are given the indirect signal to behave in tune with the market demands of the USA and other big powers. The method of wealth creation and re-distribution of wealth in the new world order is going to determine the status of the second generation of human rights across the world; but as of now, the standard of living as found in developed countries and poor countries varies in the ratio of 1:14. The human economic rights of a Westerner for instance is fourteen times better than the standard of living of a poor Indian or, Latin American or, Africaner.

The new world order is presently witnessing the emerging science and technology in the West like the new Physics of nano-technology, robotics, automation, space sciences, electronics, super conductors, super-computers, polymers accompanied with new forms of smart weapons and also new Biology like genetic engineering, cloning, neuro-biology, neuro-surgery, IVF, organ transplantation, genome projects, transgenesis, accompanied with unprecedented military capability of altering the molecular biology and structures of the man and machines in enemy countries. Some technology is found to be helpful to human rights promotion, but several areas of the new technology pose direct threat to human survival of mankind. The NPT renewal in 1995 for an indefinite period has empowered the 5+3 nuclear weapon powers of the world to bring the apocalypse to every doorstep the world over. In May 1998, India and Pakistan became nuclear weapon states. In this context, the constructive use of the political and civil liberties till the world is completely disarmed is gaining ground as the human obligation of every citizen. Human rights need not be confined merely to the orthodox domain like the exercise of political and civil liberties, which are also equally important in adverse circumstances.

The status of the third generation of human rights like the right to environment, right to development, right of people to self-determination, right to common heritage of mankind, among others, as endorsed by the respective bodies of the United Nations in the new world order, is found to be of utmost importance to the third world countries. The third generation has not been fully crystalized and it has to be adequately developed in the twenty-first century. This cannot be achieved without the support of the developed countries.

Human rights law and international humanitarian law are two viable normative global frameworks within which is constructed, a standard by which the human life, liberty and property should be protected in times of peace and armed conflicts. These are two levels of evaluating the human rights standard the world over. Normally, our concern is shown towards the protection of human rights in stable situations; however, the old and new world orders are not devoid of armed conflict situations. Millions of human lives were lost, millions have been wounded and injured and several lakh have been missing during the last world wars. Post-war world witnesses Somalia, where millions die out of hunger, Rwanda where millions die during the tribal feuds and Bosnia, among others, where millions are lost and killed in the ethnic-cleansing process. Low-intensity conflicts like wars of national liberation, proxy wars, ruthless terrorism, communal infernos and other similar armed conflicts are still visible. Nobody can justify lack of global or regional concern to these hard realities, because the victims are human beings, children, women, disabled and old age people, among others.

The safeguards required for the protection of human rights in the situations of armed conflict are enunciated by the four Geneva Conventions, August 1949 and the two additional protocols of June 1977. The common Article no.3 of the four Geneva Conventions stipulates that the human lives, property, dignity and the lives of the *horse de combat* have to be protected to the fullest extent. Common Article no.3 is *Jus Cogens* and non derogable.

Till the world is relieved of wars, international humanitarian laws have to be strengthened, since man and war can not alienate from each other, save in pious and non-real political statements about the eradication of all wars from the human civilisation. Human rights transcend rhetoric and diplomatic manoeuvres. The theme is connected with the super-eminent principles of justice, without whose integration with law, remains mere official formalism and a bureaucratic norm.

A new development worthy of mention in the field of international humanitarian laws is the creation of international criminal jurisdiction viz., Yugoslav tribunal and Rwanda tribunal by the United Nations and ICC in the July 1998. For the first time in the post-war history, the United Nations has created these war crime tribunals in the spirit of the Nurenberg and Tokyo tribunals. The war lords would be held personally liable and accountable for the transgression of human rights and crimes against mankind under these jurisdictions. The International criminal court could become a reality in the 21st century. More than 80 states have given signatures to the international criminal court treaty in 1999.

Domestic and UN jurisdictions

National jurisdictions over human rights are constituted on a large scale under the aegis and encouragement of the UN machineries at the fag-end of this century. The United States of America, which till the other day refrained itself from accepting international human rights instrumentalities like the ICCPR, 1966 has started accepting these global human rights obligations, while countries like Pakistan etc. keep themselves away from signing the human rights covenants of the UN, 1966. World conference on human rights held in Vienna in June 1993 has strongly urged upon all the member states of the UN to sign and ratify all the international human rights instrumentalities invariably. In this context, the republic of India is equally obliged to sign and ratify, the optional protocol to the International Covenant on Civil and Political Rights 1966, among others. The union government of India has signed the Anti Torture Convention 1984. It however, evades from signing the two additional protocols to the Geneva Conventions 1977.

The twenty-first century envisages that each and every country of the world should arrange its national and domestic jurisdictions so as to match literally with the global standard as set by the world community through the medium of the UN and other regional bodies. The Asian region, unlike Africa, the Americas or, the Arab nations or, the European Union, has not yet done spadework so as to mould Asian consciousness of human rights into a consensus and install Asian Human Rights Commission and Asian Human Rights Court or, Asian parliament. Europe has adopted even common currency — EURO.

The Asian statesmen, being engaged more in conflicts and disharmony largely of their own making, are yet to apply their mind towards appreciating these basic structural requirements of human rights. Asian unity itself is a positive structure beneficial to the region and in the promotion of Asian concept of human rights. We strongly urge upon the leaders and decision-makers to pay heed to the legitimate human rights structure, which is long overdue. It is also true that several hitches and nitty-gritty have to be sorted out first at the political and economical levels, as Asia lacks a Jean Monnet or, an acceptable leader within Asian vision.

The periodic reporting obligation of the member states under Article 40 of the ICCPR 1966 to the UN Human Rights Committee is by and large found defficient and casual. The reporting obligation may be tightened up and in the process, the national governments would use the national NGOs in finalising the national reports. Transparency and fairness have been found missing in this aspect.

The national human rights institutions are most likely to be strengthened with popular support and participation in the next century. In case of India, the National Human Rights Commission, is installed under a national Act in 1994.

The performance level of the NHRC of India could be fairly assessed in the 2000 or 2010 AD, considering the fact that the institution will be in the teething stage. The judicial activism of the Supreme Court of India in the protection of human rights has been appreciated elsewhere. Technicalities and frivolous procedural constraints did not prevent the Supreme Court from doing justice in class and affirmative actions. The NHRC is not, however, empowered to investigate in human rights violations committed by the Indian security forces.

In the last few years, the Supreme Court has re-emanciated state liability in torts thereby gradually eroding the age-old British concept of sovereign immunity. Along with the activism, it has also evolved the norms of payment of compensation to citizens, whose fundamental rights have been infringed upon by the state machinery in terms of unlawful detention or custodial death, among others. However, the trend is not firmly established since the Supreme Court has not yet universalised the compensatory doctrine for violation of fundamental rights, as it qualifies the relief in 'appropriate cases'. However, the trend is emerging. While the Supreme Court is pro-activist, Indian bureaucracy, executive and the law enforcement machinery by and large, are institutionally apathetic to the human rights protection . They smell like the British rulers. Even under TADA 1985 as amended in 1993 and which has culminated on May 23, 1995, nearly eighty thousand farmers, minorities and political opponents of the ruling party had been dumped along with just a few hundred of terrorists. The state is apologetic about the blunder, but it does not come out *suo motu* for providing compensatory relief to these seventy thousands improperly and wrongfully arrested citizens. Indian state looks like a big jail.

On the legislative front, some of the draconian and emergency laws, which are espoused by the emotionalists, like the Armed Forces Special Powers Act 1958 invoked in the North Eastern states of India deviate visibly from the universal human rights standard, as enunciated by the ICCPR 1966 and as accepted under treaty obligations by the union government of India. Sections 4, 5 and 6 of the above mentioned Act 1958 are not only found incompatible with the relevant provisions of the ICCPR 1966 by the UN Human Rights Committee in 1991, but are also criticised widely by global and national fora, because these sections legalise extra-judicial murder and provide immunity to those who committed extra judicial murders in the name of emergency unproclaimed. Similarly, sections 3,4,5,15,16,19 and 21, among others of the TADA 1985 as amended in 1993 have been found to be in blatant violation of the established norms of criminal and constitutional laws. It reminds us of Jurists, who once said that the English parliament has the prerogative to make laws to declare male to be female so on and so forth, but it smacks of insanity of the collective wisdom i.e. cannibalisation of the human conscience in the name of misconceived positivist legalism. Established natural law and procedure contradict these aberrations as untenable. The Supreme Court of India, however, defended the black Law—AFSPA on 27 November, 1997. It lost the opportunity to strike down black laws.

The domestic national jurisdiction on human rights protection can not and should not be overstretched on the basis of the medieval political theory of absolute sovereignty, as the sovereignty concept is shrinking all the more in the twenty-first century and with the progressive political devolution of powers, global economic integration is gaining momentum. In this context, the far-fetched assumption of the absolutist' concept of sovereignty and trade protectionism could be treated blasphemous in the next century. When the domestic laws including patent laws have to be re-drafted in order to match with the WTO prerogatives, the wild dream of enacting patent laws independent of the global consensus could be ridiculous and pernicious as well. The anachronistic attitude is poses a direct threat to the growing global interdependence and it cannot claim to be an accepted standard. The mind-set of isolationism will drag the states to the scaffold of the medieval-age-island, hostile states. The meaning of peace and security in the world is re-interpreted in terms of active cooperation, and not in terms of absence of hostilities in their exclusivity.

An important UN human rights machinery is the UN High Commissioner on Human Rights, which has been installed in 1994. Some Asian countries objected to the proposal for the installation of the Human Rights Commissioner due to an inbuilt fear that their ongoing human rights violations would be brought under international jurisdiction, but the international opinion prevailed upon this feeble opposition. The office of the Commissioner and its institutional achievements are yet to be examined, as it has no track record so far for evaluative purposes. The institution would flourish in the next century, considering the growing global thrust directed at human rights standard setting. The arrangement has a couple of indices. Firstly, the jurisdictions of the theme mechanisms and human rights rapporteurs should not overlap with the Commissioner's jurisdiction. They have to be complimentary to each other. Secondly, the Commissioner has to carve out a place of its own by opening up dialogues with governments and coordinating all the human rights agencies under the UN and elsewhere. Thirdly, the human rights supervision is brought under one centrally organised UN Commissioner.

International politics

The locus of human rights in the intersecting coordinates of the global-power equations is yet to be ascertained with precision. The difficulty arises out of certain apparent contradictions like the sacrosanctity of human rights within the proximity of politics, which has been conceived as the best art of the possibilities. Human rights cannot remain a distinct entity, completely isolated from political *apartheid*. The post-cold war unipolarity or, multipolarity as well as the balance of power and equilibrium of power-centres affect the standard and materialisation of the human rights. The co-relation of power and justice also varies in two ways viz., justice of power or, power of justice. The ideal aspect of human rights lies in the powers of justice, but *realpolitik* shifts its locus within the justice of power.

Looking back into the human rights of the Mileans of Milos with respect to the aggressive and hegemonistic Athenians in the period before Christ, the Mileans refused both the options, offered to them by the Athenians — surrender to the superior Athenian power and live happily or, vanish yourselves completely. Milos vanished, but its spirit survives for good. Power can vanish human rights and can retain them also. The contemporary power has not changed much either and it is not going to change substantially in the twenty-first century. Power equations at macro and micro levels may change. The macro-states are under international obligation to respect as many as 90 micro-states.

Power relationship considers basic parameters of the contemporary civilisation like population explosion, technology, information explosion, hunger, disease, war, low intensity conflicts, border and territorial disputes. These variables influence the response of states to the standards of human rights, accepted as such within their jurisdiction. The next century will not at all rule out conflicts and power dis-equilibrium and the perception about human rights would be altered accordingly. The UN outlaws 'war', but war is a reality and demolition of human rights on a massive scale in war is also another concomitant reality. Human right is to be promoted in the midst of the reality.

The United Nations has committed by the provisions of the UN Charter to secure peace and security on earth - the goals which are always evasive. Terrorism of all kinds including private or state terrorism is branded the world over as crime against mankind. Even a universally accepted definition of terrorism cannot be laid down by the intelligentsia and legislators of the world, because there are many grey areas like political violence and just wars of national liberation, which have been consistently approved and legitimised by International Law and all the organs of the United Nations including the General Assembly, Security Council, Human Rights Committee and Commission, the International Court of Justice, specially after endorsing the de-colonisation movements by the UN in the 1960s.

Interestingly, terrorism is a crime against mankind, while National Liberation Movements are subjects of International Law; and while exercising the right of people to self-determination, the people can lawfully exercise force in self-defence , but the force applied by the terrorists are unlawful and reprehensible. Herein lies the significance of justice of power and power of justice on the other hand. The dichotomy is not country-specific or culture-or region-specific, but it is universal. The situation of human rights in an unstable situation or conflict zone has to be assessed with the perception. Frail minds fail to identify the dichotomy.

Another interesting dimension of politicalised human rights is the politics of foreign aids. The USA evaluates the human rights standards of any aid-recipient country at the time of granting American aid to other countries. The evaluation of the standards is done by using American values and yardsticks.

How far the American or European strategic interest has not been considered within the bounds of its hidden agenda is a question, which constitutes the vital component of power-politics. In this sense, all the nations do play the same game and human rights are not completely dissociated from these exercises. The perception, however, would not degrade the universally accepted standards of human rights to the political function of expediency and convenience; we may accept the situation at a permissible level of pollution so long as the pollution does not render the environment hazardous. Once we venture a statement that India is an exception, it would be an absurdity *prima facie*.

Politics and power equations have their own space in the domain of human right, but human right by itself is not politics, since it is the inalienable essence of man. The UN system, regional power structures, member states of the United Nations and organised bodies including the NGOs have increasing global responsibility to set the standard, enforcement pattern of and for constant monitoring of human rights. The ultimate beneficiary in exercising the responsibility is none other than 'man'.

A score of independent small states are emerging in the twenty-first century as the international community closes the chapter of de-colonisation process. the human rights format in the emerging states would include challenges to their sustainable development, security and developmental issues, besides the lurking danger of re-colonisation in a new attire.

7

Rights of HIV-AIDS Persons

The World Health Report 1998 - 'Life in the 21st Century — a vision for all', released by WHO[1] has perceives healthier lives in the next century. In 1997, the report notes that 2.3 million died of HIV and AIDS.

The pandemic-plague of the post-industrial society has invaded deep inside the very fortified building blocks of the modern man, who is left almost defenceless, once his immune system has been dismantled form within. We need concerted global strategy, coalition-action, pooling of resource-technology and a consensual legal regime, governed by global AIDS law. It appears that there would not be a substitute for unwavering and firm global resolve in such a situation.

The multi-disciplinary approach, while re-endorsing WHA 41.24 resolution, 13 May, 1988, London summit of world ministers, January 1988, Geneva Consultation[1a], 28 July, 1989 and subsequent UN[2] resolutions and responses, pleads for hammering out global AIDS law[3] either on the basis of the existing human rights[4], treaty laws and UN instruments or, by complementing them with the proposal for framing an elaborate UN instrument with the sole objective of fighting out pandemics including the HIV-AIDS demolition squad. WHO regional office for Europe, Eastern Europe and Central Asia held three consultations on HIV and law reform in 1995. International guidelines are also issued in 1996 by UN High Commissioner for Human Rights.

The global village is alarmed by the militant terrorism of the HIV retrovirus[5] and its disguised invasion into the host DNA by nesting countless number of budding retrovirus, which ultimately sabotage and destroy the human immune system. The cyber-space and information super-highway man has been caught off the guard[6] and confused by even misleading notions, which market the idea that AIDS would check demographic explosion of Africa.[7]

Laurice Garrett's bestseller - 'The Coming Plague—Newly Emerging Diseases in a World Out of Balance' (1995) has unnerved[8] the powerful White House of the USA. Powerful governments have been caught napping by the militant HIV-retrovirus. The global sensibility is now awakened towards fighting out the intruder-retrovirus.

The Indian Health Organisation[9] estimates that by the year 2000 A.D., 10,000 Indians will die a day and 20,000 children will become orphans a day. AIDS conference, held in September 1995 in Thailand[10] projects that by 2,000 A.D., AIDS will infect more Asians than the rest of the world and as a result, Asian development will remarkably recede.

At present, HIV-AIDS infects 13 million people and would infect 40 to 110 million by 2001 A.D. 1 million children have already lost parents and millions of them are going to be orphaned in the near future.[11]

As on January 1,1994, 11,287,000 men, 8,737,000 women and 2,175,000 children have been infected by AIDS (total - 22,200,000). In the 1996 projection[12], HIV would infect 33,330,000 people. India[13] would have 50,000 full-blown AIDS cases. NACO report, 31 May, 1995 indicates that out of 25,07,908 samples screened, 18,291 have been confirmed by Western Blot test. It may also be noted that some HIV strains escape detection in the test and also that the samples do not reflect the real picture of the retrovirus impact.

Reportedly, HIV-AIDS infection has waned[14] in the USA and Europe due to secure blood supplies and community-vigilance, yet HIV subtype 'O' (for Out tier), largely found in Cameroon are found missing from the current stage of blood-screening test.

In Africa, all the known HIV-I subtypes are found prevalent; in Asia, subtypes B,C and E; in Europe, all the subtypes except E; in north America, subtype B and in South America, subtypes B, C, and F. Africa and Europe are the reservoir of nearly all the HIV-I subtypes.

Global AIDS strategy would not be solely based upon frenzied and hysterical alarmism[15], since the situation has not outstripped the final reach of the post-industrial man, equipped with the state-of-the-art technology and sciences. However, in the absence of a concerted global perspective, premises, strategy and action, the pandemic[16] by default, has the inbuilt potential and readiness to generate a new mutant retrovirus plague[17], because of the increasing global inter-dependence, migration, population movement, problems of millions of refugees and displaced persons.

Public emergency

Municipal jurisdictions and national legal regimes have not considered the pandemic intrusion as a public emergency situation. Municipal jurisdictions vary from country to country. In the Afro-Asian context, the pandemic may assume near-public emergency situation, due to the lackadaisical attitude of national governments.

In the context of India, the union government seems to be unprepared to draft or, enact AIDS law in order to supervise and control the ramifications of the HIV-AIDS war.[18] WHO has not directed the government of India to enact a national AIDS law. The AIDS Prevention Bill of 1989[19] had been introduced in the Council of States of India on the 18th August, 1989 and has also been placed before the Joint Select Parliamentary Committee. The AIDS Bill suffers from deficiencies like discrimination and coercion etc. As per the UNDP programme[20], AIDS resulted to 50% absenteeism in the organised industrial force. WHO[21] reports that Bolivia, Zambia, Lebanon and India have succeeded in health plan like the reduction of the impacts of HIV-AIDS. Bangkok[22] AIDS conference presents a dismal picture of Asia, since AIDS would substantially affect and retard Asian development, which was on the rise otherwise. Right to development of individuals, communities and states are impaired by AIDS impact.

The country-specific national strategies may not be found uniform and could be aimed at attaining global standard, from which standard local variations may be made. The Western companies, investors and research laboratories pick up the Western HIV subtypes for preparing vaccine that may be on the anvil for clinical trials and would have to be market and capital - friendly. The inbuilt lacunae of the thesis is that the dreaded retrovirus would simply jump out of immigration laws and political geography.

The reason behind harbouring national or country - specific bias in perceiving the global AIDS policy and strategy for action may be influenced by several preponderant parameters like — the gap in the national resources, uneven levels of R&D achieved, cultural-customary constraints, variations in population control and explosion, deep-rooted institutionalised underdevelopment of the South, variation in the BTF pattern or sexual behaviour, gender injustice, impacts of drug addiction, lack of health care and factors, among others.

Within a country, the fall out of HIV-AIDS invasion in different states differs. In India,[23] HIV spreads very rapidly from high-risk area to the general population. In Assam[24], a survey reports that rural women, illiterate women and Muslim women in large numbers are ignorant of as to how AIDS has been transmitted.

National laws differ in several aspects. Right to health and health-care is a basic inalienable right of citizens in Cuba, whereas in rich countries like the USA and the West, it is private right unsupported by the state. Right to development has not been affected by the HIV-AIDS invasion in the USA, but right to development is substantially cut to the root by the HIV pandemic in the developing world. UNDP Report 1995[25] — 'The Impact of AIDS on Human Development' on Asia and the pacific states that in measuring HDI - the Human Development Index, HIV-AIDS has already retarded Asian development since 1980s. In Asia, the retrovirus is considered to be the public enemy number one.

The national policy, laws and strategy of the individual states call for a global standardisation within the framework of global AIDS strategy and law.

Global AIDS law

Global AIDS law should incorporate Paris AIDS Summit, 1 December, 1994 norms, UNCHR Resolutions of 1994, UN Minority Committee Resolutions 1995, Bangkok Declaration, September 1995 and New Delhi Declaration 1995, among others.

As the need for formulating global AIDS law is being widely and increasingly felt or for that matter the need for an omnibus anti-pandemic law in blanket term is perceived, the possibilities for framing such a law have to be consistently explored through inter-disciplinary and inter-governmental efforts. Prima facie the International humanitarian law[26] has not much direct relevance in the war against HIV terrorism. Several aspects and components of the international human rights law[27] are found relevant in the current rights - retrovirus interface. In this context, two basic issues[28] have been considered :

I. The issue of discrimination and the danger of creating new set of minorities and structures for discrimination;

II. Everyone's right to equitable access to health care. Global consultation AIDS[29] accepts the following premises:

A. At present, there is no cure and vaccine against AIDS HIV inspite of the fact that current vaccine research and clinical trials can show us the light at the end of the tunnel;

B. The economically underdeveloped states cannot afford elaborate systems for screening blood and blood products at a time when the HIV remains a monster with enormous impregnable killing power;

C. The HIV test occasionally provides false results and hidden strains escape notice;

D. By themselves, domestic laws do not succeed in altering the behaviour pattern in drug-taking and sexual activities;

E. Several national laws have led to the marginalisation and deprivation of the human rights of the HIV-AIDS infected minorities due to discrimination, misconceptions, stigmatization and legal sanctions.

The global consensus as indicated by the summits, conferences and wide range of public opinion provides a pointer that international human rights standard should be worked out and maintained in the process of fighting out HIV-AIDS aggression inside the building blocks of man.

Specific departures[30] from the global human rights standard on the ground of public health and protection of the rights and liberties of the others may, however, be judiciously mooted :

"(a) By a specific law which is accessible and which contains foreseeable standards as opposed to administrative policy or individual discretion not based on legal rules;

(b) By such a law which in the circumstances could be shown to be strictly required to achieve a legitimate purpose of society for which a pressing social need could be clearly shown and;

(c) In measures strictly proportional to the achievement of the pressing objective so defined and to any harm inflicted, and which are the least intrusive and restrictive measures available."

Public health exceptions call for rationalised qualifications and cautious appraisals, by considering the enactment of national legislative interventions on the basis of international human rights standard.

Global legislative interventions could endorse the basic premises on which the interventions could be ingrained.

They are crystallised as follows: Anti-discrimination laws, educational aspects, accommodation of cultural norms and variations, specific consideration of vulnerable sections, children and women, right to know and information and adaptation of national institutions and laws to the preponderant matrices of global strategy and AIDS law. As the primitive ideas of absolutist sovereignty have waned from the current global perceptions, the international obligations of national governments have also enhanced.

Within the global framework, the international human rights bodies viz., Human Rights Committee, Committee on the Elimination of Discrimination against women, Committee on Economic, Social and Cultural Rights, Committee on the Elimination of Racial Discrimination, along with the regional structures — the European Commission on Human Rights, Inter American Commission on Human Rights and the African Commission on Human and Peoples' Rights have responsibilities in safeguarding the human rights against the pandemic invasion. Concrete results are yet to be shown by the above mentioned bodies. For a hard-hit region Asia, such regional structures do not even exist; regional patriotism of the European or American kind has probably not pricked the conscience of the Asian leaders and think-tanks. In the absence of regional structures, however, Asia is in the need of a platform for human rights action against the ramifications of the pandemic intrusion.

States are under obligation to report periodically about their human rights performance within their jurisdiction. State obligations[31] so far witnessed in the matter of their state reporting drop out HIV-AIDS matters, which constitute the core of human survival — right to survive, to be more appropriate.

The UN Secretary General cautioned the comity of nations in 1988 against the AIDS pandemic only and 'not against people who carries AIDS'. In 1989, a special UN rapporteur advocated for education, knowledge - dissemination, adoption of human rights and principles of non-discrimination.

World Health Assembly[32], on the basis of its resolution WHA 41.24, (May 1988)— 'Avoidance of discrimination in relation to HIV-infected people and people with AIDS', calls upon WHO to take up all necessary measures and accordingly, WHO have constantly advised governments on the lines of the resolution. In September, 1988 in support of WHO's global action and to achieve effective coordination within the UN framework, IAAG — the Inter Agency Advisory Group has been constituted. UNESCO, ILO and WTO also have their educative roles in the global action[33] against HIV-AIDS pandemic. In 1996, the Second International Consultation on HIV/AIDS programmed 12 guidelines to member states of the UN.[33a] They are issued in 1998.

The need for the review of national HIV-AIDS - related laws has been felt by the UN agencies[34]. India's AIDS Prevention Bill 1989 singled out high-risk persons, provided for compulsory testing, isolation and segregation, coercive procedure, discrimination, loopholes for breach of confidentiality and left very little obligation on the part of the medical practitioners, including their duty not to use unsafe syringes. The bill then shelved, has put a full stop on India's awaited legislative intervention in this retrovirus-immune system show down. Indian steelframe of administration and the legislators have to demonstrate their resolution against the retrovirus. Some of the medical practitioners are reportedly hesitant to even come closer the HIV- infected people and their professional responsibility has been by and large abdicated. Similarly, national legislations, rules and ordinances, enacted by the developing world are characterised by enormous deficiencies, as many of them are based upon inveterate superstitious premises, misinformed fear, hidden agenda and semi-ignorance.

WHO Director General[35] in May 1990, has urged upon member states to review their national HIV-AIDS- related laws and policies with a view to removing social quarantine, segregation or apartheid of another kind and discrimination. AIDS apartheid is apparently global in nature unlike the coloured apartheid, localised somewhere in Africa.

Discrimination against HIV-infected people or peoples with AIDS: Conclusions and Recommendations, UN. ESCOR,

Commission on Human Rights (45th session) 1993 presents pressures on the member states to take steps for elimination of AIDS-related discrimination, specially of women and children. The UN Commission on Human Rights asked the UN Secretary General in January 1994 to process report in connection with measures, taken to prevent discrimination in HIV-AIDS matter at domestic and global levels. The Committee on Economic, Social, and Cultural Rights has recently considered human rights issues connected with HIV-AIDS pandemic, while discussing state reports. Specific considerations and thrust are, however, yet to be taken up.

UDHR, 1948, ICCPR,1966 and ICESCR, 1966 (specially article 12) and other UN instruments and treaties provide for the basis of framing global AIDS law either in the format of a separate anti-pandemic covenant or otherwise in other format.

The UN sponsored global strategy projects three main objectives viz., prevention of HIV infection[36], reduction of personal and social impact of HIV infection and Unification of national as well as international efforts in the concerted war against AIDS. In India, blood banking is done within the purview of Food and Drug Act of 1940, whereas blood is not a drug and out of 1,114 blood banks opened in India[37], only 581 are run by the governments. IN UK, Finland, Canada and Australia, the state runs the blood management. States should take legal responsibility in blood management by reviewing the national laws.

Vulnerable groups like women[38], children[39], infants and weaker sections need special legislative protection within the global AIDS strategy. The UN system of rights suffers from certain deficiencies in the context of the right to health and the war against HIV-AIDS. The UN Human Rights Commission and Human Rights Committee give more emphasis to the civil and political rights; and the other rights including right to health may not be listed in their agenda. The other elementary rights too find little mention in their business. The Human Rights Committee, while handling article 6 of the ICCPR, 1966, as regards the supremacy of right to life focuses more on the reduction of infant mortality and increase in life expectancy. The Committee of ICESCR, 1966 addressed itself to right to health as provided in article 12 of the same covenant; but it does not insist upon the reporting states to submit specific and pointed reports on their compliance with the specific standards, as required in the control and elimination of HIV-AIDS pandemic.

In formulating the global AIDS law or, in lieu of that anti-pandemic law in blanket terms to meet any eventuality of similar kind in the future, human rights standard and right-liberty regime[40], would be extended to the casualties and victims of the HIV-AIDS invasion.. The AIDS - law regime should re-affirm and incorporate: right to life and health, right to liberty, privacy, to know and information, right to security, work, education and to marry to set up family, right to freedom of movement and right to social welfare and security.

In contemporary jurisprudence of the developed legal regimes, the issues on RIGHTS, PRINCIPLES, JUSTICE AND WELFARE POLICY dominate the legal mind either severally or in communion. Contradictory legal philosophy undermining the rest characterises the polemic. Rights-regime is one of the seriously endorsed theme of the legal enterprise. We do not bring in the polemic herein, but endorse the relevance of the rights regime in proper context.

The protection of the right and life of the 'many' *vis-a-vis* the non-discrimination of the HIV- infected minority is the proposition of the public health rationale. National laws have de-legitimized the normal life of the HIV-infected minority along side the majority on the grounds that public health is being jeopardised. The degree of jeopardization in the case of concealment of the infection for fear of stigmatisation and social apartheid would suffer from a quantum jump and the existing opportunity to fight out the pandemic concertedly would be found missing, since the infected victims would become a party to the pandemic. AIDS-related limitation of individual rights would be discriminatory. Misconceptions run deeper even in the mind of the professionals and health workers. Professionals would make attempts to evade professional hazards in the same way as some signals of this kind have been already picked up in hospitals. Professional bodies and councils should also accept the professional hazards by removing the loopholes of their in-house regulations. The global AIDS law should reflect on this aspect in no smaller degree.

Article 29 of the Universal Declaration of Human Rights, 1948 (UDHR), articles 4,12.3,13,18.3, 21,22.2, of the International Convenant on Civil and Political Rights, 1966 (ICCPR) and Articles 4 and 8.1(a) of the International Covenant on Economic, Social and Cultural Rights, 1966 (ICESCR) provide for restrictions on human rights in favour of vital times like national security , public order, safety and morals, general welfare and protection of lives and liberties of others. The states which would enact domestically such restrictions should justify that their legitimate social interest prevails upon the general framework of rights. Legitimate social interest would be more endangered in the event of restricting the rights and liberties of the HIV-infected persons. It would be preposterous to attribute all immunity and innocence to the HIV - infected people in blanket terms, as some or many of them may also nurture motives, malafide intentions to spread the infection on a larger scale in the hope that common grievance would lighten his mental burden. Criminal jurisprudence takes adequate care of the *mensrea* and the evil intentions. Blanket extension of criminal immunity to each and every HIV - infected person is total abdication of criminal law liability. Wilful spreading of the pandemic by interested HIV - infected people should draw the attention of the law enforcement agency and criminal laws. The HIV - infected individual has the legitimate right to protect his own right, but lacks the privilege to wilfully deprive others of their legitimate rights. When restrictive laws are enacted, the above mentioned components need careful legislative and judicial scrutiny.

On the part of the states and municipal governments, there should not be pre-mature declaration of public emergency, until and unless the very survival of the state is directly and commensurately threatened by the pandemic intrusion. Public emergency by itself is an evil and its necessity should not be based upon hasty judgement and mere alarmism.

In another context, some of the above mentioned framework of rights apparently constitute the emerging set of *Jus Cogens*, from which derogation is not permissible. In spirit, they carry the weight of *Jus Cogens* in an otherwise shifted context.

National laws relating to health care, confidentiality, privacy, information, media, food and drug, blood and blood products, personal-customary norms, right of child and woman, immigration-emigration-extradition, refoulement, scientific-pharmaceutical experiments, membrane engineering, gene-splicing, genetic-engineering, clinical trial of AIDS-HIV vaccines, bio-medical-legal profession and health workers, among others, should be reviewed by national committees, preferably under the supervision of UN-WHO-WHA monitoring committees or special rapporteurs.

It deserves mention that in 1991 Professor Max Essex, Harvard AIDS Institute, Boston lambasted, President Bush of the USA for the latter's discrimination against the entry of HIV infected persons on the soil of the USA. Opinion-leaders, the NGOs the world over can emulate Prof. Essex in their respective territories. National sovereignty concepts should not undermine global AIDS strategy law. Ethical considerations may be integrated with the parameters of global AIDS law and the national laws.

Principle

Certain constraints would arise in the formulation of global AIDS law, as similar constraints did arise in the scope of International law. However, these constraints assume lesser importance in the trade laws and the implementation of the free trade rules, postulated by the World Trade Organisation or, its early version — the GATT. Global AIDS law bears with itself, significant weight which will be honoured by the comity of nations. Alarmism and immediate expediency have induced national legislators to adopt hurried measures.

Discriminatory country-specific laws could have been enacted in order to contain the pandemic. Qurantine, segregation, compulsory HIV - testing, blocking inter-state migration, or immigration, denial of jobs, education and marriage characterise the matrices of national laws; but the long term implications do not justify these alarmist measures. The principles of law, justice and morality have been fairly established in the comity of nations; any eventual disregard of these humanising norms would be contradicted as countervailing the 'Rule of Law'.

Global AIDS law would re-affirm and incorporate the principles of equality, equal protection under the law, non-discrimination, consent, entitlements and restrictive application of public welfare measures.

Entitlement of the vulnerable groups in the society needs careful notice of the national governments. Women's rights including gender justice, reproductive health and reproductive right, among others have been considered by and re-affirmed in world conferences starting from Cairo population conference 1994 to UN Women's conference held in 1995 in Beijing. In a situation of HIV-AIDS pandemic and the consequences thereof, women are far more disadvantaged than men in the same situation, because of the millennia-old gender prejudices.

Increased HIV-AIDS infection in women is connected with women's reproductive health and reproductive rights. Some of the obscurantist socio-cultural systems continue the pernicious genital mutilation of women and they are exposed more to vulnerability from all infections, HIV being included. Physical safety of even the educated women are endangered because of her partner's male-chauvinistic sexual behaviour and normally, women's health status is insubordinated within the same family.

AIDS-infected woman[41] may be deprived of medical help, subjected to rejection by family and friends, cursed as 'impious' in some of the fundamentalist, oriental societies which have been treating women as chattel even today and coerce her to leave her home, young ones and children. The practice of compulsory HIV - testing[42] of pregnant women which interferes in the reproductive rights of women are found in many countries.

As mandatory testing of any individual for possible HIV-infection may be considered as interference with his right to privacy, voluntary testing, encouraged by awareness, education; and informed consent, protected sufficiently with maintaining confidentiality of the test, has been preferred to.

Litigations about HIV testing are liberally found common in the USA, although they may not be common in the developing world. A young woman Kimberly Bergalis contacted AIDS via the oral surgery in 1991 from her dentist David Acer. House Committee on Health[43] in USA, heard the parties and stated that doctors and health-care workers should be subjected to HIV-testing. As per the CDC guidelines, health-care workers with HIV positive status should be prevented from undertaking 'exposure prone procedures'. By following common law in the USA, HIV-mandatory testing is not a new practice; but judicial scrutiny[44] may not necessarily approve of mandatory HIV-testing. Leading medical associations endorse that mandatory HIV-testing is unnecessary and unwarranted.

Another principle supports that the HIV-test should not be leaked out to a third person without the consent of the tested person. In rare and exception cases only, the medical confidence maybe breached under prescribed guidelines of law. Making HIV-AIDS a notified disease may not be considered as intrusion into privacy of citizens.

Notwithstanding country-specific laws, which call for review, compulsory blood test, quarantine or compulsory detention in a colony constitute transgression upon liberty and security of the individual.. Subject to exceptional public health grounds and periodic scrutiny of independent judicial tribunal, detention of a known patient in case of emergency or, of a HIV-infected person who wilfully makes attempt to infect others are justified. Wilful infection or spreading of the disease should be attributed with penal liability. As reported by Father Michael Kennedy[45], an AIDS-infected lady in Ireland deliberately slept with as many as 80 males for spreading her AIDS-infection to other people. The vulnerability of the induced kind has to be taken into in drafting laws.

Expulsion of persons or, curtailment of freedom of movement of HIV-infected persons in blatant violation of the standard as prescribed provided by the relevant international and human rights instruments is unjustified. On the whole, the above principles, which have been derived from firmly established norms of Rule of Law and civilised jurisprudence could be reflected in the global AIDS law and the national laws.

When national human rights institutions are set up in conformity with the mandate of the UN instruments and conventions, national institutions[46],these may be mandated so as to assist in 'reviewing existing or proposed legislation'. The new legislation has to incorporate international human rights standard into the domestic municipal laws. There are corresponding obligations and duties with the concerned enforcement governmental or professional bodies. The global opinion on the need for achieving the north-south interdependence in all fields of life would be equally applicable within the province of global AIDS law as well.

As a result of the consensus, the developed north has obligation to transfer their high-technology, scientific know-how about eliminating HIV-AIDS along with other resources to the developing south, which has been hard-hit by the retrovirus and terrorism. The West admits that they have the advanced-laboratories. Only advance laboratory research[47] will conquer HIV-AIDS and intractable infections.

Enforcement

It is obvious that narrow nation-specific, isolationist approach to the HIV-AIDS infection would not be a match for the pandemic. The global AIDS law and strategy could be materialised by working out viable and essential conditionalities that ought to prove the global solidarity and interdependence. Broad consensus has to be judiciously cultivated in order to facilitate the enforcement of the AIDS law.

Firstly, the clear evidence of global coalition lies in the idea of sharing, empathy and mutual vulnerability. The state-of-the-art Western know-how in the field of medical science, membrane and genetic engineering, microbiology, epidemiology and vaccine manufacturing should be extended to the developing world, which also make their own efforts to cope with the infection. The strategy, policy measures and joint ventures have to be worked out at the global level, while keeping working space for regional measures as well.

As the resource crunch has disabled the developing countries to move forward in fighting out the pandemic, the developed west and USA or, G-8 countries should ensure that at least 1% of their annual GDP be utilised for the benefit of the developing countries. The principle has already been given acceptance in the creation of GEF after the Rio summit in 1992. The retrovirus onslaught is focused on mankind and not against one community only.

The above collaboration could be achieved in the field of preventing and curing the HIV-AIDS infection. Dr. John Salks who developed polio - vaccine while working for AIDS vaccine[48] states, "We want desperately now to move forward." Vaccine trials are taking place in advanced laboratories. FDA of the USA has approved large scale trial of vaccine on 5,000 volunteers. The various subtypes and strains of the retrovirus render the preparation of a single universal vaccine for the HIV-AIDS to be chauvinistic. By taking up some evidence and examples in the above context, it is noted that HIV-I subtypes are prevalent in India[49], but subtype B is prevalent in the state of Manipur and subtype C in Maharashtra state. While the current vaccine efforts are concentrated on a single subtype B, vaccine prototypes have to be based upon the subtypes prevalent in developing countries.[50] Pallava Bagla[51] writes, that with the establishment of NARI - 'National AIDS Research Institute' in Pune in collaboration with John Hopkins University, Maryland, India is making efforts to develop AIDS vaccine and evolve preventive strategies too. Admittedly, the thrust on the AIDS vaccine research has been given only to the 'Western strains of the virus'[52] by the eminent researchers and scientists elsewhere. Science has been localised.

Max Essex[53], chairman of Harvard AIDS Institute writes in his piece - 'The Hunt for an AIDS Vaccine', "My own estimate is that, if the public and private sectors cooperate, they can bring such vaccines to market within three to five years." Given a grace of another decade, the HIV-AIDS pandemic is likely to be won. Western vaccine manufacturers[54] and researchers have global responsibility towards manufacturing vaccines for all subtypes of HIV for the simple reason that HIV-AIDS retrovirus is not as much chauvinistic as some the Western manufacturers and traders are. However, at present, there is no two opinions about the incurability of the HIV-AIDS pandemic.

Concerted global AIDS law and strategy, as discussed above, remains the imperative need of all people and states, who are equally vulnerable to the fatal invasion of the HIV-AIDS retrovirus on Man. The 12 International Guidelines issued by the UN[55] in 1998 may form the basis of national and international HIV/AIDS legislation and legal enforcement. The government of India has adopted paradigm-shift in meeting the menace.[56]

References

1. Nirmala Ganpathy, 'By 2050, fewer will die by 50, but AIDS, cancer, TB will kill more', The Asian Age, 11 May, 1998. BBC service. London, 13-14 September, 1998 broadcasts that 1% of Indians has contacted AIDS.

1a. UN, Report of an International Commission on AIDS and Human Rights, Geneva 26-28 July 1989, NY, 1991. The background document is widely used in this chapter.

2. UN, UN Action in the field of Human Right, NY, 1994, p.246.

3. HIV zooms particularly on CD 4 cells at the first pre-emptive strike. Simian, bovine, and feline immunodeficiency viruses, as found in the animals have apparently not caused disease to them See TOI (Times of India), 6.9.1995.

4. See UN, Human Rights Compilation of International Instruments, NY,1983.

5. Frank Nouchi, For an AIDS Vaccine, in FL (Frontline), 2.8.91, p.89. Jaya Shreedhar states that HIV-I and HIV-2 emanated from African sub-human primates in the last 50 to 100 years, FL, 8.9.95, p.94. CDC — Centre for Disease Control in USA gave the present definition of AIDS based on three parameters. For the general interest, the *modus operandi* of the HIV invasion in man is given as :

   Human immune system has cells - phagocytes, T-cells and B-cells. HIV attacks T-cells on CD 4 receptor of helper T-cells by locking with HIV surface protein molecule - gp 120. The HIV peels off the coat, reverses its RNA into DNA with the help of enzyme called Reverse Transcripts. Viral DNA becomes part of the host DNA (of the would-be-infected individual) and by budding releases multiplied mature HIV particles which on their turn shall finish off the host DNA. As the immune system collapses due to the HIV sabotage from within, the patient would be infected by opportunistic diseases and he will succumb to death.
6. It was circulated in 1987 that the CIA had used AIDS as biological weapon released from Maryland, but the Soviet scientists denounced the motivated propaganda. See Toffler, Powershift, 1991, p.269.
7. Paul Kennedy, Preparing for the Twentyfirst Century, 1993, p.28.
8. Statesman, 13.9.1995, p.7
9. Saturday Statesman, 2.9.1995.
10. North East Observer, 18.7.1995.
11. NACO data, 31 May, 1995, in FL, 8.9.1995, p.91.
12. Span, AIDS, December 1994.
13. D.D. Rishi, Drugs. The Noose tightens, ND, 1995, p.48. With a record 15.94% HIV positive cases, Manipur leads the AIDS infection in India.
14. Newsweek, 22.81994, p.42.
15. Jaya Shredhar, AIDS, Apocalypse Now, FL, 20.12.1991, p.117. See also The AIDS Alarm, FL., 31.8.1990, p.33.
16. Jaya Shredhar, AIDS Beyond the Medicine, FL, 23.9.1994, p.57.
17. Reportedly, Delhi University biochemists have developed 10-sec. AIDS blood test to detect antibodies to HIV, Sentinel, 15.9.1995: In secret vaccine trial, HIV-infected people has been used as guinea pigs — TOI, 6.9.1995.
18. Hindustan Times, ND, 16.3.1995, p.10.(HT)
19. Gazette of India, part II, 18th August, 1989.

20. HT, 23.8.1995, p.18.
21. HT, 13.8.1995, p.17.
22. NE Observer, 18.9.1995.
23. National Family Health Survey, Population Research Centre, Gauhati University, IIPS, Bombay, June 1995, p.190.
24. Ibid. p.191. In Assam state, only 8% of ever married women age group 13-49 heard about AIDS and the knowledge among women age 13-24 is just 5% (very very low). In the North eastern region of India, Assam is the top most industrialised state.
25. HT, 15.9.1995, p.9.
26. UN, Human Rights Fact sheet 13, International Humanitarian law and Human Rights, July 1992.
27. UN Consultation, *supra*. fn. I, p.15.
28. Ibid. p.2.
29. Ibid. p. 13-15.
30. Ibid. p.15.
31. UN, Manual on Human Rights Reporting, UN, 1991; See also UN, Workshop on International Human Rights Instruments and Reporting Obligations, Report 26-30 August 1991, Moscow.
32. United Nations Action in the Field of Human Rights, NY, 1994, p.246.
33. UN, Yearbook of Human Rights for 1998, NY, 1992, pp.32
33a. UN Action, 1994, op. cit.p.246.
UNDP Guiding principles are, among others : para 3. Policies relating to HIV/AIDS must encompass and be accepted by all sectors in a society. Those affected by the pandemic should be involved in the policy dialogue — para.5. Collaboration and coordination among all participants is essential for an effective national response:- para 7. The power imbalances in interpersonal relationships and in society, which create women's subordination must change — FL, 20.5.1994, p.79
35. Ibid.
36. All India Institute of Medical Sciences, ND, found 5% of blood donors infected with Hepatitis C - HT, 4.9.1995, p.10.
37. Id.
38. UN, Human Rights Fact Sheet No. 22, Discrimination Against Women, Geneva, 1994.
39. UN. Human Rights Fact Sheet No. 10, Right of the Child, 1990.
40. See Background Document, annex III., in UN Geneva Consultation, op. cit. See f.n. 332 *supra*: One of the 12

International Guidelines issued states - " States should review and reform public health legislation to ensure that they adequately address the public health issues raised by HIV/AIDS, that their provisions applicable to casually transmitted diseases are not inappropriately applied to HIV/AIDS, and that they are consistent with international human rights obligations." (p.12). India's public health laws call for review.

41. Sofia Gruskin, 'Negotiating the Relationship of HIV/AIDS to Reproductive Health and Reproductive Rights', in American University Law Review, April, 1995, p. 1196.
42. Ibid. p. 1197.
43. Mark D. Johnson, ' HIV testing of Health Care Workers. Conflict between the Common Law and the Centre for Disease Control', in American University Law Review, Vol. 2, 1993, p. 479.
44. ibid. p. 501.
45. Telegraph, 15.9. 1995, Calcutta, p. 4.
46. Centre for Human Rights, UN, Professional Training series No. 4 National Human Rights Institutions, NY, 1995.
47. D.J. Weatherall, FRS, 'The New Genetics and Clinical Practice', in Ranbaxy Science Foundation, Molecular Genetics and Gene Theraphy, 1995, p. 3.
48. Time weekly, Feb. 4,1995, p. 48.
49. FL,8.9.1995, p. 92.
50. Ibid. p. 93.
51. Span, December, op. cit. p. 11.
52. FL, 2.8.1991, p. 91.
53. Span, December 1994, p. 7. A note on vaccines-current status: Vaccines would prevent the HIV from bonding to the host cell. Two surface molecules of glycoproteins which cover surface of virus i.e. gp. 120 and gp. 41 (together gp.160) do the binding process. Antibodies, which are released from the body are designed to block gp. 120 molecule. As Max Essex writes, Tu-Hou-Lee, Harvard Professor of Virology mapped and located all the sugar positions on gp. 120. Another approach is the use of the technique of genetic engineering to delete the areas of gp. 120 molecule that induce useless antibodies. As of now, multiple vaccines may be required.

    Professor William HaseLine, Danafarber Cancer Institute, Boston has identified structural genes in HIV viz., gag, pol, env, tat and five other regulating genes. The opportunity of vaccine trials in advanced laboratories raise some hope among the HIV-AIDS infected people and the rest of the society.

WHO has given green signal in phase III recently to a committee to adopt human trials of vaccines on a big scale in developing. countries. The discriminatory signal is that without consent, such trials could not be done in developed countries. Global AIDS law disfavour discrimination at any level.

54. HT,6.9.1995 reports that when Interleukin-2 was administered to HIV positive peoples, the number of CD 4 cells increased by 50% in 12 months.

Professor Daniel Zagury of Curie Institute, Paris tries vaccines on the basis of his research on gp. 160 recombination virus.

It is reported that current HBV vaccine is 85 to 97% effective (AULR, 1993 op. cit.). Reportedly, BIV vaccine is one of 42 candidate vaccines in the USA, proposed for human trials. India is also making efforts to manufacture vaccines.

55. See *supra* f.n. 33a: The 12 guidelines cover national framework, supporting community partnership, Public Health Legislation, Criminal Laws, Anti- discrimination and Protective Laws, Regulation of Goods, Services and Information, Legal Support Services, Women, Children, Vulnerable Groups, Education, Training and Media, Development of Public and Private sector standards, State Monitoring and Enforcement of Human Rights and International cooperation.

56. The union cabinet has decided to adopt effective steps — The Hindu, 1 September, 1999, p.11.

The steps are — decentralisation from NACO to state government, control of STD, reduction of blood-born transmission of HIV to less than 1 %, targeted intervention through NGOs, protection of right to privacy and employment of patients, notification of sexual partners. Mandatory testing would be discouraged strictly.

8

Indigenous Peoples' Rights

Emerging paradigm

The indigenous peoples' perception of half a century of Indian independence would not be as optimistic as the government would make it out to be ; and their consciousness would not be matching with either the dogmatic class-definition or, the hierarchical value-system of the outworn classical social structuration. Their perception cannot be fully explained by stereotype political, economic or, cultural categories, as prescribed by ideological regimes. However, the middle-class-dominated (in Verma's idiom, criminalised politician's regime) Indian state gives recognition to their aboriginal existentialist entity. The HDR (Human Development Report) 1999 places India's place in the Human Development Index as the 134th country in order of human development. HDR evaluation is multi-parametric and holistic, besides having an ethical rationale. HPI (poverty index) of India is fairly high.

The indigenous peoples are direct source of our primary knowledge experience and they bear the testimony of what development really meant to them. The government of India, specially, the clever bureaucracy and leadership could be said to have perfected the art of regimented, totalitarian administration in a style, not much different from what the white colonial regime had offered, in the guise of formal democracy and highly capital-controlled media-regime—the best representative of official democracy and functional totalitarianism. A small point would substantiate the drama.

The government of India pontificates the World Bank that India has substantial indigenous peoples, who need close attention of the Bank. On the contrary, the same establishment in its conscientious duplicity would deny and negate itself before the United Nations Working Group of Indigenous Peoples in 1995 and recent times by stating that there are no indigenous peoples exclusively in India, who deserve the charter of Indigenous People's Rights, as enunciated in the 'United Nations Draft Declaration on the Right of the Indigenous Peoples'. The draft has been endorsed by ECOSOC by resolution 1995/32 of 25th July, 1995. The faithful media, academic and opinion-leaders replay the official doublespeak, lest the totalitarian regime under the garb of liberal democracy should have been politically swayed over by principles of equality, justice and radical humanism.

The ideological state is not going to whither away, albeit the rise of post-nations and market-driven conglomerates that transcend boundaries. Macro-states or, micro-states are emerging out of historic compulsions and the empire-states like India cannot justify their very existence without undergoing metabolic changes because of the problems of management. The criteria of critical management is decisive and determinative. The indigenous peoples, long forgotten to be reckoned with in the midst of well-articulated, drama of the powerful, the affluent and the engineers of the world-orders, regional paradigms and the powerful THOUGHT POLICE in every dispensation, could resurface in the contemporary cognitive scheme of the human family, the UN and the power-elite. Questions may arise if the indigenous peoples are candidates for alternative or, rival nationhood to the existing European model state-paradigm. There is no easy answer yet emerging except that they are recognised entities in the present day scheme of things. Indigenous people's state is very rare in India. The North-Eastern states as a cultural-geographical entity is invariably an indigenous people's ancestral domain. Their collective fear-psychosis is fairly articulated by the phenomenological-existential questions posed in their reflective collective psyche on the one hand and also by the challenge - threat perception to their self-preservation on the other hand. The

UN sponsored trans-national agenda admittedly embodies the issue into the universal discourse. Indigenous peoples are evenly distributed in the rest of India.

The political, cultural, economic, sociological and legal languages, as understood in the dominant ideological, political linguistics, do not fully match with the language, they want to elaborately communicate with the outside world. The languages are different and the failure of the language does not lead to failure of mind nor that of the existential sensibilities. Half a century of Indian independence, while being a fair and eloquent demonstration of political linguistics of contemporary dominance, hegemony, sectarian meritocracy and elitism, presents more or less a stony piece of silence and monologue at the best to the indigenous sensibilities. Even in the language of a modern state-structure, 'Tripura', as a representative miniature model of the other North-Eastern states, has long ceased to be Tripuri ancestral domain except leaving the imperishable ethnic memories which are nightmarish and haunting the Tripuri indigenous mind. The survival of the indigenous people elsewhere is at stake.

The Indian mainstream 'Esperanto' and linguistics cannot be further mellowed down, as the linguistics of conquest and dominance scar away any semblance of audibility among the indigenous. The mainstream linguistics not only occasionally gives wrong signals but also triggers and sensitize internecine, inter-ethnic bloody strifes. The 'hawkish — the ruling class, who anticipates Pavlovian reflex after showing the occasional gift packages are too self-fulfilling with self-indulgent complacency. The Babel is merely self-assuring. The colonial governance is considered to be the master of the ceremony in either hanging all the indigenous peoples jointly or, hanging them separately. The imperialistic, diplomatic nitty-gritty and nuances of the erstwhile ox-bridge or, their surrogate masters of the hanging ceremony would neither loosen the noose nor delay the patriotic task of pulling the rope. The common destiny of the aborigines had been already written in page number one of the chapter - 'Tripura' and once the fly page is opened, the other pages would follow in quick succession. The wise call it 'Domino effect' and the lesser, a dwindling house of cards for the aborigines — the vanquishing people in India.

The power-elite, their most powerful instrument — the totalitarian-sectarian media and 'thought-police' are yet to accept UN Special rapporteur Martinez Cobo's working definition of the UN-protected indigenous people(s). The excerpt : "Indigenous communities, peoples and nations are those which having historical continuity with pre-invasion and pre-colonial societies that developed on their territories, consider themselves distinct from other sectors of the societies now prevailing in those territories, or parts of them. They form at present now-dominant sectors of society and are determined to preserve, develop and transmit to future generations their ancestral territories, and their ethnic identity, as the basis of their continued existence as peoples, in accordance with their own cultural patterns, social institutions and legal systems". The indigenous peoples constitute a separate category in the universal nationality — discourse, which need not essentially coincide with the conventional category of states.

The United Nations discourse is reflected by the UN Draft Declaration on indigenous peoples,1995, which is in the wait for approval by the General Assembly. They constitute a nation, a community in their ancestral domain on their own terms and choice, and they are emerging *'subjects of International law'* in the UN discourse. The existing political, ideological, linguistic structures and universal grammar have to belatedly learn from a scratch, the indigenous people's political linguistics, lest the habitate without inhabitants would be as incomplete as anybody can ever think of independence that sans the independence of the native bears no contextual meaning and purport. The native is waiting for a twig on the brink just to hold on.

Background

The United Nations and the member states of the UN have celebrated the year 1993 as the year of the Indigenous Peoples of the world. The United Nations General Assembly made efforts to make a Declaration on the Indigenous Peoples and possibly a Convention on the same subject. An estimated 300 million Indigenous Peoples (IP) who settle in more than 70 countries have remained the most neglected and most vulnerable group, who have not received justice from the international community and the member states.[1]

The Indigenous Peoples of the world have demanded justice from the international community as regards their land, self-government and self-development, resources, environment, culture, language, education, health, social and economic conditions, among others. In order to awaken the international obligations, the theme- "Indigenous Peoples - a New Partnership" has been community to their international selected for promotion of global consciousness of the legitimate aspirations of the Indigenous Peoples (hereafter IP).[2]

The government of India has found itself unable or inexpedient otherwise to define and identify who the IP are in the demographic mapping in the republic. The World Bank on its own, however, classified in 1991 the scheduled tribes as IP of India.[3] Dr. B.R.Ambedkar, the architect of the Constitution of India, in his writings and political statements, had all along cited the Dalits — renamed as Backward Classes or Scheduled Castes, as the IP of ancient India. It may be fairly said that many of the under-privileged communities or vulnerable ethnic groups in India constitute the IP in India, considering the historical facts of both external and internal colonisation of the vulnerable groups in the past. The margin of error will be minimal in the value judgement, as the IP had not been fitted into the higher echelon of the hierarchical society of India. The hierarchical militancy and social terrorisation is a social fact even today, which fact occasionally leads to counter-terrorisation from the vulnerable groups. They react with the most modest means at their command.

The IP in the international community constitute the descendants of conquered peoples, tribal population and analogous ethnic formations, certain categories of national minorities, historically distinct categories, and scheduled tribes, among others.[4] The North-Eastern states of India for historical reasons, happen to be the pristine homeland of the IP till the union government of India dramatically overturned the demographic picture of these states for her political reasons, by inviting millions of aliens from across the border and thereby threatening the political, social-economic and cultural status of the IP. The over-all accountability of the present state of affairs happily lies with government of India.

Although the *Adivasis, Dalits* — the IP of India are scattered, the IP of North Eastern region remains in compact states since time immemorial. The history of the region clearly suggests the reality of IP status of the people. In retrospect, the present and pre-fragmented Assam had been annexed to British India in 1826 A.D. The states of Manipur and Tripura had been annexed to the new Indian dispensation and republic on October 15, 1949, two years after Indian independence following the territorial expansion at the time of the passage of Indian Independence Act 1947. The rest of the North-Eastern states have emerged out of Assam.

Several legal and political problems in the NE states have been one way or other interwoven with issues relating to the native IP vis-a-vis massive refugees and illegal migrants, several millions of whom have been settled by the union government of India in the small states leading to eventual economic backwardness which has further worsened, as the IP was made out to be artificial minorities in relation to the colossal influx which constitute the majority in the democratic decision-making process.[5] Had the government of India redistributed the influx population in all the states of India in proportion to their intake capacity, territorial size and resource pool, the IP in the NE states should not have remained as political minorities incapable of deciding their own political destiny. The colossal multimillion influx, lacks constitutional legitimacy. It is in this context faithfully reported that the union government of India is directly accountable for the ETHNOCIDE and MINORITIZATION of the ethnic IP in their own ancient homelands. The government of India is, therefore, unable to define the

Indigenous People (IP) at least in the context of the NE states, whereas the World Bank had already done it in 1991.

Status of the IP

The working group, constituted by the UN Economic and Social Council, the organ of the UN Sub-Commission on Prevention of Discrimination and Protection of Minorities had reviewed national developments and considered the need for developing international standard concerning rights of IP.[6] The working group prepared a draft Declaration on the rights of the IP for proclamation by the UN General Assembly. The draft includes, among others, preservation and development of ethnic and cultural characteristics and distinct identies, protection against genocide and ethnocide, self-government and autonomy in their own internal and local affairs, the honouring of treaties and agreements concluded with the indigenous peoples, ownership and possession of indigenous lands and resources; participation in political and economic life, rights relating to religion, language and culture, so and so forth.[7]

The IP have to take frequent recourse to the '1503' procedure, established by the Economic and Social Council to look into gross and consistent violations of the human rights of the IP and procedure established under the Optional Protocol. The ILO had adopted Convention No. 107 and Recommendation No. 104 for the protection of the IP, yet certain flaws had been pointed out in these ILO procedures[8] as well.

The Geneva Seminar (16-20 January, 1989)[9] on 'The effects of racism and racial discrimination on the social and economic relations between indigenous peoples and States' had deliberated upon the *de jure* and *de facto* racism, racial discrimination, conflict between individual and collective approaches to the indigenous rights, state obligations to the IP, accountability and compensation for past violations of the indigenous rights, informed consent, emergence of 'peoples' as international legal personalities, the invalidity of *terra nullius* and conquest of indigenous lands need for national ombudsman for the IP, need for revision of ILO Convention No. 107. It has concluded that colonial laws and concepts are illegitimate, theory of territorial acquisition of indigenous lands unless redressed had been wrong, states should negotiate with IP and that IP's collective rights as well as right to self-determination should be honoured.[10]

Among several rights of the IP elaborately cited in the 'Study of the Problem of Discrimination against Indigenous Population' by UN special rapporteur Jose R. Matinez Cobo, the political rights of the IP appear to be relatively high in the priority list, although all the other rights are equally significant and important. Some of the important ones are reproduced below:[11]

***Para* 265**

It is beginning to be acknowledged that indigenous peoples have their own national identity based on historical realities that transcend mere solidarity vis-a-vis discrimination and exploitation.

***Para* 266**

Respect for the forms of autonomy called for by the indigenous people is the necessary condition for guaranteeing and ensuring these rights.

***Para* 270**

Broadly speaking, indigenous peoples have the right to self-determination which will enable them to continue to exist in dignity, in keeping with their historic right as free peoples.

***Para* 277**

In the widest sense of its " external" connotations of this right means the right to constitute a State and includes the right to choose various forms of association with other political communities.

The right to self-determination for all historical nationalities and peoples is a universally recognised right.[12] The member states of the United Nations who had signed, acceded and ratified the two major Covenants of 1966 are under Charter and international obligation to honour the 'right to self-determination of peoples'. Peoples are either nations, nation states or states.[13] The exercise of this right by the peoples in the North Eastern states is a concern of the current international legal and constitutional studies.[14]

Another major right of the IP, which deserves immediate attention of all policy-makers is the 'Right to Development' of the IP,[15] besides the green rights, cultural, socio-economic and linguistic rights and rights to original lands, occupied by non-IP. The draft Declaration[16] of the Rights of the Indigenous People have been discussed by the Working group of CHR. Of the 45 articles, two have been adopted. Article 3 of the Draft provides, "Indigenous peoples have the right of self-determination. By virtue of that right they freely determine their political status and freely pursue their economic, social and cultural development."

While the states argued in favour of restricting self-determination right in colonial context only and for recognising 'internal self-determination', the representatives of the indigenous peoples argued for 'true self-determination' including the right to secede. It was Finland which proposed to insert 'internal' before 'self-determination'. The Draft could be successfully hammered out and approved in the near future by the international community.

The existing UN dispensation should have entrusted the colossal refugee problems in the NE states to the province of the UNHCR, who could have taken recourse to the voluntary repatriation of the millions of refugees to their countries of origin. The states or, the countries of origin of the massive alien refugees also are under international obligations to receive the refugees, who are their own legitimate nationals and citizens. The survival of the IP in the NE states and rest of India is at stake because of the apathetic attitude of the union government of India to the ethnic IP and the loss of the historical identity of the IP at the hands of other jurisdictions.

The union government of India, the United Nations and the appropriate international agencies of the UN have to take timely cognisance of the inalienable, historical rights of the Indigenous Peoples in India; and the IP should be allowed to exercise their rights, which had been widely or universally recognised by the contemporary International law and human rights jurisdictions. The union government of India has its responsibility in this jurisdiction, as it has accepted state responsibility, the obligations under the UN and other international obligations towards the maintenance of 'peace' and 'security' in the 'New World Order'. The laws and Constitution of India should make the IPs rights more explicit and legitimate. A permanent Forum for the IP in the UN is on the anvil.

References

1. Shiladitya Dev, UN double-talk on the status of the Indigenous Peoples, Link weekly, Sept. 6, 1992. p.37.
2. Ibid. p.38-39.
3. UN News Letter, New Delhi, August 8,1992.
4. ibid. cf. commission on Human Rights, UN Discrimination against Indigenous Peoples, 31 July, 1995, 15 August, 1996, Human Rights of Indigenous Peoples, E/CN.4/Sub.2/1997/17, 20 June, 1997.
5. Naorem Sanajaoba, Socio-Legal Problems and Developing Society, Deep & Deep, New Delhi, 1986, p.81
6. UN Fact sheet 9, The Rights of the Indigenous Peoples, 1990, p.7 Study Series 10, Protection of the Heritage of Indigenous People, UN, 1997.
7. ibid p.8.
8. ibid. p.14-15.
9 See Annex UN Human Rights, Geneva Report, 1989.
10. op.cit. p.8
11. Jose R. Martinez Cobo, Study of the Problem of Discrimination against Indigenous Population Volume V. Conclusions, Proposals and Recommendations, p.20-21. See Alfonso Martines, Study on Treaties, 1999; Erica — Irene A Daes, Standard - Setting, 1996

12. Aureliu Cristescu, Special Rapporteur, The Right to Self Determination-Historical and Current Development on the Basis of the United Nations Instruments, UN, 1981. See also CHR, UN, E/CN.4/1997/102, 10 December, 1996 for self-determination of IP.
13. op. cit. p.39-41.
14. Naorem Sanajaoba, Right to Self-Determination, Principles and Practices, seminar paper of Regional Seminar on Human Rights, May 1992, Gauhati University. For constructive criticism of Alfonso Martinez, see CORE, Manipur, Submission, March, 1999.
15. UN Human Rights, The Realization of the Right to Development, Global Consultation on the Right to Development as a Human Right, UN, 1991, p.33
16. See also UN , United Nations Action in the field, Adrein-Claude Zoller ed., human rights monitor, No. 39-40, 1997, Geneva, p.23-24, No. 43, 1998, p. 9-11.
    See UN Economic and Social Council, CHR, 'Indegenous Issues', E/en.4/1997/102, 10 December 1998,n p.57-66, debate on self-determination.
17. ECOSOC has approved the Commission on Human Rights proposal for setting up the Forum — See UN, CHR, E/CN.4/1998/
18 7, Supplement no. 3, 1998, p. 20.

9

Humanitarian Laws of Early India

Human rights law has been legislated with the adoption of multilateral treaties and UN conventions. Diplomatic conferences have adopted Geneva conventions and protocols in order to codify the customary laws of war and consolidate the scattered conventions of the past. Sometimes these laws overlap.

International humanitarian law, as it is known as such following the outlawing of war by the Charter of the United Nations since 1945 and the eventual obsolescence of the laws of war, is a normative framework by which armed conflicts — international and non-international are humanely regulated. The four Geneva Conventions, 1949 and the two additional Protocols, 1977 provide the canvas in which, unlike the human rights structures and instruments, super-eminent, protectionist principles of life, property and security of the vulnerable sections as well as the non-combatants or *hors de combat* have been raised to the non-derogable norms comparable to the *Jus Cogens*. *Manusmriti* records that, in the past, *hors de combat* had been protected during war.

Hindu epics like *Mahabharata*, *Ramayana*, other writings and positivistic manuals like *Manusmriti* and *Arthashastra* provide for the proto-humanitarian laws or, the laws of armed conflict in early Bharata or, India. The Chinese like the Hindus had evolved manuals of war millennia before Christ. Despite occasional violations of the law, as it will be discussed hereafter, the laws had to be complied with.

We would appreciate further crystallisation of pacific movement on the one hand and application of the laws on the other hand. The historical perspective of India in the evolution of the humanitarian laws could be evaluated in the context of the humanitarian laws as accepted at present.

War or armed conflicts or hostilities have been a part of human life and save the transformation in forms and manifestations, they would remain so. Nobody could ever dream that the basic essence of man would shed off the conflict-gene. After the last world war, every reasonable soul on earth has been disgusted with the world war. But the reality is different. Futurologists like Toffler's states with remarkable authority: "In fact, in the 2,340 weeks that passed between 1945 and 1990, the earth enjoyed a grand total of only three weeks that were truly war free." (I:p.14). New forms of war are emerging (I:III). We do reaffirm Albert Einstein's speech: "We all know that power politics, sooner or later necessarily leads to war, and that war, under present circumstances, would mean a mass destruction of human beings and material goods—"(2:145). To Bertrand Russell, war represents the recrudescence of primitive human combativeness.(3:127). War is going to stay in one form or another.

Kautilya's *Arthashastra* dwells upon deeply into the foreign policy, International law, neutrality, diplomacy and war. The armed conflict i.e., war is entrenched in his foreign policy. Kautilya's six approaches to foreign policy are :Peace, War, Neutrality, Marching, Shelter and Dual policy. Instruments of diplomacy are-Conciliation, Gift, Dissension and Force. The four powers of a would -be- conqueror are: Bravery, Treasury, Army & Knowledge. In a changed era, Rajinder Puri would point out : "In his defence Godse (Nathuram who assassinated M.K. Gandhi) blamed Gandhi for approving army action in Kashmir which was violent." (4:57). No politician could refrain from the temptation of war.

The early human institutions were not found to be invariably barbaric without having any shade of compassion. Besides the religious motivation, altruistic thoughts had been evolved by Plato and Greek thinkers, among others. (6:199). Saint Augustine left an enduring legacy through his words: "Wars may be called just when they are waged to punish unjust acts." (5:45). The Hindus evolved the idea of just wars in their concept of *Dhramayudha*. In another ideological framework that of Marxian culture — Lenin and later on, Mao Dze Dong discriminated just wars from unjust wars. Holy wars also occur. The early forms of humanitarian laws in early Bharat had been considerably developed. Kautilya distinguished *Dharmayudha* from *Kutayudha* in his study of four forms of war.

Indian tradition had been found pluralistic in all aspects, yet the *herrrenvolk* or dominant culture emerged from early Hindu thoughts. The sources of early humanitarian laws of the *Bharatavarsha* are found in *Shrutis* (four Vedas — Rig, Yajur, Sama, Atharva), the *Smritis* viz., *Dharmasutras* left by Gautama, Baudhayana, Apastamba, Harita, Vishnu and *Dharmashastras*, *Manusmriti* containing 2,694 verses, the synthesized *Yajnavalkya Smriti*, Narad Smiriti, Puranas, 112 mystical *Upanishads* and the commentaries (7:334). Besides the Charvaka school and materialistic Indian tradition, early Bharatavarsha had evolved Buddhist and Jain traditions. Essentially, these two strong early Indian traditions opposed Brahmanical Vedic-orthodoxy (8:67), as they by and large, espoused the upgradation of the downtrodden, the warrior Kshatriyas, Vaishyas and Sudras (8:68). These two non-Vedic traditions not only espoused the absolutist forms of humanitarian laws of that time, but also went upto the extent of outlawing any loss of life under one pretext or other.

When Prithvi Raj Chauhan lost the war, Islamic tradition had also joined the prevailing streams of *Bharatiya* humanitarian laws for centuries; it had further been enriched by the Western characteristics of humanitarian laws. The latter could be better described in terms of Clausewitz and Machiavelli. War has become an extension of politics. Machiavelli as well as his predecessor Vishnugupta or, Kautilya had evolved the positivist doctrine of war. Humanitarian laws had been diluted by the rationale of exigency.

At present, the government of India is a signatory of the four Geneva Conventions only. The historical perspective, therefore, remains largely of academic importance; yet some of them may be usefully studied for the purpose of enriching and developing the contemporary humanitarian laws (see common article 3 of Geneva Conventions, *infra*.)

While re-examining the important themes of the historical perspective, the Indian plural tradition has to take note of the significant contributions of the Dravidans, the Aryans and the Mongolians (the Sinic race) in different stages of the evolution of plural India. (9:12). Suniti Kumar Chatterjee explains the pluralism that was, The classical law of India has been based upon *Dharma*, *Dharmasutra* (10:19) and *Dharmashastra* (10:73). The major sources of early *Bharatiya* humanitarian laws, as espoused within the vedic framework are *Manusmriti*, *Arthashastra*, *Agnipurana*, *Shantiparva* of *Mahabharata* and *Gita* episodes, among others. *Sukraniti* prevents the murder of child, youth, woman and a lonely person.

The Vedic and post-Vedic sources within their specific frameworks, developed the laws of war, different forms of war — both just and unjust — diplomacy, treaty-making, conquest, occupation, enemy-targets, attitude to incapacitated warriors, civilian subjects, property and land, among others. Although, *Matshanayay* (law of big fish eating the small ones) and Dansdaniti had been prevalent, Manu explained the laws of war :

"While fighting in a battle, he should not kill his enemies with weapons that are concealed, barbed, or smeared with poison or whose points blaze with fire (11:137)."

Similarly, the king could not kill one, who has climbed mound or is impotent or folds hands in supplication or one asleep or without armour or one who is engaged with some one else (11:38). The six tactics to be observed by the king viz., alliance, war, marching, camping, dichotomy, and seeking refuge were written by Manu. (11:145). Manu in his time (14 Manus existed) had evolved the elementary forms of contemporary concept of *horse de combat* (7:341). Chapter seven of *Manusmriti* dwelt upon laws of war and conduct of war in that age. Chapter XI of *Arthashastra* examines war; Kautilaya had separated law from religion.

Arthashastra of Kautilya elaborately dwells upon defence and war in part XI (12:675), foreign policy of the government in part X (12:541) and covert operations in part IX (12:498). The basic principles of Kautilya are : augmentation of resources by the king, elimination of the enemy, identification of friends, prudence, preference of peace to war and justified behaviour of the king. (12:546). Nearly one fourth of the comprehensive 5,391 sections of the *Arthashastra* manual is devoted to laws of war and diplomacy. The relevant chapters are the state, covert operations, foreign policy, defence and war. It includes secret services as well. Some major highlights are furnished as follows:

> A weak ruler has to quickly submit with an offer of peace (13:235). Kautilya's *'Mandala'* is a circle of twelve. It is for defence and expansion. Pledging their words, treaties had been honoured like *Pacta Sunt Servanda* (13:237). The wise ruler of Kautilya operated within a *'Mandala* of 12 which identified friends, foes and future alliance.'

In the Kautilyan version of Hindu wars, there had been four forms of wars: Diplomatic wars (*Mantrayudha*), just war (*Dharmayudha*), evil war (*Kutayudha*) and also covert war (Gudayudha). In the Hindu heritage of laws of war, the *Shantiparva* of *Mahabharata*, Kautilya, Manu and also Gautama, Baudhayana and Apastamba provided for the laws for the protection of the civilians, non-combatants and the injured combatants. Some of them had been considerably analogous to the norms of the Geneva Conventions, 1949 which the government has signed.

Open war i.e. *Sammukha yudha* was a form of the just *Dharamyudha*. In Manu's conduct of war, the weapons have to be carried in the open and poisonous weapons could not be used. Chapter XI of the *Arthasastra* is exclusively on the laws of Hindu war. The early Bharata was protected and defended by these norms of Kautilya. The

Chinese counterpart of Kautilya would be found in Sun Tzu of China before 2,400 years (see Samuel Griffith, Sun Tzu).

How the just war had degenerated to unjust war forms and led to violations could be understood from several examples. A particular scene has been significant and spectacular— the lord Krishna stood for unjustifiable violation of the law in a situation, where his alliy, the Pandavas were nearly doomed. We reproduce the *Karnabadha* (murder of Karna) from the *Mahabharata* (see Dutta, Mahabarata). Stuck up in the mud, Karna should not have been even touched by Krishna's friend Arjuna, but they struck Karna dead just to win the war. The dialogue follows:

> Karna : "O Partha (Arjuna), wait for a moment till I extricate my wheel" (stuck in the mud and he was not ready to fight).

> Karna said:" Brave and pious heroes never shoot their arrows at persons with dishevelled hairs, at those who fly away from the battlefield, at Brahmana (Brahmin caste), at him who clasps his hands, at him who surrenders, at him who prays for quarter, at one who throws off his weapon, at one whose arrows are all gone, at one whose weapon has fallen off or been broken."

Karna should not be touched at the time when he was not ready to shoot arrows at Krishna and Arjuna. The righteous of that time save the cowards was not ready to violate the law at that moment. Karna cited the law for all.

Arjuna took off his arrow *Anjalika*, which was fatal as the rod of Death. Thereupon, Krishna ordered to *Partha* (Arjuna):

> "Cut off with this arrow the head of your enemy before he gets upon his cart." Together they did it and won the war they were supposed not to win but for the *Kutayudha*.

Immunity was extended to the envoys (13:243). The king in the immediate proximity is the enemy (13:245). The confederation or, configuration of states need breaking through peace offer, money or by whichever means. (13:246), however, a broken ruler shall not be harassed. Open warfare is righteous, while other two forms of war like concealed and secret wars also were resorted to (13:250).

The soldiers of the enemy camp who had fallen or surrendered, or turned back were given protection. Kautilya recommends treacherous war at that time, when open warfare becomes inappropriate (13:253). This conduct is widely used by major powers in the twentieth century, yet it is in derogation of the accepted humanitarian laws. King Ashoka stood for the Law of Piety (24:203).

The conqueror of the war has the responsibility to honour the customs and rights of the subject people he has occupied in the war. The bilateral relations of the state varied on the basis of the identification of the status viz., *ari*(antagonist), *shatru*(enemy), *mitra*(ally), *ari-mitra*(ememy's ally), *mitra-mitra*(friend of the ally), *ari-mitra-mitra*(friend of enemy's ally), *parshnigraha*(enemy-in the -rear), *aakranda*(friend in the rear), *antardhi*(weak intervening king), *udhasina*(neutral king) and *madhyama*(middle king), among others (12:551-552). The variation in the conduct and laws of war had varied on the basis of these parameters. Some forms of protection of non-combatants and injured combatants had been substantiated by Gautama, Baudhayana and Apastamba etc., the verocity of which had been testified later on by Megasthenes and Hiuen Tsang. The concept of protection given to the POWs or , captured enemires had also been enunciated by the *Mahabharta*. Slavery was not recognised by the *Puranas* and Kautilya conceded the release of POWs (12:347). Kautilya stated for release of POWs, Manu and Kautilya stood for fair treatment of subjects found occupied territories.

The author, however, observes that the covert murders of Meghanath or, Karna, stuck up without arming for a fight, Bali the other monkey monarch, Aswathama, Jayadratha and several other deified heroes, might not be easily defended in the name of *Dharmayudha*, although Kautilya might retrospectively justify it under his complex manual of war. Notwithstanding the equivocal alarmist protests raised against war, the humanitarian laws have to coexist with the recurrent human phenomenon known as 'armed conflict' in the new language of the post-Geneva conventions. The International humanitarian law is also developing fertile areas on use of prohibited weapons (14:58), international responsibility of states (14:87) and the complex area of non-international armed conflicts.

It may be noted that treaty on International Criminal Court has been adopted on 17 July ,1998 at Rome and the court would become a reality.

The contemporary International humanitarian law is universally accepted (15:450). In the case of India, it has signed Geneva Conventions 1949 in 1950, the Hague Convention, 1954 in 1958 and Weapons Convention, 1980 in 1984. The government of India is yet to sign both the Geneva Protocols of 1977 along with the Declaration on the Protocol. The ICRC movement has to continue (16:447).

Preventive diplomacy, peacekeeping and peace-building draw the global attention (17:351). It appears that ICRC insists upon peace-enforcement, besides the peacekeeping, which is seen to be very costly and lackadeaisical. Lesser respect had been shown by the belligerents to the humanitarian laws during the cold war period. (18:215). Although the provisions of the common article 3 of the Geneva Conventions are non-derogable in nature, it would be absurd to assume that states have been literally enforcing the common article. Bosnia and Rwanda, just to cite one or two instances, demonstrate as to how far states reach out to violate the humanitarian provisions manifestly and blatantly. The very rationale of constituting the 'Yugoslav and Rwanda Tribunals' by the UN Security Council furnishes a clear testimony to the transgression of the Geneva Conventions (22:605).

The author has briefly discussed the pluralistic and stratified historical evolution of early humanitarian laws in early India. Notwithstanding blatant violations of laws of war and the Machiavellian justification of unjust wars as act of state, the ideal standard of Indian humanitarian laws had been identified with the conduct of war within the framework of *Dharamayudha*. Some of the significant norms of the *Sammukhayudha* and *Dharmayudha* are found to have been incorporated into the contemporary humanitarian laws.

Early Indian humanitarian laws are prelude to the creation of contemporary humanitarian laws, which are also in the process of development. In India like the UK, international laws have to be transformed into municipal laws. Customary international laws, state practices and peremptory norms like the *Jus Cogens* are invariably non-derogable under all circumstances as long as India is in the comity of nations, and the United Nations. The laws of war, that the early Indian ruling clique had adopted, contains a treasure of contemporary humanitarian norms.

References

1. Alvin and Heidi Toffler, War and Anti-War, 1994. See Samuel B. Griffith, Sun Tzu The Art of War, OUP, 1971, "Those skilled in war cultivate the *Tao* and preserve the laws..." p. 88.
2. Ideas and Opinions by Albert Einstien, 1979.
3. K.L.Julka, Political Ideas of Bertrand Russell, 1977.
4. Rajinder Puri, Rediscovery of India, 1989.
5. International Review of the Red Cross, No. 298, 1994.
6. International Review of the Red Cross, No. 299, 1994.
7. L.R. Penna, Armed Conflicts in ancient India, International Review of the Red Cross, August 1989.
8. Romila Thapar, A History of India Volume I, 1966.
9. Suniti Kumar Chatterji, Kirata-Jana-Krti, 1974.
10. Robert Lingat, Classical Law of India, with additions by D.Derrett, 1973.
11. The Laws of Manu, Penguin Classics, 1991.
12. Kautilaya, The Arthashastra, Penguin, 1992.
13. V.K.Gupta, Kautilyan Jurisprudence, 1987.
14. Hans-Peter Gasser, International Humanitarian Law, Haupt, 1993.
15. International Review of Red Cross, No. 302, October 1994.
16. International Review of Red Cross, No. 307, August 1995.

17. International Review of Red Cross, No. 306, June 1995.
18. International Review of Red Cross, No. 305, April 1995.
19. UN Instruments, Convenants and Literature relating to Humanitarian Laws.
20. See N. Sanajaoba, ed., Human Rights, Omsons, New Delhi, 1994. See his book, Right of the Oppressed Nations, Omsons, 1996.
21. N.Sanajaoba, Human Rights in the 21st century, in Jawahar L.Kaul, ed., Human Rights, Regency, 1995.
22. International Review of the Red Cross, No. 321, November December,1997 (see IRRC No. 322, March 1998 about International Criminal Court).
23. See recent developments in Dieter Fleck, The Handbook of Humanitarian Laws in Armed Conflict, OUP, 1995 and also M.K. Balachandran, Rose Varghese, ed., Introduction to International Humanitarian Law, Delhi, 1997. See Humanitarian Debate in IRRC, March, 1999 Volume 81.
24. G.I.A.D. Draper, The contribution of the Emperor Ashoka Maurya to the development of the humanitarian ideal in warfare, International Review of the Red cross, March-April, 1995

GENEVA CONVENTIONS

12 AUGUST, 1949 (FOUR) COMMON

ARTICLE 3

In the case of armed conflict not of an international character occurring in the territory of one of the High Contracting Parties, each Party to the conflict shall be bound to apply, as a minimum, the following provisions:

(I) Persons taking no active part in the hostilities, including members of armed forces who have laid down their arms and those placed *hors de combat* by sickness, wounds, detention, or any other cause, shall in all circumstances be treated humanely, without any adverse distinction founded on race, colour, religion or faith, sex, birth or wealth or any other similar criteria.

To this end, the following acts are and shall remain prohibited at any time and in any place whatsoever with respect to the above-mentioned persons:

(a) violence to life and person, in particular murder of all kinds, mutilation, cruel treatment and torture;

(b) taking of hostages;

(c) outrages upon personal dignity, in particular humiliating and degrading treatment;

(d) the passing of sentences and the carrying out of executions without previous judgement pronounced by a regularly constituted court, affording all the judicial guarantees which are recognized as indispensable by civilized peoples.

(2) The wounded and sick shall be collected and cared for.

An impartial humanitarian body, such as the International Committee of the Red Cross, may offer its services to the parties to the conflict.

The Parties to the conflict should further endeavour to bring into force, by means of special agreements, all or part of the other provisions of the present Convention.

The application of the preceding provisions shall not affect the legal status of the Parties to the conflict.

10

Humanitarian Laws in the Peripheral States

We have cited at the ratification of the four Geneva Conventions, 1949 by the union government of India and also at the long felt need for the same government which is yet not given signature to and ratify the two additional Protocols, 1977, that invariably constitute the part and parcel of the four Geneva Conventions.

Out of 185 members of the United Nations and 188 parties to the Geneva Conventions, as many as 148 states have ratified the Protocol I additional to the Geneva Conventions and 140 states have ratified the Protocol II. Considering the importance of India as a leader of the NAM and as a responsible regional power, actually, she should have been one of the first few states which signed the Protocols.

Admittedly, there is peripheral secessionism in the North-Eastern states and Jammu-Kashmir in the republic of India. Several organisations have been declared as unlawful secessionist bodies under the Unlawful Activities (Prevention) Act 1967. The security forces, which are deployed in disproportionately huge numbers for five decades are empowered under the Armed Forces (Special Powers) Act 1958 to shoot down anybody to death and destroy any property and immunity is apparently granted from prosecution to the forces. On 27 November 1997, the Supreme Court has upheld the above mentioned statute and laid down certain guidelines without stipulating a monitoring, supervisory mechanism. Other equally repressive laws including Punjab Security of State Act, 1953 National Security Act are also invoked by supplementing the Armed Forces Special Powers Act. Cases of massive violation of human rights are reportedly and un-reportedly piled up, whereas the National Human Rights Commission has the least jurisdiction over the excesses, committed by the security forces.

There is by all counts a perennial situation of armed conflict in the insurgent states (NES). It may be considered as non-international armed conflict as the government would label it or, as international armed conflict as the belligerents would like it to be classified as such. Humanitarian laws are, therefore, applicable in this situation.

The armed conflict which occurs due to historical, political and economic reasons. The insurgents claim that their states had remained independent of India before the series of annexations in the 19th and 20th centuries took place. The government upholds that they have been integrated and integration can not be reversed; hence, the belligerency and the colossal problems of human rights violations and ongoing victimisation of the civilian, unarmed population.

The Geneva laws and the Hague laws have been accepted as customary International law even before they were codified into the Geneva Conventions. The United Nations laws reinforce these laws of humanitarian nature. The ICJ in Nicragua vs. USA in 1986 further reaffirms their status as customary International law. The humanitarian laws become enforceable in varying degrees in armed conflicts in the insurgent states like the NES. The Hague laws had in the past stipulated some of these norms.

Under article 22 of Hague Regulations 1907, "The right of belligerents to adopt means of injuring the enemy is not unlimited". Article 6 of the Convention for the Amelioration of the Condition of the Wounded Armies in the field, 22 August ,1864 had provided long back —" Wounded and sick combatants to whatever nation they may belong shall be collected and cared for". Besides, *Martens clause* as found in Haque Convention no. IV, 1907 has been widely accepted as customary International law; it stipulates that

"Until a more complete code of the laws of war has been issued, the High Contracting parties deem it expedient to declare that in cases not included in Regulations adopted by them, the inhabitants and belligerents remain under the protection and rule of the principles of the law of nations, as they result from the usages established among the civilized people, from the laws of humanity, and dictates of public conscience."

Article 35 of Protocol I provides,"In any armed conflict, the right of the parties to the conflict to choose methods and means of warfare is not unlimited" These laws have been given sufficient notice by the United Nations and its agencies.

By resolution no. 237 of 1967, the UN Security Council stressed that all parties to the armed conflict should respect the human rights and the parties should fulfil all the obligations, they have accepted as per the four Geneva Conventions. Teheran Conference held in 1968 also upheld that the humanitarian laws be followed during the armed conflicts. By resolution no. 2444 (XXIII), the UN General Assembly laid down the principles that (i) the parties do not have unlimited means to injure the enemy, (ii) it is prohibited to launch attacks on the civilian population and (iii) civilian population should be spared by distinguishing them from the persons taking part in hostilities.

The General Assembly in a series of resolution adopted since 1970 took up similar stance and also affirmed that-participants in resistance movements and freedom fighters should, if arrested, be treated as prisoners of war. These norms have the essential bearing in the North Eastern region.

The union government for India being a party to the four Geneva Conventions is under obligation to abide by the established norms of International Humanitarian Law in the situation of armed conflict. The established principles of qualifying the military necessity which is not absolute, principles of proportionality, restriction, reciprocity, humaneness, limited rights of the belligerants, and principle of state liability for any breach of the Geneva Conventions are applicable. The principles are reinforced by the rules for the respect of *hors de combat*, surrenderees, protection of medical personnel, and captured insurgents or combatants, judicial guarantees, prohibition of any form of torture of combatants or insurgents, and restriction to legitimate military objectives, among others. The individual commanders bear the responsibility for strict compliance of these rules, lest the issue for the breach of Geneva Conventions should be raised.

In order to define unarmed civilians, the combatants are distinguished by the customary law. Further, article 43 (2) of

Protocol I defines thus — "Members of the armed forces of a Party to a conflict... are Combatants." The combatants have the privilege to participate directly in hostilities. (article 43).

The difference between human rights regime and regime of humanitarian laws is that the latter is *non-derogable* and is accepted as the peremptory norms of *Jus Cogens*, whereas the former is not elevated to that non-derogable status. Increasingly, the individuals are accepted as subjects of International law and international duty. Individual as a subject of International duties has been established in war crimes, Genocide, Crimes against humanity and Crime against peace, among others. (*See* UN, Status of Individual and Contemporary International Law, by Erica-Irene A. Daes, NY, 1992,p. 40-41)

Individual liability in the event of the breach of humanitarian laws has been established by the International military tribunal in 1946 and the principles of Nurenberg had been confirmed by the UN General Assembly on 11 December, 1946 by its resolution no. 95 (I). The individual responsibility for commission of crime against peace, war crimes and crimes against humanity as decided by the IMT on 8 August, 1948 is by now, a principle of the UN. Article 6 provides that the leaders are responsible for the commission of crimes and article 8 provides that *superior order is no defence* save that it mitigates the punishment. The subordinates had to obey only the lawful orders of the commanders. These principles are worthy of the attention of the armed forces in action.

Security council

The UN Security Council reserves its power to install *ad hoc* war crime tribunals under chapter VII of the UN Charter. It can do so whenever it feels it appropriate as in the cases of Yugoslavia and Rwanda. The NES could also be considered a focal theme like any other place in the world.

The ICTY (International Criminal Tribunal for Yugoslavia) has been installed as per Security Council resolution no. 807 and 827, 25 May, 1993. The ICTY has jurisdiction over the grave breach of the four Geneva Conventions, 1949, violations of the laws and customs of war, genocide and crime against humanity. Several political and military leaders have been booked for prosecution. The ICTR (International

Crimes Tribunal for Rwanda) installed as per the Security Council resolution no. 955 of 8 November, 1994 has jurisdiction over genocide, crimes against humanity, violation of common article 3 of the four Conventions, 1949 and additional protocol II, 1977. Common article 3 of the Geneva Conventions (*supra*) is now considered as customary International law and every state party or, state is under obligation to invariably comply with the common article 3. The union government has not been excluded from this common article's purview.

The Nurenberg and Tokyo tribunals had set the precedent for prosecuting and punishing civilian and military leadership of the erring countries. The ICTY has formally indicted half of the 60 suspects in custody. The great Bosnian leader of Serbs Radovan Karadzic and general Rakto Mladic, who are in the wanted list found absconding from the ICTY. 23 of the 32 suspects including His Excellency prime minister Jean Kambanda, was sentenced for genocide by the ICTR. ICTR on the 4th September, 1998 ordered prime minister Kambanda to serve life-term imprisonment for committing genocide.

The Security Council could have set up a number of tribunals in different parts of the world including countries in South Asia — Combodia etc. It takes political decisions favourable to itself. The adoption of the multilateral treaty for setting up the first permanent - ICC (International Criminal Court), also known in common parlance as war crimes tribunal on the 17th July, 1998 at Rome by the international diplomatic conference is a major historical breakthrough in international criminal law. The status of humanitarian laws has also been not only elevated but also strengthened to a considerable extent with the emergence of the ICC, which will become a reality after the ratification of the treaty by sixty states. The obsolete academic, puritanist concept of absolute sovereignty will no longer hold water, as the human security is taking precedence over other narrow political absolutes of the medieval period. The NAM and third world look upon India to give a lead by signing and ratifying the treaty.

Any country either a party or non-party to the treaty would be brought under the ICC jurisdiction with the consent of the territorial country, where crime has been committed or, that of the country of the accused or, by the Security Council independent of other considerations. The German draft for compulsory, universal jurisdiction of the ICC has however, been diluted in hammering out a *via media* on the subject of the jurisdiction.

The humanitarian laws are being progressively evolved by the UN agencies, *ad hoc* tribunals and the ICC, as adopted so far.

International Criminal Court

The first ever permanent International Criminal Court of the global village would hold trial of individuals, who are accused of committing crimes of genocide, war crimes, crimes against humanity, forced pregnancy (to alter ethnic and racial composition, as it was done in Bosnia) and aggression. Aggression would be within the scope, when it is finally defined by the international community. As regards, war crimes, a state party after putting its signature may opt out of the ICC jurisdiction for a period of seven years. This being transitory provision would not affect the text of the treaty, which otherwise accommodates no reservation.

The 1994 ILC draft has been whittled down by removing treaty-based crimes like hijacking, hostage taking, torture, apartheid and drug-trafficking outside the ICC purview. The efforts of the USA and India to induct opt-in mechanism in the jurisdiction have been internationally isolated and voted down. The last ditch efforts of Dillip Lahiri of India to enlarge the ICC jurisdiction to include nuclear weapons and terrorism had also been scuttled down as hypocritical by the plenipotentiaries. The domestic jurisdiction has been retained for investigation and relevant powers. The UN Security Council can refer cases to the ICC and can defer cases involving matters of peace and security for one year at a time, provided the P-5 takes a consensual resolution on the subject.

The omnibus ICC jurisdiction, when established would reach out to any individual (or official), who is accused of committing crimes like genocide, crimes against humanity, aggression in the states and who is also accused of committing war crimes anywhere. When the transitory provision runs out. Naturally, there is no alternative than strengthening humanitarian laws in the region by all the parties concerned. The ICC which would be financed by the UN would address itself to not only prosecution, trial of accused, conviction and imprisonment of the convict upto a maximum of thirty years (death penalty not being favoured by the civilised civil society), but also to imposing fine and redressing the victims. The treaty could be placed before the review conference after seven years of its operation.

Aggression is evading a final definition for several decades due to the ideological polemic. However, ILC draft definition of aggression has been available. In 1974, the UN General Assembly by its resolution no. 3314(XXIX) of 1974 has adopted an eight article definition of aggression. The first article defines it : "aggression is the use of armed force by a State against the sovereignty, territorial integrity or political independence of another state or in any other manner inconsistent with the United Nations Charter, as set out in this definition ." The global village would be able to hammer out the ultimate definition of aggression along with the installation of the ICC for humanitarian purposes.

Peripheral secessionism

The five-decade-old insurgency in the North-Eastern states and elsewhere has been considered as militancy, separatism and also loosely as terrorism by the government. The insurgents and belligerents claim that they are exercising their right to self-determination by way of conducting national liberation movements. Whereas the government considers it as internal violence, the latter considers that their movement partakes the character of international armed conflict between them and the government forces. This being the polemic, humanitarian laws have assumed the status of customary International law, *Jus Cogens*, general principles and codified laws. Humanitarian laws are, therefore, applicable in varying degrees in the insurgent states in the country.

The humanitarian laws as prevalent in today's contemporary global community are explicit about the contentions and conflicts. The existing international norms and principles are, therefore, assessed in the light of the armed conflicts.

Non-international armed conflict

The government has treated the armed conflicts in insurgent states as internal violence or, non-international armed conflict, as several metropolitan powers did in the past in similar situations. In that event, the ICRC (International Committee of Red Cross) is empowered to take initiative for a role and the government shall open the door for that initiative to fully materialise. (See Marion Harroff-Tavel, Action Taken by the International Committee of the Red Cross in situation of Internal Violence, Review of the Red Cross, May-June ,1993).

The union government could set up a 'National Committee' for implementation of Humanitarian laws, to which the National Red Cross Society may extend its fullest cooperation. The role of the national society remains totally undefined for five decades in the North-East and they made their presence least felt in the conflict situation. The national committee could have established a link with the ICRC. These paramount steps have not yet been taken up so far and the humanitarian laws have to remain the first casualty of the apathy of the government and national societies.

Protocol II is specifically meant for non-international armed conflict and the signature of the government of India could have been on it two decades ago.

Common article 3 of the four Geneva Conventions and Protocol II are cumulatively applicable in the scenario. Common article 3 is *Jus Cogens* — the peremptory norm, from which no derogation could be made by any state. International Court of Justice in Nicaragua vs. USA (1986) has accepted the same as customary international law and also as codified law. The Armed Forces Special Powers Act, 1958, Punjab Security of State Act 1953 and other repressive laws are found to be in blatant violation of the common article 3. The Supreme Court has upheld the 1958 statute on 27 November, 1997. The statute is akin to 1942 ordinance of the British colonialists in a changed context and with this instrument, the British wanted to make the last ditch efforts to save her empire from cracking up. The law rather ironically hastened the break-up of the British empire.

Protocol II, which supplements common article 3 of the Geneva Conventions has recognised, for the material field of application, the armed conflict between the armed forces of the government party and the *'dissident armed forces* or other organised armed groups.' (Article I.I of Protocol II). Humanitarian laws could not be applied in the way it ought to have been, because of these blatant lapses and apathy of the government, which under article 51 of the Constitution is responsible for the promotion of international peace and security. 'Dissident Armed Forces' could be used in lieu of media-cliche like militants etc.

Liberation movement

The insurgents in the peripheral secessionist states in India claim their movement as legitimate national liberation movement by obviously stipulating historical, political and economic reasons. The government has outlawed them under the Prevention of Unlawful Activities Act 1967 for their separatist and secessionist activities, found to be prejudicial to the Indian national interest. The government has opened political dialogues with some of them and continues the same as ongoing process. By taking the paradigm, the movements partake of the characteristics of international armed conflict. Despite the difference in perceptions, the movements have to be assessed from the established international standard and practices, if we have to make dispassionate and objective study of the conflicts. But such dispassionate attempts are not only arduous but also considered political to one party or the other.

Insurgents are subjects of International law and even third parties may give recognition to them by making unilateral declaration. Since the adoption of the Protocol I, NLM (National Liberation Movement) has been accepted as international armed conflict. At present, it is as good as an universally approved instrument. A few countries hold up the signature to Protocol I. The government has to sign and ratify the Protocols in order to render her international commitment literally significant. The national NGOs and pressure groups would no longer allow their government to choose a path of self-isolation for such a long time.

Article 4 (2) of the Third Geneva Convention, to which the government of India is a party provides for according POW (prisoner of war) status to the members of the 'organised resistance movements' — the organisations, banned under Unlawful Activities Prevention Act 1967. The provision has to be fully implemented by the government.

Protocol I defines the general principles and scope of application in article I. Article I (2) is equivalent to *Martens clause*; it makes no difference if a state has signed the Protocol or not. The state party cannot derogate itself from 'established custom, from principles of humanity and from dictates of public conscience.' The situations covered by the Protocol I and *Martens clause* equivalent in article I (2) is wide enough to cover the liberation struggles:

Article I (4)

The situations referred to in the preceding paragraph include armed conflicts in which peoples are fighting against colonial domination and alien occupation and against racist regimes in the exercise of their right of self-determination, as enshrined in the Chapter of the United Nations and the Declaration on Principles of International Law concerning Friendly Relations and Co-operation among States in accordance with the Charter of the United Nations.

Treaty relations involving the 'authority representing a people engaged against a High Contracting party in an armed conflict of the type referred to in Article I, paragraph 4' are stipulated in Article 96 (3) of Protocol I. Humanitarian laws do recognise the national liberation movements and the government which abides by the humanitarian laws is under humanitarian obligation to recognise them as such and enforce these laws on their own.

Besides the humanitarian laws, the UN laws since 1973 give official recognition to the legal status of combatants struggling for exercise of their right to self-determination. The essence of the UN laws is furnished by Human Rights Fact Sheet no. 13 (UN, July 1991 p. 10-11). The excerpt :

> Such struggles are legitimate and in full accord with the principles of international law.

> Attempts to suppress struggles against colonial and racist regimes are incompatible with the UN Charter, the Universal Declaration of Human Rights and the Declaration on the Granting of

Independence to Colonial Countries and Peoples as well as with the Principles of International Law concerning Friendly Co-operation among States. Such attempts constitute a threat to peace and security.

Captured combatants are to be accorded the status of prisoners of war under the Third Geneva Convention.

The use of mercenaries against national liberation movements is a criminal act.

Violation of the legal status of combatants entails full responsibility in accordance with the norms of international law.

The essence of UN laws, as cited above from UN Fact Sheet constitutes humanitarian laws, which along with the Geneva Conventions and Protocols, *Martens Ccause*, customary International law provide the elaborate corpus of the humanitarian laws, as accepted the world over.

The Geneva conventions

The first three Geneva Conventions, 1949 address to the protection of and for safeguarding the humanitarian rights of *hors de combat*, wounded enemy soldier, and captured combatants. Even resistance movements are also covered by the third Convention. The fourth Convention is for the protection of the civilian population in occupied territories. This prevents the use of civilian as shield and collective punishment as meted out by the Punjab Security of State Act 1953 to the innocent people of the insurgent states. The municipal statute like the Punjab Security of State Act 1953 contradicts India's ratification of the Geneva Conventions and so, this statute could to be repealed.

Torture, which has been prohibited in the strictest term ever by the Conventions, coupled with the Anti-Torture Convention 1984 of the UN, has been religiously followed by the security forces while extracting informations from the captured insurgent-combatants and many of the captured combatants die after receiving repeated electric shocks and relentless de-humanizing tortures conducted by the special squads in special camps inside jungles and even in urban enclaves. NGO reports testify the torture-culture.

Death penalty which cannot be given to children below the age of 18 years under the Conventions are routinely meted out whenever the young ones fall into the security dragnets. The wounded insurgents have never been spared from being liquidated by the state forces, who could have believed that insurgency would be wiped out after executing all the young ones, associated with the movement.

The *Corpa delicti* have been elaborately enunciated by the Protocol I (article 85). The superior officers are not absolved from the breach of the Conventions (article 87, Protocol I). Compensations have to be awarded to in case of violations of the law (article 91). Article 89 and 90 envisage a role of the United Nations in the event of serious violations of the Protocol I.

Usually, on the breach of humanitarian laws, national obligations to the Geneva Conventions, the national forces that breached the laws should have been punished; but that do not happen in India. Besides, individual responsibility has not also been fixed due to the irregularities found in the judicial process, which could have been corrected on the initiative of the executive wing of the government. The Geneva Conventions Act, 1961 has been practically shelved from putting incase.

Interestingly, the claims and counter claims, published by the government and the insurgent parties in papers as well as non-papers (which are abundantly available in the media also) take a polemical turn. The freedom of press that India promotes removes opacity to a considerable extent.

The government of India has its material basis on the 1950 Constitution. Article I of the 1950 Constitution provides that-"India, that is Bharat, shall be a union of States". The insurgent parties, as the government perceives, are cracking up this article and the union of states and hence, they should have to be liquidated with the help of the Armed Forces Special Powers Act 1958, that empowers the soldiers to shoot down any body at pleasure with impunity and immunity.

The belligerent, insurgent bodies make a counter-claim that their territories have been occupied by using force and other devious means and their populace remain under occupation of a hostile army. Article 42 of 1907 Haque Regulation defines occupied territory : "Territory is considered occupied when it is actually placed under the authority of the hostile army." Geneva Conventions endorses this view point.

The humanitarian laws permit the insurgent guerrillas to go underground. There are conditions attached to the guerrilla and combatant also. They have to comply with common article 3 of the Geneva Conventions and other practices. In this respect, many of them are found wanting in their business. The Fourth Geneva Convention is virtually a constitution or, bill of rights for the civilian population.

The combatants including the NLM guerrillas are under obligation to abide by article I of the Haque regulations 1907 and the Geneva laws. They have to be commanded by a responsible person, to have distinctive emblem, carry arms openly before their engagement in the contact zone and have to carry operations by customs and laws of war. These rights, privileges and duties are exclusively meant for the privileged combatants, not for the terrorists, who are criminals *per se*. Mercenaries and spies are also not protected persons unlike the civilians. The NLM combatants and guerrillas are also under obligation to prove to the world that they are not terrorists in both words and deed.

The polemical turn, as discussed above could only be resolved either by ICRC initiative or, third party mediation or some other mechanisms that would be acceptable to both the parties in engagement. A better alternative could also be suggested. Under article 90 of the Protocol I, an *'International Fact-Finding Commission'* can be constituted in order to clarify the facts as alleged. The process would remove any undesirable allegation made against the government and at the same time bring the NLM guerrillas to the humanitarian platform. Nobody would be a loser in the event of constituting an *'International Fact-Finding Commission'* for probing into the facts in the insurgent states and placing them across the board.

The government has to promptly sign and accede to the two additional Protocols, 1977 to the Geneva Conventions. It has to accede and ratify the 1998 Rome treaty for installation of International Criminal Court. The national courts have to be revamped so as to punish the individuals, who have committed the breach of the Geneva Conventions, to which the government is a party. The insurgent parties too should not lag behind and should sign common article 3 of the four Geneva Conventions and comply with the accepted practices of the humanitarian laws. Unless the most minimal tasks ahead are taken seriously by the parties concerned, humanity would always remain as the helpless casualty of the armed conflicts.

References

1. Hans-Peter Gasser, International Humanitarian Law, Haupt, 1993.
2. Dieter Fleck, ed. The Handbook of Humanitarian Law in Armed Conflicts, OUP, 1995.
3. C. de Rover, To serve and Protect, ICRC, 1998.
4. International Law concerning the conduct of hostilities ICRC, 1996

11

Rights of the Child in Armed Conflicts

The accession of the UN Convention on the Rights of the Child (CRC hereafter) on 11 December ,1992 and the subsequent enforcement of the CRC on 11 January, 1993 by the union government of India makes an obligation for the government to submit periodic reports' on the measures, they have adopted which give effect to the rights' as per article 44 of the CRC - the Convention.

The very fact that the union government of India has not yet constituted a statutory 'National Commission of the Child' inspite of the inbuilt deprivation and denial of the basic human rights of the child on a colossal scale, lends credence to the feeling that the rights of the child are not in the top priority of the successive governments at the federal level. Besides, the periodic reports submitted by the government happen to be the routine desk-work of inefficient post-colonial civil servants who are the masters of the statistics and paper-works. They do not give material result.

The rights of the child in the North-Eastern states (NES) are sinned against two evils. Firstly, the ongoing armed conflict between the state forces and the non-state forces continued since 1949 till today. The delicate and tender mind-set of the child under 18 years of age have been profoundly disturbed because of the armed conflict and huge military presence for decades. Physical and material damage also take place.

Secondly, the rights of the child are at the receiving end in the NES even in the period of normalcy or peace time. In this context, the rights of the child in the NES call for closer attention on both counts, whereas the rights of the child in the rest of India have been marginalised or faulted exclusively on only one count. The psychic pressure, built up on the mind of the child and the youths, more particularly in the state of Manipur induced several thousands of the Manipuri children under 18 years of age to adversely sublimate the pressure by way of taking to drugs and facing the eventual death due to HIV/AIDS infection. It is tantamount to then forced extra-judicial massacre of Manipuri children, allegedly designed as a counter-insurgency arm of the strategic decision-makers. The fallout is steadily noticeable in other parts of the NES, although Manipur happens to be the ground zero or, epicentre of the Drug-AIDS bomb of the strategists of all hues. In a tiny population of 2 million, 30,000 Manipuri children are booked for the body-bags in the coming decades. The NES or peripheral areas face the same fate of Manipur. It is, in this context, felt that the rights of the child in the NES need the close scrutiny of the union government of India and in equal measure, that of the UN committee of the rights of the child, constituted under Part II of the CRC. Unless emergency measures are adopted on this front, the NES may lose entirely the next generation; even if there is a next generation, they may remain misfits, destroyed totally from within.

The state of the rights of the child in India is deplorable. It has been endorsed by the SAHDOC report, submitted to the UN Human Rights Committee. The report testifies that India's estimated 200 million child labourers work in agricultural lands, care for siblings, do domestic chores; several hundreds of them are bonded labourers forced into servitude to pay off their parents' debt (1:93). The Child Labour Regulation and Prohibition excludes the child agricultural labourers (1:94). 'Millions of child labourers, street children and children caught in internal armed conflict situations continue to be denied primary education' (1:19).

1991 UNICEF report has an estimate of 75 million children in India, who are out of school (1:95).

The union government of India has given more emphasis on engaging itself in wars with neighbours and others while denying millions of children their fundamental right to primary education, by way of diversion of resources and national attention from the right of the child to avoidable wars and armed conflicts. Tribal children suffer from starvation deaths (1:91). The civil servants take the least notice of starvation deaths and manifold miseries. They are excellent in submitting reports and justification of human misery.

The UNICEF and NHRC admit that child labour and bonded labour are on the rise and the Supreme Court by its judgement given on 10 December, 1996 has emphasised that the state chief secretaries would be personally liable in the event of non-filing of detail affidavits (1:60). How far the affidavits are found true and reflect the reality on the ground are not clear. There is no supervisory mechanism to oversee the affidavits which are normally submitted as the routine desk-work. Any chief secretary — even a Tom, Dick, Hary can easily draft a defensive reply in English; but this would rather perpetuate the evil which the Supreme Court desires to ward off.

'Thousands of children have been forced into prostitution. Countless girls from Nepal and other parts of India have been sold in brothels in Bombay, Calcutta and Delhi' — the report states. 'The Government of India, by strictly limiting the scope of discussion to bonded labourers, has indicated that it has little concern for the thousands of girls trapped in the brothels across India.' (1:60). The National Commission on Women has not taken up the issue either. Child prostitution in India, compounded by widespread HIV/AIDS infection is a neglected issue. Child marriage and dowry deaths are rampant in India and the National Commission of Women remains a helpless spectator, as it does not have adequate powers and will to fight these crimes out.

The SAHDOC report records that thousands of refugee children suffer from malnutrition and disease (1:74), only

Indo-Aryan refugees have been given citizenship purely on racial grounds by denying the same to Mongolian Chakma refugees etc. (1:96) and tribal children are socially segregated in Indian schools (1:90). Why *apartheid* still operates in the social fabric of India at all levels is enigmatic and the government is yet to give answers for this social *apartheid* (2:120). On this subject every Indian is well conversant and no courtroom evidence is necessary for the perpetuation of the crime. The young minds are tortured, destroyed from the early stage. The government of India is yet to evolve a concrete race-relation policy in the country inspite of defending the paper laws on equality in the Constitution, which is officially free from racism. The SAHDOC report could be taken seriously, as it comes from the Indo-Aryan expertise themselves and not from the Mongolian scholarship.

The violation of human rights of the child in India is also reported by the Amnesty International in clear violation of article 24(1) of the ICCPR, 1996(3:74). Three lakh girls below the age of 15 years do not survive in India due to gender discrimination — reports the UNICEF document on May 30, 1996 (Times of India, May 31 ,1996). It may be seriously noted that 17 Manipuri children had been physically liquidated by the security forces. Their names, photographs, details and age groups are clearly given by the COHR (4:5-46). In the Manipur hills and hills in the NES, involuntary disappearance has become common and death bodies are seen in obscure places. The rights of the child in the North Eastern States are at stake in both peace time and more so periods of turmoil.

The convention in practice

Amnesty International observes, "As an especially vulnerable group, children tend to have less defence against human rights violations than adults, and are unable directly to access the legal system to seek remedy for violations. Amnesty International has reported several cases of violation of the rights of children, in India, despite the government having acceded to the UN Convention on the Rights of the

Child in 1992 (5:20) . Amnesty International records the extra-judicial murders of children and urges the government of India and the government of Manipur to 'publicly demonstrate its opposition to extra-judicial executions and deliberate and arbitrary killings by giving a clear message to members of the security forces that such violations will not be tolerated'. (6:15). The same phenomena occurs in the NES, apart from Manipur.

The CRC having the force of national and international law has to be literally implemented and its successful implementation has to be monitored. The UN working groups and machineries including the 'Working Group on Contemporary Forms of Slavery' have to oversee the implementation of the CRC (7:6). The CRC provides for a wide range of human rights for the child. The child in a situation of armed conflict is to be given full protection as per the provisions of the article 38 of the Convention (7:26).

Article 38

> (1)States Parties undertake to respect and to ensure respect for rules of international humanitarian law applicable to them in armed conflicts which are relevant to child.
>
> (2)States Parties shall take all feasible measures to ensure that persons who have not attained the age of fifteen years do not take a direct part in hostilities.

The union government has to ensure the 'protection and care of children who are affected by an armed conflict' (article 38.4) in the NES and other parts of India. Article 39 provides for psychological recovery and re-integration of a child-victim of exploitation or armed conflict. (7:26). The union government should take all appropriate legislative, administrative and other measures to implement the CRC (8:11). 'Mechanisms may be introduced at the national and local levels to coordinate policies and monitor the implementation of the Convention, including through an ombudsman's office' (8:12).

The Vienna Declaration and Programmes of Action, 1993 of the United Nations has emphasized the 'continued work on the improvement of the functioning, including the monitoring tasks, of the treaty bodies' in regard to the approach taken by the Committee on the Rights of the Child (9:27) and the world conference also asked, in imperative sense, the states to accede to the Geneva Conventions of 12 August, 1949 and the two additional Protocols thereto for their 'full implementation'. The union government is yet to pay heed to these Protocols to the four Geneva Conventions. The Vienna Programme of Action stipulates:

> 'The World Conference on Human Rights strongly supports the proposal that the Secretary-General initiate a study into means of improving the protection of children in armed conflicts. Humanitarian norms should be implemented and measures taken in order to protect and facilitate assistance to children in war zones... The need for aftercare and rehabilitation of children traumatized by war must be addressed urgently...'(9:21)

The above mentioned tasks have to be taken up with a strong sense of urgency in the NES, by the governments of the centre and the state, considering the regimentation and resultant traumatization of the children in the NES due to the armed conflicts between the huge and mighty security forces and the non-state forces. The world conference elaborately works out the details to be incorporated in the 'national action plans' (9:21).

The United Nations High Commissioner for Human Rights has in 1996 clearly identified the areas of priority for the protection of the human rights of the children; the UN machineries like the UNICEF, ILO, Committee on the Rights of the Child, the Special Rapporteur, Centre for Human Rights and the experts preparing a study on the situation of children affected by armed conflicts, the working group on Contemporary forms of Slavery have to coordinate their activities. (10:28). The representatives of the union government, who function in the UN machineries have to undertake co-ordinated efforts so as to espouse the rights of the child in all the fronts in both peace time and situation of armed conflicts in the NES and other regions of the country.

The third periodic report of India, submitted to the UN Human Rights Committee has furnished the positive steps taken up by the government for the protection of the rights of the child. (9.27 see pages 28,29,34 and 36 also). However, the members of the UNHRC raised several issues in the discussion of the India report and some of the lapses could be identified despite the tall claims of the government. Reactions are briefly cited below.

Mr. Ando, member of the UNHRC raised issues with Mrs. Chadha and Mr. Desai on the child prostitution (12:17). Mr. Kretzmer questións as to why the government of India 'made no legal declaration of a state of emergency under article 4 of the Covenant' before the Armed Forces Special Powers Act 1958 was promulgated in the NES (12:17). Mr. Desai has replied to the query about the Juvenile Justice Act 1986, that the 'Law Commission of India was currently studying the definition of the child' (13:11). Mrs. Medina Quiroga questioned about the India Report's studied silence about the problem created by the traffic in women and girls and also about the girl infanticide and abortion of female fetuses in India. (14:3). Mrs. Evatt also asked about the fate of compulsory education of the child and also about the loopholes of the child labour (prohibition and regulation) legislation (14:7). The *devdasi* system was also disputed by Ms. Medina Quiroga (15:9).

The UNHRC deliberation focused some of the achievements of the government of India and exposed the wide gap between officially sponsored rhetoric (propaganda) and the failure or lapses as found on the ground. The government and civil servants have to make up the visible gap with urgency after going through the detail deliberations of the UNHRC. The MEA (Ministry of External Affairs's) *web-site* worldwide propaganda offensive in defence of 55 million Indian children going to workplace instead of the school is considered to be an issue of poverty, tradition and function of socio-economic development; the offensive has been seen as an undertaking of the Indian ruling class and elite (16:78). The *web site* or INTERNET info-tactics may promote Indian market outside, but the evil of child labour would remain as such inside the country but for initiating a radical political resolve and time-bound agenda.

The UN Human Rights Committee has made concluding observations for the follow-up action to be taken by the government of India. The committee expressed regrets about bonded labour, child prostitution, practice of *Devadasi*, street children, and child labour law (17:8). Despite the committee's request for wide dissemination of the committee's concluding observations to the large Indian public (18.72), the 1 billion Indians are kept totally dark about the observations in this age of information and media-autonomy as offered by the *Prasar Bharati*. The law has changed but the minds of the Indian civil servants remain stagnant for half a century. The deplorable state of affairs should be rectified on a war footing (19:99). From the UN and global perspective, the community of nations and individual state has to implement the 10 points action plan, laid down by the World Summit on Children in 1990 (20:235). Amnesty International observes: "children are often victims of indiscriminate killings by security forces in their operations against suspected members of armed opposition groups" (22:8). It has urged upon central government and state governments to implement the CRC and ensure protection of children (22:10).

Child in the armed conflict

The union government and the state governments in the NES promulgate *de facto* emergency and allied laws without formal declaration of emergency like Unlawful Activities (Prevention) Act, Punjab Security Act 1953, Disturbed Areas Act, National Security Act and the draconian Armed Forces Special Powers Act 1958 (as amended in 1972). Admittedly, the ongoing situation of armed conflict between the state security forces and the non-state forces had made deep inroads into the sanctity of human rights, personal liberty, property and mental stability of the populace. The impact is more profound and directly vulnerable to the child in the NES. The rights of the child call for non-derogable protection in the North Eastern States by the state and the non-state bodies (2:259). The writer has dwelt upon the theme in his other books.

As discussed above, the state has the treaty, UN and International law obligations to abide by the International Humanitarian Laws in order to safeguard the child, trapped in or around the situation of armed conflicts. The CRC to which India has been a party also elaborately provides for this protection and in this context, the International humanitarian law is non-derogable unlike other human rights laws. The four Geneva Conventions 1949, the additional Protocols 1977, *Martens clause*, judgements of the International Court of Justice and the Indian law - the Geneva Conventions Act 1961 unambiguously and invariably reinforce the existing state responsibility and international obligations of India.

The non-state bodies like the guerrillas, the insurgents and the belligerents may not have state responsibilities under the prevailing law of the comity of nations; however, by practice and civilised norms, they have to invariably abide by the common article 3 of the four Geneva Conventions which constitute *Jus Cogens* for all. The protection of the rights of the child should also be complemented by all institutions, non-state bodies and individuals, leaving apart legal arguments about state responsibility or otherwise for the simple reason that the CHILD is the future Man, destiny of mankind and precious capital that no other resource could ever vie with.

Geneva conventions, protocol, 8th June, 1977

1. Children shall be the object of special respect and shall be protected against any form of indecent assault. The Parties to the conflict shall provide them with the care and aid they require, whether because of their age or for any other reason.

2. The Parties to the conflict shall take all feasible measures in order that children who have not attained the age of fifteen years do not take a direct part in hostilities and, in particular, they shall refrain from recruiting them into their armed forces. In recruiting among those persons who have attained the age of fifteen years but who have not attained the age of eighteen years, the Parties to the conflict shall endeavour to give priority to those who are oldest.

3. If, in exceptional cases, despite the provisions of paragraph 2, children who have not attained the age of fifteen years take a direct part in hostilities and fall into the power of an adverse Party, they shall continue to benefit from the special protection accorded by this Article, whether or not they are prisoners of war.

4. If arrested, detained or interned for reasons related to the armed conflict, children shall be held in quarters separate from the quarters of adults, except where families are accommodated as family units as provided in Article 75, paragraph 5.

5. The death penalty for an offence related to the armed conflict shall not be executed on persons who had not attained the age of eighteen years at the time the offence was committed.

Article 77 — Protection of Children

Article 78 - Evacuation of Children

1. No Party to the conflict shall arrange for the evacuation of children, other than its own nationals, to a foreign country except for a temporary evacuation where compelling reasons of the health or medical treatment of the children or, except in occupied territory, their safety, so require. Where the parents or legal guardians can be found, their written consent to such evacuation is required. If these persons cannot be found, the written consent to such evacuation of the persons who by law or custom are primarily responsible for the care of the children is required. Any such evacuation shall be supervised by the Protecting

Power in agreement with the Parties concerned, namely, the Party arranging for the evacuation, the Party receiving the children and any Parties whose nationals are being evacuated. In each case, all Parties to the conflict shall take all feasible precautions to avoid endangering the evacuation

2. Whenever an evacuation occurs pursuant to paragraph 1, each child's education, including his religious and moral education as his parents desire, shall be provided while he is away with the greatest possible continuity.

3. With a view to facilitating the return to their families and country of children evacuated pursuant to this Article, the authorities of the Party arranging for the evacuation and, as appropriate, the authorities of the receiving country shall establish for each child a card with photographs, which they shall send to the Central Tracing Agency of the International Committee of the Red Cross. Each card shall bear, whenever possible, and whenever it involves no risk of harm to the child, the following informations:

(a)surname(s) of the child;

(b)the child's first name(s);

(c)the child's sex;

(d)the place and date of birth (or, if that date is not known, the approximate age);

(e)the father's full name;

(f) the mothers' full name and her maiden name;

(g)the child's next-of-kin;

(h)the child's nationality;

(i) the child's native language, and any other languages he speaks;

(j) the address of the child's family;

(k)any identification number for the child;

(l) the child's state of health;

(m)the child's blood group;

(n)any distinguishing features;

(o)the date on which and the place where the child was found;

(p)the date on which and the place from which the child left the country;

(q)the child's religion, if any;

(r) the child's present address in the recieving country,

(s) should the child die before his return, the date, place and circumstances of death and place of internment.

DECLARATION ON THE PROTECTION OF WOMEN AND CHILDREN IN EMERGENCY AND ARMED CONFLICT

Proclaimed by the General Assembly of the United Nations on 14 December, 1974 (resolution 3318 (XXIX)

The general assembly

Having considered the recommendation of the Economic and Social Council contained in its resolution 1861 (LVI) of 16 May,1974,

Expressing its deep concern over the sufferings of women and children belonging to the civilian population who in periods of emergency and armed conflict in the struggle for peace, self-determination, national liberation and independence are too often the victims of inhuman acts and consequently suffer serious harm,

Aware of the suffering of women and children in many areas of the world, especially in those areas subject to suppression, aggression, colonialism, racism, alien domination and foreign subjugation,

Deeply concerned by the fact that, despite general and unequivocal condemnation, colonialism, racism and alien and foreign domination continue to subject many people under their yoke, cruelly suppressing the national liberation movements and inflicting heavy losses and incalculable suffering on the population's under their domination, including women and children,

Deploring the fact that grave attacks are still being made on fundamental freedom and the dignity of the human person and that colonial and racist foreign domination. Powers continue to violate international humanitarian law,

Recalling the relevant provisions contained in the instruments of international humanitarian law relative to the protection of women and children in time of peace and war,

Recalling, among other important documents, its resolutions 2444 (XXIII) of 19 December, 1968, 2597 (XXIV) of 16 December, 1969 and 2674 (XXV) and 2675 (XXV) of 9 December, 1970 on respect for human rights and on basic principles for the protection of civilian population in armed conflicts, as well as Economic and Social Council resolution 1515 (XLVIII) of 28 May, 1970 in which the council requested the General Assembly to consider the possibility of drafting a declaration on the protection of women and children in emergency or wartime,

Conscious of its responsibility for the destiny of the rising generation and for the destiny of mothers, who play an important role in society, in the family and particularly in the upbringing of children,

Bearing in mind the need to provide special protection of women and children belonging to the civilian population,

Solemnly proclaims this Declaration on the Protection of Women and Children in Emergency and Armed Conflict and calls for the strict observance of the Declaration by all Member States:

1. Attacks and bombings on the civilian population, inflicting incalculable suffering, especially on women and children, who are the most vulnerable members of the population, shall be prohibited, and such acts shall be condemned.

2. The use of chemical and bacteriological weapons in the course of military operations constitutes one of the most flagrant violations of the Geneva Protocol of 1925, the Geneva Conventions of 1949 and the principles of international humanitarian law and inflicts heavy losses on civilian populations, including defenceless women and children, and shall be severely condemned.

3. All States shall abide fully by their obligations under the Geneva Protocol of 1925 and the Geneva Conventions of 1949, as well as other instruments of international law relative to respect for human rights in armed conflicts, which offer important guarantees for the protection of women and children.

4. All efforts shall be made by States involved in armed conflicts, military operations in foreign territories or military operations in territories still under colonial domination to spare women and children from the ravages of war. All the necessary steps shall be taken to ensure the prohibition of measures such as persecution, torture, punitive measures, degrading treatment and violence, particularly against that parts of the civilian population that consists of women and children.

5. All forms of repression and cruel and inhuman treatment of women and children, including imprisonment, torture, shooting, mass arrests, collective punishment, destruction of dwellings and forcible eviction, committed by belligerents in the course of military operations or in occupied territories shall be considered criminal.

6. Women and children belonging to the civilian population and finding themselves in circumstances of emergency and armed conflict in the struggle for peace, self-determination, national liberation and independence or who live in occupied territories, shall not be deprived of shelter, food, medical aid or other inalienable rights, in accordance

with the provisions of the Universal Declaration of Human Rights, the International Covenant on Civil and Political Rights, the International Covenant on Economic, Social and Cultural Rights, the Declaration of the Rights of the child or other instruments of international law.

References

1. South Asia Human Rights Documentation Centre, Alternate Report, to the UN Human Rights Committee, July 1977 (SAHDOC);
2. Naorem Sanajaoba, Right of the Oppressed Nations, 1996, New Delhi;
3. Amnesty International, INDIA, July 1997, London;
4. Right to Life in Manipur, A Report, COHR, February 13, 1997, Imphal;
5. Amnesty International, Amnesty International and India, 1996;
6. Amnesty International, India Official sanction for killing in Manipur, April 1997;
7. United Nations, Fact Sheet No. 10, The Rights of the Child;
8. United Nations, Fact Sheet No. 10 (Rev.), 1996 December;
9. United Nations, General Assembly, World Conference on Human Rights, Vienna, June 1993, Vienna Declaration, 12 July, 1993;
10. UN, The High Commissioner for Human Rights, 1996;
11. UN, CCPR, Addendum India I (Third report), 17 June ,1996;
12. UN, CCPR, 29 July, 1997;
13. UN, CCPR, 31 July ,1997;
14. UN, CCPR, 7 November ,1997;
15. UN, CCPR, 21 November, 1997;
16. Praveen Swami, Child Labour, The MEA's children, Frontline, February 6, 1998;
17. UN, CCPR, Human Rights Committee, 4 August ,1997;
18. UB, Report of the Human Rights Committee vol. I. General Assembly, 52 session, New York, 1997,
19. Naorem Sanajaoba, ed. Human Rights, 1994, New Delhi;
20. UN, United Nations in the Field of Human Rights, New York, 1994;

21. AI, Children in South Asia: Securing their rights, April 1998;
22. AI, India — Manipur: the Silencing of youth, May 1998. The military commanders should be conversant with ICRC's book 'To serve and to Protect', 1998, Geneva, p.455.

12

Human Rights

India's Third Report, 1995

Parties to the International Covenant on Civil and Political Rights are accountable to the UN Human Rights Committee for maintaining the universal standard. India's third periodic report, which was due in 1992 and submitted on 29 November, 1995 has been placed before the UN Human Rights Committee in July 1997 for deliberation of the committee. The fourth report is due by 2001 A.D.

The UN Human Rights Committee in its concluding observations, has appreciated some of the positive aspects of the India report viz., installation of the National Human Rights Commission in 1993, other national commissions for scheduled persons, for women in 1992, for the minorities in 1993, the lapse of TADA in 1995, and reservation of one third of elected seats in local bodies for women, among others. These contributions are positive.

The Committee, however, has expressed deep concern over other commissions and omissions of the government of India in other fronts — the Optional Protocol to the political covenant, reservations made in regard to several provisions of the political covenant, the continuing reliance on the Armed Forces (Special Powers) Act, the National Security Act, on clause 19 of the Protection of Human Rights Act just to cite a few. The third report has several lapses.

The union government of India's official electronic media - DD-I has effectively telecast in 1995 a theme- 'Human Right is not the monopoly of terrorists', in addition to a routine range of similar themes, like 'K-File', 'Ajanabi' and endless — propaganda-ridden info-tainment. The propaganda offensive being conceived to be explicitly and manifestly sectarian, a huge majority of Indian populace has been induced apparently to equate human rights with terrorism and ironically, terrorism with the unsavaoury saviour of their unfulfilled human rights. Because lopsided propaganda is a two-edged weapon, it may reverse the intended direction and boomerang. As we are not going deep into the merits of the massive official propaganda in whatever circumstances it has taken for a ride, we pick and choose the brasstacks and nitty-gritty of contemporary debate on human rights in India. The erudite coffee-house ideologues also ideologise Human Rights, without their own logic.

In the present discourse, we choose the 'Third periodic report' on human rights, submitted by the union government of India in November 1995 to the United Nations Human Rights Committee (UNHRC), in Geneva. The Third report (hereafter report) was long overdue in 1992, but the inordinate delay in its submission gives rise to suspect in the efficacy of the government in paying adequate and basic attention to the safeguarding of human rights in India.

The Third report has been processed for deliberation and the CCPR documentation is available. The United Nations General Assembly examined and endorsed the report and deliberations of the UNHRC, after the report was placed before the General Assembly.

The UNHRC had deliberated upon India report on article by-article basis of the International Covenant on Civil and Political Rights, 1966 (ICCPR). It is not improbable that due to institutional opacity and official obstruction of free-flow of information, the UNHRC would have applied its mind exclusively to the official version of the Human Rights situation in India but for the stray and piece-meal disorganised, informations oozing in from other vague sources. In other words, the UNHRC had only one exclusive field-view of its agenda. The reason is not far to seek. Right to information, open government and transparency, which are the basic pre-requisites of a democracy worth its name have remained permanent casualties in India so far.

Two articles of the ICCPR, 1966 have a direct nexus with the volatile imbroglio in the North Eastern states. The positive aspect of the report is found in the creation of a few commissions, whose findings are not binding to any authority.

Article 4, ICCPR

Third report, India (UNHRC, Geneva, 1996) has justified the continuous invocation of emergency laws and extraordinary laws like the Armed Forces Special Powers Act, 1958 (AFSPA) TADA, 1985 and National Security Act 1987 (NSA) on the grounds of loss of several lives in the insurgency movements in the North Eastern States, Punjab and Kashmir.

The report does not at all indicate :

(i)The state repression or, state terrorism, let loose on the unarmed civilian populace under military siege,

ii)The fact that AFSPA had been enacted by the parliament with an assurance in the house that such a draconian law would cease to exist after shortly in 1958,

iii) TADA has been repealed on the recommendation of the National Human Rights Commission, and

iv) The fact that several thousands of citizens deplore, repudiate and curse the black laws as often as they can. The protest demonstrations are routine affairs in the North Eastern States.

The treaty obligation of India to furnish periodic report under the reporting obligation of article 40 of the ICCPR arises out of India's ratification of the ICCPR, 1966, UN Charter obligations and state practices.

The international obligations demand the country — its government in particular, to improve its human rights report in between the submission of the previous and the subsequent periodic reports and fulfil the recommendations of the HRC made in the 1991 HRC session, duly endorsed by the UN General Assembly in 1991. The process recurs.

The UNHRC in 1991 had strongly urged upon the government of India to surgically remove the de-humanizing section 4 of AFSPA, 1958 (army's licence to shoot down any citizen in North Eastern states merely at the slightest suspicion) and section 6 (virtual immunity of the force from prosecution for the extra-judicial murders), on the ground that the obnoxious sections of the so called Indian laws had been found incompatible with the provision of ICCPR, 1966.

The Third report fails to explain as to why the government dishonours the UNHRC recommendation, specially at a time when an *ex* Chief Justice of India sits in the UN Human Rights Committee. The defence given by the government by stating that the British also enacted emergency laws does not hold water, since British threw open an Irish parliament in 1971 and offered the Downing street declaration, December 1994 by accepting in principle, the right of self-determination of the people of Northern Ireland. The political package need not be overlooked in high lighting British emergency law, which unlike AFSPA, is of a short span and is a collateral aspect of self-determination arrangement. Besides, the government has worked out an agreement in April 1998 at Belfast.

It may be recalled that NHRC chairman Justice Ranganath Misra took steps to recommend the repeal of AFSPA, 1958 and the onus of scrapping the infamous AFSPA happily lies with the successor Justice Venkatachaliah. The human history gives foolproof testimony to the fact that the barbaric laws cannot overturn the cause of human history, as even the laws of the third Reich, which had been as good and clear as the AFSPA failed to twist the history at the choice of leaders.

Article 1, ICCPR

India's Third Report, 1995 (UNHRC, 1996) dwells on the exercise of the Right of Self-determination by people(s) by indicating that:

—Right of Self-determination is a positive legal right and India is not derogating from it notwithstanding the reservation;

—At times, the import of the legal right is uncertain; and

—The people (meaning those represented by insurgency movements in North Eastern states and Kashmir who are not named as such in the report) cannot exercise both internal and external self-determination;

—Territorial integrity of India should not be impaired.

In the Third report, the government uses the term ' terrorism' in the context of Article 4 of the ICCPR and 'insurgency' in the context of Article 1 of the ICCPR — which term is a valid and widely accepted legal term in contemporary international law. Undoubtedly, terrorism is a crime, unlike insurgency (or national liberation movement) which is a valid term, while being a subject of International law. The Third report clearly states that right of self-determination by people cannot be exercised in order to impair the territorial integrity of the country. It is fair to note that an irreconcilable situation of two contending rights co-exist in the presentation of the Third report.

As India report frequently cites history (history of India as a compact monolith), the facts have to be re-assessed. Manipur and Tripura came to the Indian territorial fold in 1949 and Kashmir in 1947. Assam came to British India in 1826, otherwise it had been an independent country in history. People of Tripura and Nagaland also demand the right of self-determination. The loss of territorial integrity of Manipur or Tripura or Kashmir has been contested by the ongoing insurgency. The issue is political in essence.

The Third report has repeatedly cited the history of India barring the factual, and objective history of expanding the territory of India. It appears that Indian representatives ignore history and it also seems that the UNHRC has been ignorant of facts.

In India report, 1991, reservations had been made in regard to the exercise of the right of self-determination by people(s). It states that such a legal right could only be exercised by people(s) under alien, colonial and foreign rule or domination. The exhortations made by national liberation and insurgency movements in the peripheral states of India, as cited above clearly demonstrate that as they belonged historically to alien and racially different people and Hindustan had been constantly alien to them. The polemic remains unresolved.

In the above context, we clearly visualise the imbroglio in the North Eastern states and Kashmir as a lingering political crisis, which cannot and should not be misrepresented as an ordinary internal affair, law and order problem of India. They carry the unmistakable stamp of international issues which affect the peace and security of the world. The conflicts in the peripheral states assume international character.

Private terrorism (Albert Camus's idiom from his book — REBEL) or, state terrorism pose obvious threats to the maintenance of standard of human rights, as accepted the world over. As stated above, contemporary International Law, coupled with established state practices dichotomise* ordinary criminal terrorism from international armed struggle for national liberation movement.

When armed conflicts occur, International humanitarian law, as accepted by national jurisdictions renders innocent lives to be sacrosanct. (*see* Common articles 3 and 4 Geneva Conventions). The Indian state and its security forces are accountable for loss, enforced disappearance and torture of innocent lives, under the humanitarian laws and the insurgent groups could be made accountable for similar offences. Responsibility arises out of the UN Charter, treaty

* See N. Sanajaoba, Right of Oppressed Nations, 1996, Omsons, pp. 195-235, 245-258; UN Resolutions on de-colonisation since 1960; GA resolutions 37/35 of 1982, 52/78, 10 December, 1997, among others.

law and customary international law obligations for the subjects of international law.

A discourse on moral domain for the occurrence of armed conflicts between state forces and non-state or, organised armed groups should have to focus on norms of consent, free will, authority, force, strength, justness and justice. The confrontation between the authority of the state and free will of organised groups of people could be reduced to legitimacy that emanates from the consent of the governed. In this moral front, in the present context, the state is placed on the defensive. Under all circumstances, neither the state nor the opposition armed forces can defend themselves in the deprivation of lives, more particularly those of the unarmed, non-combatant civilians. On the same ground, ethnocide, ethnic-cleansing or, low scale genocides remain as crimes. The Third report has not elaborated the details that lead to conclusions.

By shifting the responsibility at both national and international jurisdictions, the state cannot evade its responsibility in the event of loss of lives at the hands of its own armed forces or, at the hands of the opposition armed groups or, insurgents or, even ordinary criminals. There is a 'State' to protect lives and property of citizens unlike other entities. However, insurgent groups, whose existence have been officially recognised by the state bear responsibility under the prevailing international humanitarian laws in the event of murder and loss of lives of innocent civilian populace. It is considered ideal that no armed conflict should ever happen in any corner of the world; but in reality, the idealism has undergone head-on collision with the ground realities.

Human rights in both peace time and time of armed conflict situations are sacrosanct and when the sacrosanctity has been violated, responsibility arises. Politicians judge events by the tangible description of events, while statesmen can easily hunch and intuit the root - cause of the events. India's Third Report, 1995 (1996 in UNHRC) being a clean job of politicians of this age, is yet to reveal the whole truth about Human Rights.

Notwithstanding certain positive achievements of the union and state governments in their efforts to attain the universal standard of human rights as stipulated in the international covenants, the human rights situation in the country is far from reaching the benchmark. Institutions have been set up but the impact of the institutions are not significant and resources have not been fully utilized. The union government is placed under international obligation to withdraw the reservations made in regard to the human rights covenants and has to strengthen the creatures of the Constitution in order to improve the human rights, civil liberties and also to make errant officials both officially and personally accountable. The over all achievements in this front have been dismal.

References

1. UN Human Rights Committee, INDIA (29 November,1995), CCPR/C/76/Add. 16-17 June, 1996. 32 pages covering 27 articles of the ICCPR, 1966.
2. UN, Human Rights Committee, 1603rd, 1604th, 1605th, 1606th meetings, Geneva, July 1997. CCPR/C/SR. 1603, 29 July ,1997 etc.
3. UN, Human Rights Committee, Consideration of Reports submitted by State Parties under Article 40 of the Covenant: Concluding Observations of the Human Rights Committee - INDIA, CCPR/C/79/Add. 81, 4 August, 1997. The concluding observations and UNHRC set the material agenda for India.
4. South Asia Human Rights Documentation Centre, Alternate Report and Commentary to - India's Third Periodic Report, July 1997. The SAHDOC alternate report in as many as 110 pages presents facts and figures regarding grave violations of human rights by the state.
5. Amnesty International, INDIA Submissions to the Human Rights Committee.., July 1997, AI Index: ASA 20/27/97.
Amnesty International has urged upon the government of India to ratify the Optional Protocol to the ICCPR, and the Convention against Torture and Other Cruel, Inhuman and Degrading

Treatment or Punishment, to review the Protection of Human Rights Act 1993 and the Armed Forces (Special Powers) Act 1958 and National Security Act, 1980 among others.

6. Alternate Report to the Third Periodic Report ....India, COHR, Manipur, India, February 1997.
7. U.S. Department of State, India Report on Human Rights Practices for 1997, by Bureau of Democracy, January 30,1998.

13
Right to Life in Peril

The human rights defenders around the world have been projected by the persons in power through the powerful multimedia as proxy terrorists till the United Nations has resolved in early April 1998 that the human rights defenders should also be defended from the crimes, likely to be committed by the state agencies. Even the state commissions on human rights would conceive the government officials to utter the voice of the people. The reason is very simple: the commission may be one of the defenders of the state at a time, when the state is in the readiness for commission of state terrorism and state repression in some of the states. We do not impute motives to the state human right commissions, which lack teeth since birth. At present, state commissions provide cosmetic service and act as locai post office at best.

The universality and indivisibility of human rights that had been enunciated by the Universal Declaration of Human Rights, 1948 and two complimentary Covenants of 1966, which the union government of India had ratified for faithful compliance, have once again been reaffirmed and re-endorsed with a concrete programme of action, by the Vienna Declaration in June 1993. On the pressure from the United Nations and international community and also partly as pressurized by the Indian NGOs, the National Human Rights Commissions and a couple of state human right commissions have been constituted under the Protection of Human Rights Act 1993.

The commissions render service to a minimal extent in several aspects excluding the RIGHT TO LIFE, which is extremely precious. In this context, there would be no two opinions about the utility of the commissions on several counts except their institutional incapacity to make legitimate enquiry into the crimes, committed by the security forces, who are put into border-security service during the un-proclaimed *de facto* emergency-situation in the North Eastern region for half a century. The attention of the international community has been drawn recurrently towards this pathetic situation of right to life, by the human rights NGOs.

The United Nations General Assembly had established the post of UN High Commissioner for Human Rights on 20 December ,1993 and Mr. Jose Ayala Lasso has assumed the charge on 5th April ,1994. Ms. Mary Robinson has succeeded Mr. Lasso in 1997. Ms. Mary Robinson, the UN High Commissioner in her address to the Oxford University has dispassionately pointed out the deficiency in national jurisdictions. In her words, "I do not propose to detail here the range of international instruments and mechanisms developed since 1948, but that body of substantive international human rights law is there because domestic protection of vulnerable individuals or groups is either absent or insufficient." The mandate of the UN High Commissioner has been defined by a UN General Assembly resolution as regards the promotion and protection of all human rights, international cooperation for the promotion of human rights, reaction to situations challenging human rights and the adaptation of the UN human rights machinery to the evolving needs. Human rights are indivisible and invariable.

It has been insisted that the Indian legislature and also the National Human Rights Commission should enlarge the commission's jurisdiction and make the commission's verdict enforceable like the order of the court. Even a munsiff's order is enforceable, but the commissions's is not. Even the existing Act does not enable the commission under Section 19 of the Act to investigate into crimes, committed by the security forces without a permission from the union government, which would not literally issue it. The National

Human Rights Commission and the state commissions have statutory powers, as defined in chapter III of the 1993 Act to make broad recommendations for preventing human rights violations including recommendations to repeal Section 19 of the said Act, so as to bring the security forces under its compulsory jurisdiction and the recommendation to repeal the controversial Armed Forces Special Powers Act 1958, considered to be a black law. The Commonwealth Human Rights Initiative (CHRI), has recommended on 20 August, 1998, the repeal of the section 19. In November 1996, Justice Ranganath Mishra felt the need to recommend the repeal of the draconian Act of 1958, but his term shortly expired. However, the union government has repealed the TADA on the recommendation of the National Human Rights Commission. The repeal of the Armed forces Act 1958 is the justifiable, as it contravenes established Rule of Law.

After half a century of engaging the defence forces against the civilian populace in the N.E. region, the union defence ministry appears to have undertaken a paradigm-shift in this aspect. Defence minister George Fernandes has stated that army should not deal with insurgency. (Asian Age, page 1, 21 March ,1998). The defence minister of India has once again categorically announced in Imphal city on April 4,1998 that he stands for the repeal of the Armed Forces Special Powers Act 1958. In his own words : "I believed that the army should not be used against its own people". No judicious cabinet could ever brush aside the defence minister's categorical statement, as because the army has been used for too long against the civilian populace in the region. Even the British never did so during the peak of their brutality against an alien race and people.

'Right to life' is the uppermost in the mind of the citizens of the region. We may recall the proceedings of the House on 18 August, 1958, when discussion took hardly three hours. Inspite of home minister Gobind Ballabh Pant's assurance to the parliament that the 1958 Act was meant for a short duration to deal with Naga hills district, the Act has not only outlived but has also catalysed the conflagration from one tiny district to all over the seven states; and the region has been fully militarised, because of the terror, let loose by this process. The monster-genie ought to be inserted back into the bottle.

Human rights protection is no longer confined to the exclusive domain of the domestic jurisdiction, as we have reported the position of the UN High Commissioner of Human Rights. The UN Human Rights Committee has to oversee India's strict compliance with her international obligation and national commitment. It has to periodically report on her level of compliance and in this regard, the human rights commission and other national institutions do share the responsibility. Universities and NGOs are also effective national institutions, which the responsible state commissions have to consult with dignity and confidence, whereas it has not been done so far because of the deep-rooted elitist-culture, and inveterate feudal outlook.

The UN Human Rights Committee has urged upon the representative of government of India in 1991 to urge upon the government to sign the Optional Protocol to 1966 Covenant and remove all reservations to the 1966 political Covenant. In the last session of the HRC, held on 27 March, 1991 at Geneva, the Attorney General of India assured the committee of removing the reservations. In his words, "And the second apprehension, concern was about the reservation. I will convey to my Government seriously to consider about the reservations, and you all know that it is a political decision." (minutes of the HRC, UN, Geneva).

While considering the Armed Forces Special Powers Act 1958 in 1991, the UN Human Rights Committee found the impugned Act to be incompatible with the right to life provisions of the ICCPR, 1966, which instrument the government of India has signed and ratified for compliance. The UN Human Rights Committee after considering the Third Report of India in its 1603rd and 1606 the meetings held on 24 and 25 July ,1997 at Geneva, made several observations on the pathetic human rights situation in India. The human rights commissions in the country could see that these chronic malaise and slur on humanity be removed by way of their active intervention.

In para. 18 of the observations of the UNHRC, the committee considers terrorism in India and 'armed insurgency' as 'essentially political in character' and hence, they should be 'fought with means that are compatible with the Covenant'. (See UN, CCPR/C/79/Add.81 4 August ,1997, p.4). The political crisis of armed insurgency should be resolved by the union government by applying the universal human rights standard, as defined by the Covenant and human rights cannot be deprived in disregard of the norms of the Covenant. Humanity does not deserve a thorough beating and brutalisation at the hands of the arrogant executive and its armed instrumentalities for one reason or another. Life in the N.E. region has been brutalised for half a century and that is enough for a civilised civil society. The concept of treating the region as a benign concentration camp is reprehensible.

The right to life and security remains the undisputed primary right, which would be complemented by other substantive human rights. The institutions of the government established under law, are duty bound to abide by the 'rule of law' and its subsequent crystallisations, made by the apex court of law. Responsible state officials have been frequently found to be ignorant of the laws and the covenanted rule of law.

Enforced disappearance of citizens and children, custodial deaths, torture are the crimes of the government officials against its citizens. The Supreme Court in its judgement in D.K. Basu vs. State of West Bengal 1996 laid down the rule that the police personnel carrying out arrest and handling interrogation should bear accurate, visible and clear identification and name-tags with their designations. They shall prepare an 'ARREST MEMO' to be attested by at least witnesses who may be either the member of the family or respectable persons of the locality. Other elaborate procedures are also prescribed in order to ensure the safety of the arrested person. The state human rights commissions are under statutory obligation to ensure that security forces are educated, trained up in the light of the indispensable safeguards; but they seem to take more interest in other matters of secondary importance by way of accepting the impunity by default.

In Nilabati Behra judgement, the Supreme Court in 1993 has ordered that any citizen could claim compensation for illegal arrest and detention under article 21 of the Constitution. In 1997, judges S.N.Mullick and S.K. Tiwari of Calcutta High Court have ordered the acquittal of Chakarvarti in November 1997, directed the state government to pay a compensation of Rs. 1 lakh to Chakaravarti and recover the amount of Rs. 1 lakh from the police personnel, who illegally arrested him. Not being content with this package, the court observed that the appellant should proceed against the erring police personnel for civil and criminal remedy. The apex court has consistently developed the *victimology* jurisprudence and rule for compensation since Rudal Shah judgement in 1983 till today. Personal liability of the erring officials has also been consistently ascertained, but the lower courts have to widely apply the law, as provided by Article 141 of the Constitution. This area of law is fast developing.

Custodial deaths are immoral and condemned the world over as the remnant of barbarism of the medieval age. But they occur as a matter of routine in India and the region to be more specific. Supreme Court bench, constituted by B.P. Jeevan Reddy and Subhas Sen ordered on the 6th February 1997, the government of Manipur to pay Rs. 1 lakh compensation each to the families of Lalbeiklin and Saikaplein — two members of the Hmar Peoples Convention, who were killed in false encounter by the police. The Supreme Court passed strictures against *'Administrative liquidation'* by the government and its forces. PUCL complained that the two persons were taken by police in a truck and shot dead. The state routinely shirks responsibility.

The Supreme Court bench, constituted by chief justice J.S.Verma and Justice S.P. Barucha awarded on September 18 ,1997, a compensation of Rs. 1.25 lakh each to the mothers of Thockchom Lokendra Singh and Kangujam Loken Singh, who were picked up by the army on

September 23 ,1980 and returned to an unknown destiny forever. Any other criminal liability of the respondents would not still be affected by the award. In the N.E. region, permanent disappearance of citizens has become customary.

The Armed Forces Special Powers Act 1958 has been challenged by writ petition Nos. 5328/80 and no. (Crl.) 550 of 1982 before the Supreme Court in 1980. A bench consisting of J.S.Verma CJI, M.M.Punchhi, S.C.Agarwal, A.S. Anand and S.P.Bharucha, JJ upheld the constitutional validity of the black law along with a set of guidelines, furnished by the Attorney General of India. *Para*. 56 and 57 of the judgement stipulate the do's and don't's to be obeyed by the security forces which act in aid of the civil administration in disturbed areas. Guidelines cover the actions before operation, action during operation, action after operation, among others. The civil and military authorities have to supervise so that the guidelines are being religiously observed. Immediately after the issuance of these guidelines, students and children in the region have been allegedly abducted by the security forces and the orders of the High Court, issued to top the brass to produce the children and persons abducted are not at all honoured by the top brass. The conflagration escalates and fire fighting is made nearly impossible because of the intransigence and belligerent attitude of the military-machine.

Besides the primacy of the right to life and civil, political and socio-economic rights, the human rights agenda include the collective rights of the women, child, disadvantaged groups, indigenous people, oppressed nations and people, entrenched by colonial and neo-colonial trappings and bondage. It may be added that International humanitarian law is applicable in situations of armed conflicts. The injured, arrested, soldiers or insurgents *hors de combat* have to be honoured, protected, and given medical and other relief by both the parties. Following the experience of the Yugoslavia and Rwanda tribunals, installed by the UN Security Council on the lines of the Tokyo and Nurenberg war-crime tribunals, the International Law Commission has submitted the draft for ICC (International Criminal Court) to the Pre-com in 1994. The Rome conference has adopted to the text in July 1998.

References

1. South Asia Human Rights Documentation Centre, Alternate Report to the UN Human Rights Committee, July, 1997.
2. National Campaign Committee against Militarisation, Proceedings of the workshop, August, 1996 New Delhi.
3. National Campaign Committee, where 'peacekeepers' have declared war, April 1997, New Delhi.
4. COHR, Right to Life in Manipur, 13 February, 1997
5. Amnesty International, INDIA Submission to the Advisory Committee established to review provisions of the Protection of Human Rights Act, 1993, October, 1998 — ASA 20/26/98.

14

Armed Forces Special Powers Act, 1958

The extra-judicial executions of innocent civilian-populace and other forms of naked human rights violations remains a fact of life in the North Eastern states in India for the last four decades. Two contentious stances are being advanced by the state, which has rationalised the enactment and enforcement of demoniacal law like the AFSPA 1958 (Armed Forces Special Powers Act 1958 — AFSPA, hereafter) and by the defenders of the human rights, who not only defy the apparent legitimacy of such a law, but also raised the politico-historical basis of the upsurges, that characterise the North Eastern life. The apex court upheld the statute on 27 November, 1997, by overlooking the gross human rights violations since 1958 whereas it could have struck down the black law.

Indian state, unlike the Indian nationhood is a nascent British-created entity, which has passed through diverse — and even, non-complimentary historical experiences. A nation-in-the-making that India is, Manipur state and Tripura state have been brought to the fold of the nascent state after two years of Indian independence ; the other states of the region remained parts of Assam, which on its part, joined the British Indian mainstream in 1826.

Now, politically speaking, the sub-terranean faultlines[2] are cracking up and Indian state persists in quick-fixing the deep-structured faultlines with the help of the powerful Indian army and state repression, which would loose legitimacy without having demoniacal laws like the AFSPA, and the Punjab Security Act 1953. Occasional patchwork and cosmetic reforms apart, the deep-structured political contradictions are shelved beyond the reach of bold and visionary stroke of statesmanship, which itself is a missing word in the colonial legacy.

The tangible political repercussions of the invocation of the AFSPA demonstrate the following phenomena : Firstly, the correlation of the demoniacal law with corollary of such a law, is found in a subsequent political fallout. The AFSPA's predecessor — the Armed Forces Special Powers Ordinance 1942 — had been enacted in order to neutralise quit-India movement. It was hundred per cent a colonial instrument, used for legitimisation and continuation of colonialism. Nearly 50 nation-states are awaiting for independence in the 21st century. [see UN and UNPO papers]

The 1942 demoniacal ordinance, among others, had expedited and facilitated the passage of Indian Independence Act 1947. The 1958 law inherits the same powerful political potency.

Secondly, the AFSPA was enacted in order to quell the ethnic uprising in Naga hills in Assam in 1958. After four decades, like a nuclear chain-reaction, the invocation of the black law in a small range of hills spread over the conflagration domino effect in all the seven states. It has the potency of flaring-up politically sensitive issues like prairie-fire.

The state and security forces have also been conditioned to demoniacal-law-dependency so much so that the state feels deeply vulnerable/without resorting to *unproclaimed emergency* and special power laws. It is comparable euphemistically to the addict's drug dependency or ICU. The decision-makers in the state and security forces have evolved a different short of hyper-subjective perception in regard to the unresolved political question of historical importance. The distorted perceptions are indicated by the following official projections:[3]

I- The security forces are fighting low-intensity war against ANEs (Anti National Elements, as they are known to the army— the insurgents (ene for enemy);

II- In aid of the civil authority, the forces assume the power for internal security management on par with defence against external aggression;

III-The forces use military power so as to quick-fix the fault lines, inherited from colonial history;

IV-The armed forces need additional empowerment like the AFSPA and other concomitant draconian laws in order to maintain public order; extra judicial power for execution of any suspected citizen under section 4 of the AFSPA and virtual immunity from prosecution under section 6 of the same statute;

V- In doing so, the forces should not be dragged into allegations of human rights-violations; the forces have their own court-martial system;

VI-The forces, deployed by the the third largest army in the world against a few hundreds of politically motivated secessionists can not be considered to have been deployed in excess of the requirement of military necessity;

VII-Human rights violations are not atrocities,[4] but a modest inconvenience, to be born by the civilian population: these violations are a military necessity to keep India in tact.

The reasons had espoused the same set of strong arguments, advanced at the time of enactment and invocation of the colonial Armed Forces Special Powers Ordinance in 1942 by the imperial power, who desired to keep the empire in tact. The obvious contradiction lies in the fact that the justification for colonisation or, re-colonisation through colonial statute after the lapse of the colonialism is totally absurd and false. The demoniacal colonial law had to exist in order to sustain colony and conversely, the invocation of colonial statute proves that the colony survives.

The central issue, which resulted to insurgency or, national liberation movement — as it has been known to the insurgents or, in the parlance of universal de-colonisation, is the historical legacy and a deep-structured political question, which should not be addressed to the draconian law and the army, who had been given additional empowerment under the AFSPA .

The issue has been misconceived as 'law and order' or, at most 'internal security' issue, whereas it bears the intrinsic essence of de-colonisation and national liberation war — euphemistically, known as secessionism. The issue is very deep and the fault lines are profound. The sustenance of the issue for more than four decades itself indicates that human rights violations and the twisted perceptions are merely symptoms of the malaise. The Annual Report of Home Ministry, Government of India 1996-97 reports about the states most affected by insurgent activities of various militant groups. The union government, has therefore, arranged for talks with the Nagaland outfits since 1997.

The available evidence, the demands-structure, the historical facts and the pattern of union government's response to the issue make it amply clear that the decades-old political violence, as espoused by the insurgents or liberation army, has been a consequence of unresolved political question.

Historical evidence very clearly stipulates that (I) Manipur[5] and Tripura had been annexed to the Indian political fold, after two years of Indian independence; (II) Assam became a part of British India not by her choice but by the choice of Burma and British, who signed the Treaty of Yandaboo[6] in 1826; (III) the ethnic tribes who remained in the excluded hill areas of Assam fused themselves in the last five decades into nationhood and claimed independence prior to the passage of Indian Independence Act 1947 and (IV) British-created India has been a totally different entity from the original Indian nation that continued for centuries in the Gangetic basin. The British-created India has been a deliberate political creation, unlike the homogenous Indian nation, based on Aryabrata. The issue is, therefore, not secession, but about fixing the region to India by hammer and tongs.

The accords[7a] reached and breached between national groups and the government during the last four decades, being purely political issues in all sense of the term, exclude the wide arms of the apex court or, human rights commissions or, the instruments of the civil government like the army. Since 1997, the union government[8] has initiated political moves by holding dialogue with one of the liberation outfits from amongst a couple of effective outfits.

The human right violations following the invocation of special demoniacal laws and state repressions for nearly half-a-century has been inextricably associated with the political question. The issue, therefore, stands for the closest political scrutiny; however, the enactment of special laws, invocation of emergency laws without formal declaration of emergency have to be assessed on the basis of 'Rule of law' and accepted standards civilised jurisprudence.

Humanitarian law

The imperative need for the government to abide by the International bill of human rights arises out of constitutional requirement, general customary International law, common law background, state practices and above all, the union government's signature and ratification of the two convenants, 1966 on 10 April ,1979. The bindingness of human-rights law on the part of the union government and its instruments like the security forces etc. arises out of the following norms, obligations and assured compliance:

I : Articles 253,51,53,246, schedule VII list I[9] items 10-15,among others, of the Constitution of India;

II :State practices starting from India's becoming a member of the United Nations in 1945, even before two years of her independence;

III :General and customary International law, *Jus Cogens* as followed by the comity and community of nations, of which India is an inseparable part;

IV :The supreme court of India's endorsement of the human rights covenants of the United Nations in the process of evolving 'human rights jurisprudence' in several landmark public interest litigations cases ; and the apex court's endorsement of the human rights covenants by incorporation as part of particular fundamental right, is found in the apex court statement in PUCL vs. Union of India (1977) 2 JT 3/1/1) among others ;

V :Fundamental rights under chapter III of the Constitution which can no longer be suspended even during a situation of emergency, following the 44th amendment of the Constitution;

VI :Article 21, compounded with articles 14 and 19 of the Constitution that has been placed as a special class of mini-code, specially after the construction of 'due process of law'[10] meaning in the 'procedure duly established by law';

VII :Rule of law, democracy and judicial review which are the basic features of the Constitution, unlike peripheral and unsustainable special laws, which do not conform to the basic tenets of 'rule of law'.

Human rights covenants, signed and ratified by the union government of India are no longer convenient appendages, which could be dispensed with, whenever found inconvenient. They are increasingly indispensable.

The international standard of human rights, which has been defined by the Constitution and International bill of human rights has to be complied with by the union government and its civil as well as military instrumentalities. In the case of the compliance or non-compliance, the union government has been placed for reporting obligations[11] under article 40 of the ICCPR, 1966. The union government has so far submitted three periodic reports to the UN Human Rights Committee[12] and the Fourth report is due by 2001, as reported by the committee.

Besides constitutional and legal accountability, the union government is politically accountable to the comity of nations for the maintenance of *'peace'* and *'security'*, as envisaged by the UN Charter, the violation of which could be made a subject matter of the UN instrumentalities including the action of the UN Security Council. Just because India is having one of the largest army and special laws empowering the army to commit covert or, overt genocide, it does not waive its accountability towards the maintenance of peace and security in the world by resorting to naked state repression of the dependent populace.

The union government of India had recognised a number of national liberation outfits or, insurgent groups as bodies demanding secession from the country vide the Unlawful Activities (Prevention) Act 1967 and other similar laws. The statute has paradoxically given recognition to the national liberation outfits as bodies fighting war of independence and secession from the union of India.

Periodically, notice has been publicly issued to these bodies through dailies in order to lend testimony to that they mean separation from India and claim independence. The series of governmental gazettes, notices and publications, by implication, label that these outfits are merely 'goons', 'criminals', provocateurs of 'law & order' problem and both the parties, interlocked in insurgency and counter-insurgency armed conflicts endorse the same view point that the outfits demand independence from India and they use *'Any Means'* in the process of their liberation struggle. International humanitarian laws[13] become, therefore, relevant in the context of the governmental recognition of the outfits as political organisations, committed to a political cause.

The prevailing International humanitarian Laws invariably stipulate the following universal standards, which even in the event of violation, do not lose their standing legitimacy :

I : The four Geneva Conventions,[14] 1949, signed by the union government of India and Indian enactment of Geneva Conventions Act 1961 render the International humanitarian Laws applicable to India and its forces:

II :The protection of life and property of the civilians, *hors de combat* is non-derogable[15] under common article 3 of the Conventions and the two Protocols. World Court (ICJ) has endorsed this right as *Jus Cogens*[16] and the same under customary international law (Nicaragua vs. USA, (1986):

III :The non-combatants, civilians — injured, wounded or, arrested insurgents are, therefore, fully protected under the law. (*see Martens clause*). The Supreme Court Judgement in NPMHR vs. Union of India, 27 November, 1997 has laid down guidelines in para. 56-58, [see Document annexed]; these guidelines cannot be violated.

IV :The insurgents and national liberation movements had been admittedly accepted as subjects of International law, specially after the de-colonisation movements since the 1960s. Since the beginning of the 1960's — "It has been increasingly the practice among states, based on claims by the Third World and as expressed in United Nations resolutions, to consider manifestations of a people's right to self determination as an international event".[16a] Insurgents [17] are also bound by International humanitarian law. The details of the application of the law are widely known.

V :State practices indicate that *national liberation movements* are legitimate barring in the case of naked terrorism and ordinary crimes. UN resolutions passed by the GA, Security Council, International Court of Justice and UN committees make it abundantly clear that legitimate movements[18] are not terrorism *per se* and internal security matters. 35 states have emanated in this process.

VI :The use of force is not only governed by the humanitarian laws and state practices, but also by other principles, like 'Basic Principles on the use of Force and

Firearms by Law Enforcement Officials.' [UN, Professional training series No. 5, Human Rights and Law enforcement, 1997]. India could not use force against liberation movements.

VII :Since the crystallisation of International criminal law jurisdiction in Tokyo and Nurenburg war crime tribunals and in UN jurisdiction in Yugoslav and Rwanda tribunals in the recent years, crimes committed against a race or, mankind are subject to presecution, trial and punishment. Protection of civilian life and property is taken more seriously in armed conflict - situation and it is non-derogable.

VIII:The International Criminal Court, adopted in 1998 would become functional after the ratification is completed in the early part of 21st century.

As discussed above, the state has the responsibility and obligation to honour and comply with the internal and international human-rights standards in all shifting circumstances. The insurgents[18a] are also under obligation to protect civilian life and property; they have to declare that they abide by the Geneva Conventions in this regard. However, they lack the compulsory state obligations as long as they do not constitute a recognised state and become a member of the United Nations. In this sense, their obligations are more narrowed and limited than what the state had to comply with and periodically report compliance to the comity of nations. The insurgents could demonstrate their sense of responsibility by complying with common article 3 of the Geneva Conventions, 1949.

Procedure established by law

The protection of life and liberty of a person including citizen is a sacrosanct commitment of the Constitution under article 21 which states :

"No person shall be deprived of his life or personal liberty except according to procedure established by law."

The provision intrinsically is not an enabling law, but a disabling law. It can not and should not be construed so as to mean that one's life should be taken away by enacting a law. A larger bench of the apex court should - it is deeply felt - have reviewed, therefore, the 27 November ,1997 judgement. The sharp difference to be discovered between an enabling law and disabling law can be best understood only by considering the paradigm of jusuice as the basic foundation in the constitution.

The *'procedure established by law'* is construed as one of the easiest ways and methods to commit gross injustice and even genocide against an alien race. The 27 November, 1997 apex court ruling is henceforth untenable. A similar example is seen in the Third Reich,[19] which has taken several millions of human lives as tuition-fee for teaching the world that one can establish such a procedure under law and constitutionally wipe out a people [race], you dislike.

After this lesson, we learnt after paying a hefty tuition-fee, that all the constitutional and legal acts should pass through a test of profound justice, fairness and reasonableness. Not so long ago, the USA bought and cut off coloured people as they do to the vegetables and the same was repeated in apartheid regime in South Africa under *'procedure established by law.'* So, the *'procedure established by law'* of these regimes had been condemned unto the last man by the civilized world. Similarly, the parliament had enacted in 1958 according to *'procedure established by law'* — the demonical AFSPA 1958 — in order to give additional empowerment to the security forces to commit extra-judicial murders by shooting down, a race of people, who have recently joined[20] the Indian mainstream as 'distinct people.'

Ridiculously, the Third Reich had enacted lawfully. It had Nurenberg laws of September 15, 1936, Reconstruction of Law, January 30, 1934 and had witnessed Emergency Presidential Decree of February 28, 1933 under article 48 of the German Constitution. By law of March 21, 1933, special court had been set up for trial of cases of "insidious attacks against the government." The official gazette *"Reichsgesets blatt"* published the lawful government orders under "AB

Action" or, beautifully worded "Extraordinary Pacification Action "(*Ausserordenliche Befriedigungsaktion*). Intelligentsia who do not subscribe to 'one people, one reich and one faith' had been cleansed away. The third Reich and Indian parliament acted absolutely *intra vires* the constitution.

The cleansing of Germany by weeding out the Jews had not been performed without observing constitutionality and a lawful procedure. The *'Procedure established by law'* may wipe the entire populace in the North Eastern states or, the indigenous people in the region by enacting laws like the AFSPA and the apex court totally ignored complaints, till the contemplated act has been completed. However, India's apex court is usually prompt to strike down, at a moment's notice, incompatible statutes or executive action *suo moto* or, otherwise in the normal course. It did not happen to writ No. 550 of 1982 till 1997.

The *'procedure established by law'* in the context of article 21 has undergone enormous change in the process of construction. The transformation, it has undergone is crystallised below :

(I) :Justice Fazal (in minority, but in more saner way than the majority) in Gopalan vs. State of Madras (1950 SCR) stated that the word 'established ' suggests " certain principles of Justice which inhere in every civilized system of law" (p. 180). The absence of the word 'due process' in article 21 could not lead to a possible self-righteous and arbitrary use of the procedure ;

(II):The majority judgement in Maneka Gandhi vs. Union of India, A.I.R.,1978, S.C.. 597 made it amply clear that whatever procedure is prescribed by the statute "cannot be arbitrary, unfair or unreasonable" (p.622). If the procedure is arbitrary or so, the court would invalidate laws which prescribed an unjust, unfair or unreasonable procedure. The procedural 'due process' has been constructed out of the silent zone of article 21 ;

(III) :By a creative interpretation of the article 21, Justice P.N.Bhagwati enlarged the sweep of the procedure. In his words: "The principle of reasonableness, which legally as well as philosophically, is an essential element of equality or non-arbitrariness pervades Art. 14 like an omnipresence and the procedure contemplated by Art.21 must answer the test of reasonableness in order to be in conformity with Art 14. It must be "right and just and fair" and not arbitrary, fanciful or oppressive; otherwise it would be no procedure at all and the requirement of Art. 21 would not be satisfied."

(IV) :The meaning of life under Art. 21 has been progressively and more affirmatively interpreted by the apex court 21 in the subsequent PIL cases. In this context, the amplitude of 'reasonableness' is widened to the extent of saving the life from arbitrary deprivation, and statutes forestall the slightest tinge of arbitrariness even in the common sense.

(V) :The "Human Rights Jurisprudence", which all the agencies of the government subscribe to, by virtue of the International Bill of Rights and Jus Cogens blatantly censures extra-judical executions and other brutalities, committed by the state.

The near-permanent perpetuation of a 'Lawless Law' — the AFSPA — in the post-colonial period, cannot at all be justified except on the score of re-colonisation of a *'distinct group of people'* belonging to and rooted in a distinct region, who happily remained outside the geo-political geography of India for millennia, till they had been conveniently quick-fixed to the mainland in the recent past.

The *'distinct people'*,more particularly the indigenous people of the region find no other reason than considering the 'Lawless Law' as outrageously repressive.The demonical AFSPA statute[22] does not deserve to remain for a day longer in the statute book of a civilized legal system.Home Minister G.B.Pant got this statute enacted as a short term measure in

1958 after a discussion for three hours only.The justification for the immediate scrapping of such a statute are cited below:

Historical reasons

i] In the post-colonial era, no repressive law whatsoever had succeeded in resolving deep-structured political crisis. It could be Palestine case, Vietnam, Bangladesh or, Soviet Union in 1991 or situation of the Rowlatt Act 1911; and Armed Forces Special Powers Ordinance 1942 had rather hastened and expedited passage of Indian Independence Act 1947, before it was actually due in June 1948.

ii] AFSPA is a recrudescence and revival of the British colonial statute and it should not be re-enacted in the post-colonial scenario under any circumstances. AFSPA is the best evidence of sustaining colonial law in a new era.

iii]Parliament did not fully apply its mind to the passage of this black statute in 1958. The law which partook an emergency status had been enacted without formal declaration of emergency. Ostensibly, the statute was enacted for a brief while and not for the perpetuity. The United Nations Human Rights Committee addressed itself to this issue in July 1997,

iv]When the parliament briefly discussed the purpose of invoking the law in Manipur and Naga hills, among others, all the MPs of Manipur resisted the passage of the law. It had been thrust upon the helpless racial minority by a brute and tyrannical majority against the vehement resistance of the minority.

v] It has a covert agenda for genocide.

i] The initial objective of enacting the black law had been totally betrayed and frustrated. The statute was enacted so as to contain a small-scale uprising in Naga hill district of the state of Assam, which was just a tiny district among several larger districts of Assam. After four decades of invocation of the law, the insurgent flare-up has spread over in Manipur, Assam, Nagaland, Tripura, Arunachal Pradesh, Meghalaya[23] etc. 'The mightier the state repression, the wider is popular discontent and insurgency-proliferation' — is apparently the law of nature in the new epoch.

ii] The over all cost - benefit of the passage and invocation of the black law is counter-productive. It had already cost not less than 30,000 crores of poor tax payer's money, while the starving millions of Indians need a square meal from this drained - out money. In the list of HDI in 1999, India stands as the 134th in terms of human development in the world, because of this obsession. The arms race is flagged off on 11th May 1998 in South Asia with 5 nuclear weapons test by government of India.

Constitutional incompatibility

i] The declaration of disturbed area by the union government has not been guided by obvious, objective criteria. The whole exercise has been arbitrary, since *de facto* emergency had been impared without formal promulgation.

ii] The maintenance of public order and tranquillity is within the ambit of the Cr. P.C. section 129 of Cr. P.C. provides for the dispersal of assembly by use of civil force; sec. 130, for use of armed forces[24] to disperse assembly and sec. 131 for power of certain armed forces officers to disperse assembly. The existing fundamental law of the land is adequate enough to moblise armed forces in bringing peace and tranquillity in the civil order. The AFSPA is an additional, but highly repressive and oppressive empowerment of the forces.

iii] It blatantly violates the internal and international standards of human rights, as enunciated above and universally agreed upon. It negates India's conviction and commitment.

iv] Section 4 (a), (b), (c), (d), of the black law is a direct transgression upon articles 21 and 22 of the Constitution. The power to 'fire upon' to the extent of 'causing death'[25] given to the lowest rung of NCO on the slightest suspicion i.e. the power to commit extra - judicial execution is not only arbitrary, unjust, unfair but is also a legitimization of outright murder. No civilized jurisprudence would justify this additional empowerment, given to the forces to kill citizens. The apex court by its 27 November, 1997 judgement failed to give reason to refute the criticism of the powers so exercised. It has in just one or, two pages very weakly upheld section 4 of the Statute. It has run short of ammunition.

v] The apex court judgement commands respectability and bindingness according to article 141 of the Constitution. The Delhi High Court judgement — Indrajit Barua vs State of Assam (AIR 1983, Delhi 513) had the least bearing with article 141. The Supreme Court has disposed of the writ petition nos. 5328 of 1980, 550 of 1982 and 9229 and 9230 of 1982, which challenged the constitutionality of impugned black statute,[25a] on November 27, 1997 after long seventeen years of receiving the petition in 1980. After accepting a set of guidelines to be followed at the time of enforcing the law, the apex court has upheld the validity of the Armed Forces (Special Powers) Act 1958, the repeal of which has also been desired by chairman of the National Human Rights Commission in 1996.

The Constitutional bench, headed by chief justice J.S.Verma, in its 60 page judgement observed that the parliament could enact the impugned statute, under power conferred under article 248 read with list 1 entry 2, entry 97 and entry 2A, inserted after the 42nd Constitutional amendment. The verdict borders on the extreme edge of technical formalism of the crudest positivist kind, which is totally devoid of the public justice, as accepted at this stage of our civilisation. Till a full bench of the apex court (13 judges or so) decides, the positivist verdict stands in justification for a draconian law.

The PUDR rightly observes, "The court refused to go into the actual working of the Act and deemed it irrelevant for purposes of deciding its constitutionality" and the basic fact that the Constitution does not envisage long term deployment of the armed forces in civilian areas has been concealed.

VI]The apex court did not apply to mind to the relevance of humanitarian laws to the conflict - situation in the N.E. region.

International standard

All the black laws — particularly, the AFSPA, 1958 — enacted by the parliament of India are found to be manifestly incompatible with the international standard for the following reasons :

i] The United Nations Human Rights Committee[26] in 1991 found section 4 of the AFSPA and other sections too, to be incompatible with articles 6, 9, and 14 of the International Covenant[27] on Civil and Political Rights,1966, the compliance of which has become union government's obligation following India's ratification of the Covenant on 10 April ,1979 : the incompatibility has not yet been rectified by the union government;

ii] The global opinion passes strictures on the violation of human rights by the state with the instrumentality of black laws. The Amnesty International[28] in 1993 recommends that the government should review the black law and incorporate the minimum safeguards, as provided in the relevant articles of the covenant. The Amnesty further recommends in April 1997 that the government of India should "review the Armed Forces (Special Powers) Act to ensure that there are strict legal limitations on the use of force and firearms by law enforcement officials" and "remove the requirement of sanction for the prosecution of police or armed forces personnel under section 7 of the Armed Forces (Special Powers) Act."

iii]The human rights organisations in India had sent memoranda to the National Human Rights Commission[29] by censuring and denouncing sections 3, 4, and 5 of the AFSPA, which have been instrumental in the gross violations of human rights;

iv]The UNHRC in 1997 has recommended that the government of India should remove restrictions, given by article 19 of the 1993 Human Rights Act.

v] Prevention of Terrorism (Additional Powers) Act 1967 and also the 1989 Act had been inappropriately cited as reference point of United Kingdom. But they are temporary measures unlike the perpetuated AFSPA. In United Kingdom, the anti-terrorist Act of 1989 - now 1996 has been invariably followed by a political package like the *'Downing Street Declaration'* (Anglo-Irish),[30] December 15, 1994 prescribing right of the Irish people to self - determination and 10th April Belfast Agreement 1998. In British India also, the demonical Armed Forces Special Powers Ordinance 1942 was not enacted without itself being followed by the complimentary, all — healing Indian Independence Act 1947. The Brits are relinquishing Northern Ireland in phases by virtue of the 1998 Agreement.

vi] The non-self governing territories in N.E. regions need de-colonisation and a popular consultation could be arranged as it has been in East Timor on 30 August, 1999.

Way ahead

The gross human rights violations in the North Eastern states of India have been fully documented by human rights NGO's in India.[31] The Amnesty International observes that the AFSPA 1958 empowers the government to make *'de facto* derogation from non-derogable covenant rights' and it has urged upon the UNHRC to examine the factum of this derogation.[32] By criticising the black law - AFSPA 1958 and the licence to shoot and kill any citizen merely on suspicion, SAHRDOC[33] observes : "These provisions give a broad licence to extrajudicially execute" innocent and suspected persons under the disguise of maintaining law and order. It violates every norm of civilised society. The juridical conscience in the apex court and elsewhere legitimised extra-judicial massacres. This is deplorable.

The UN Human Rights Committee[34], while showing deep concern at the state's continuing reliance on the AFSPA, the Public Safety Act and National Security Act, which are incompatible with articles 6, 7, 9 and 14 of the Covenant recommends that the insurgency problems which are essentially in political in character be resolved with means that are compatible with the Covenant. Reacting against clause 19 of the Protection of Human Rights Act 1993 the UNHRC recommends that "these restrictions be removed and that the National Human Rights Commission be authorised to investigate all allegations of violations by agents of the State." The government continues illegitimate derogation of the observation.

The union government of India has already considered the insurgency as a political question and initiated unconditional political dialogue with certain section of hill insurgents[36] since August 1997 ; but it left out other effective and equally viable insurgent groups from the political dialogue on the chronic political questions. The very fact of holding political negotiation between the union government and the insurgent group on the initiative of the former has disproved the administrative misnomer in treating the political questions as ordinary law and order problem. The polemic is blatantly self-contradictory.

The Supreme Court bench[37], headed by chief justice J.S. Verma heard seven petitions challenging the constitutionality of the impugned Armed Forces (Special Powers) Act 1958, the first of which had been filed by the Manipur Human Rights Forum in October 1980. The bench upheld the law that interferes with the deep-rooted political question. India's defence Minister[38] however, calls for repeal of the black law of 1958. The continuance of this black law gives a fillip to the insurgency.

The draconian law — AFSPA 1958 — that violates the vital provisions of the International Covenants, infringes upon the basic tenets of civilised policy and *'Rule of Law'* for the last forty years ought to be scrapped from the statute book once and for all. The deep-structured political and nationality questions that characterise the turmoil in the North Eastern states[39] for half a century deserve political attention and resolution. Notwithstanding the changing political dynamics and fluidity in the discourse-pattern, the fact remains that the global human rights standard should not be at all compromised with one pretext or, another and the state responsibility in this context, leaves no room for abdication.

References

1. Alvin and Heidi Toffler, War and Anti-war, 1994.

1a. Amnesty International, INDIA, Official Sanction for killings in Manipur, April 1997, AI Index : ASA 20/14/97 ;
- Right to Life in Manipur, COHR, Imphal, April 1997.
- Amnesty International, INDIA "Operation Bluebird" A Case study of Torture and extra judicial executions in - Manipur, 10, October 1990;

- Amnesty International and India, March 1996, AI Index: ASA 20/05/96;
- Amnesty International, INDIA Memorandum to the Government of India, August, 1994 : ASA 20/20/94
- INDIA Assam : The Killing of a human rights defender, June 1996, AI Index: ASA 20/28/96 ;
- see other AI reports ;
-'India silent on annual US report on rights violations', Asian Age, 7 Feb, 1998, p. 4;

2. Phanjoubam Tarapot, Insurgency Movement in North-Eastern India, 1996; The early India was covered by 'Magadha, Videha, Kashi, Koshala, Panchalas only.
- see, Jawaharlal Nehru, Glimpses of World History, p.26 ; after 1824-26, Assam joins British India, p. 411,Glimpses;
- On Manipur and Tripura, see V.P. Menon, The Story of the Integration of the Indian States, Orient, 1961, p.288-289 and 287;
3. Army chief's statement, published in dailies, May middle, 1997 and also occasional military observations and hand-outs, as published ;
4. Casual observations in forums ;
5. PDM, Annexation of Manipur 1949, Imphal, 1995 ;
R.M. Lahiri, The Annexation of Assam, Firma, 1975 ;The indigenous Tripuris have been swamped by illegal foreign migrants, who rule Tripura now and they had been reduced to 20% of the population as a direct result of the merger with India. Minority Tripuris (not the illegal immigrants) took up armed struggle but they are vanquishing at the hands of India's ruling class.
6. See text of Yandaboo Treaty in A.C. Bannerjee, The Eastern Frontier of British India., 1943, p.405 Article 2;
7. Nicholas Mansergh, Transfer of Power, 1942-1947, all volumes; see H.V. Hodson, The Great Divide 1969, among others;

7a See Shillong Accord, 1975, Mizo Accord, Assam Accord 1985 etc.;

8. "Gujaral urges N-E insurgents to accept talks offer", Times of India headline, May 21, 1997; the Prime Minister addressed the Lok Sabha on March 4, 1997 that he has invited the insurgents for "discussions without preconditions, in order to find a political solution which would ensure durable peace in the region". One of the insurgent leaders Isak Chishi Swu addressed his ethnic HOHO

parliament in Nagaland that the "talks shall be unconditional from both sides", be held outside India, on 21 March ,1997 (NE Sun, 1-14 April 97) p.9. It reminds one of the round table talks of M.K. Gandhi with the British;

9. Art. 51: The state shall endeavour to (a) promote international peace and security .. (d) encourage settlement of international disputes by arbitration; see Constitution text for details;

10. Durga Das Basu, Human Rights in Constitution at Law, 1994, pp. 365-522;

11. Art. 40 of ICCPR; " I. The States Parties to the present Convenant undertake to submit reports on the measures they have adopted which give effect to the rights recognized herein and on the progress made in the enjoyment of those rights;"

12. India Initial Report, 4 July, 1983 to UNHRC; India Second Report,
12 July, 1989 UNHRC; India Third Report,29 November ,1995, UNHRC - See Human Rights Monitor, nos. 35-40,1997, ed.. Zoller, Geneva;

13. See Hans Peter Gasser, International Humanitarian Law, Henry Dunant Institute, Haupt, 1993 ; The Geneva Conventions of August 12, 1949, ICRC and Protocols Additional to the Conventions, ICRC ;

14. By common article 3, in armed conflict situations, 'violence to life and person, in particular murder of all kinds, mutilation, cruel treatment and torture,' etc. of civilians and wounded soldiers, or goerrillas are prohibited;

15. ibid. Even wounded soldiers, insurgents need humanitarian care, under Geneva Conventions. Only the rogue state violates this rule. Under the 4 Geneva Conventions, 1949 and the two additional protocols, 1977, insurgents and guerrillas, captured by the other belligerant party should be retained in their custody without molestation, injury or any other form of damage to their human person, which should be honoured under all circumstances till they are transferred to the POW camps. The state consistently violates the rule in the N.E. region.

16. International Court of Justice in Nicaragua vs. USA, held that articles 1 and 3 of the Geneva Conventions reflect general principles of Customary International Law;

16a. ICRC, International Humanitarian Law, 1993, p. 72;

17. Hans-Peter Gasser writes : "Insurgents, therefore, generally have the legal status of subjects with rights and obligations under

international law only if they have been recognised as such... Yet there is no doubt either in theory or practice that insurgents are bound by international humanitarian law," p. 69;

18. See for UN norms, principles in, N. Sanajaoba, Right of Oppressed Nations (and peoples), ND, 1996 pp. 82-119, 245-258. The Indian scholars and media call national liberations in the word as terrorism and stand against de-colonisation in the world;

18a. One of the viable outfits - RPF - has deposited on Geneva 1997, instrument to abide by common article 3 in order to become subject of International Law. Other outfits will follow;

19. William L. Shirer, Rise and Fall of the Third Reich, 1960;

20. *See* f.n. 5, 6 supra ;

21. *See* f.n. 10 *supra* ; recent PIL cases of the apex court, 1997;

22. South Asia Human Rights Documentation Centre, AFSPA, 1958 ; AI reports — f.n. 1 *supra* ; UN Human Rights Committee proceedings, 1039 - 1042 meetings, Geneva ; NHRC, Issue paper on AFSPA, 13 May, 1997 mimeographed; COHR, Manipur, Alternate Report on 3rd Periodic Report, India, February 1997;

23. Recently, AFSPA had been promulgated to Tripura in 1997 ;

24. Section 130 (3) Cr. P.C., " Every such officer of the armed forces shall obey such requisition in such manner as he thinks fit, but in doing so he shall use as little force, do as little injury to person and property..." The army has enough and enormous power under normal law of the land ;

25. AI reports, NGOs, UNHRC and mass of people protest against this kind of absolute licence to commit extra-judicial murders by army; the apex court holds up the writ petitions since 1980 on the subject ; so, it loses credibility in NES. It could have given its verdict in 1980 or, 1981 at the latest;

25a. See PUDR, Supreme Court judgement on the AFSPA, New Delhi, May 1998 for criticism of the verdict;

25b. ibid. p. 3;

26. UN HRC reports, GA, 46th session, New York, 1991 ;

27. Article 6 of the ICCPR, 1966 - "Every human being has the inherent right to life. This right shall be protected by law. No one shall be arbitrarily deprived of his life." *Contra* Sec. 4 of AFSPA stands for arbitrary execution even on mere suspicion;

28. *See* f.n. 1 *supra*, in details ;

29. NHRC issue paper, May 13, 1997 ; its former chairman R.N. Mishra desired to the recommend revocation of AFSPA in

November 1996 . Every right-thinking person demands its immediate revocation;

30. See f.n. 18 *supra*. p. 82 and 102 ; British premier Tony Blair offered separate parliaments to Scotland and Wales; he looks at Kashmir issue from the international law perspective as a remnant of the British colonial hangover;
31. The Committee on Human Rights (COHR), Manipur,Right to Life in Manipur, February 13, 1997 - COHR/EJE/RPT-97. The report records. "1.36 The issue of the AFSPA surfaced prominently during the discussion of the second periodic report of India under the ICCPR by the UN Human Rights Committee in 1991 in New York. The Committee members were shocked to learn that such legislation exists in a supposedly democratic country like India." Ultra-chauvinists support this law; Some of them express desire to liquidate all people in one night.
    The above report has been followed by another in April 1997- 'Where peacekeepers have declared war' in seven North Eastern states. (The Other Media has, however, misrepresented the history and geography of the states like Manipur, Assam and Arunachal Pradesh, as it is based on the Other Media's campaign for Greater Nagaland by proxy).
32. Amnesty International, INDIA, Submission to the Human Rights Committee concerning the application of the International Covenant on Civil and Political Rights, July 1997— AI Index : ASA 20/27/97, p. 38. See details on the incompatibility of the AFSPA with the ICCPR, 1966;
33. South Asia Human Rights Documentation Centre, Alternate Report and Commentary to the UNHRC, July 1997, pp. 46-47 ;
34. UN, Human Rights Committee, CCPR/C/79 Add. 81, 4 August 1997, INDIA Concluding observations of the Human Rights Committee, para, 18, p. 4;
35. ibid. *para*. 22, pp. 4-5; The Fourth India Report on Human Rights situation in India is due on 31 December, 2001, para 35, p 7 of the above report;
36. All the national dailies in India, July-August, 1997. The government of India had talked to the NSCN-IM in Paris, Bangkok, Davos, Geneva, Zurich, Atlanta and many places outside India in a bid to resolve Nagaland insurgency. PMs Narsimha Rao, Devigowda, I.K.Gujral and Vajpayee took steps. None of these governments enjoyed 2/3 majority in the parliament;

37. The Asian Age, 25 August, 1997, pp. 1-2. Even dailies like the Sentinel in Guwahati states in its editorial, dated 24 September, 1997:
"This is the kind of power (sec. 4 of AFSPA) that a dictator of a banana republic may hand over to his military chief. It is high time, therefore, that the Armed Forces (Special Powers) Act and the Disturbed Areas Act were repealed without any loss of time, and our army instructed to grapple with insurgency with the same kind of laws that the armies all over the world are subject to when placed in similar situations." p. 4, Sentinel daily, Guwahati. *See* ' Amnesty Slams Ultras for Targeting Civilians', IANS, Sentinel daily, 10 February, 1998, p.4;
38. George Fernande's statement in Imphal, on 4 April, 1998, Telegraph, 5.4.1998, p.7. His union cabinet remians silent;
39. N.Sanajaoba, Constitution and Ethnic Aspirations, GUTA seminar, 6 May ,1998 ; NE Daily, 14-15 May, 98. *cf.* His advocacy for repeal of AFSPA, National Campaign Committee, Guwahati, 23 May ,1998;

FURTHER READINGS

Author's Publications on Human Rights

1. Right of the Oppressed Nations and Peoples, Omsons, New Delhi,1996.

2. `Human Rights in the 21st Century', in J.L. KAUL, *Ed.* Human Rights, 1995.

3. Human Rights, Principles and Practices, Omsons, 1994.

4. Human Rights - Myth and Reality, NS., 10 December, 1982.

5. Ambulance Justice, NS,2 June ,1983.

6. Human Rights in India, Vera Lex, New York, 1&2, 1983.

7. On Human Rights, NS, 10 December ,1984.

8. Earth Watch : Panorama of Human Rights, GUJL, 1985.

9. Destabilising Indian Apartheid, *Souvenir,* National Seminar on Ambedkar, New Delhi, 1987.

10. Human Rights Commission, *Assam Tribune*, 10 December, 1992.

11. Human Rights Violations, *North East Times*, 6 May, 1993.

12. Human Rights Enforcement, *Assam Tribune*, 29 & 30 October, 1993.

13. Right to Self - Determination, *News Front*, 10 December, 1991 & also in NET, etc.

14. Right to Self Determination, UGC Seminar, May 1992, GU.

15. Human Rights Advocacy, Seminar, Banglore, 1993.

16. Human Economic Rights, CLEA, Bangalore, 1993.

17. National Liberation-Terrorism Dichotomy, Asian Chapter, Commonwealth Legal Education Association Seminar, Rohtak, 1994.

18. Genocide in Bosnia, International Centre of Legal Science, the Hague, July 1994 (Invited to chair a session).

19. Right of the Child during Armed Conflicts, International Conference, ILI, New Delhi, March 1994.

20. Human Conditions in Manipur and Global HR Standard, PDM, 4 Dec. 94.

21.to 41. Human Rights Thematic serials, *Chingkhẹi Hunba* monthly January 1994-1996 (separate themes - 22 elaborate series).

22. Indo-Nazi Apartheid, *Explorer Weekly*, Imphal, March 1994 (15 series).

23. On Racism and Human Rights, *Imphal Times*, April 1997 (series).

24. Human Economic Rights, *Freedom daily*, April 1994 (20 Series).

25. UN at Fifty plus-Human Rights Benchmark, *Assam Tribune*, 18 December 1995.

26. Peoples Law vs. Anti-People Black Law, Freedom, 24-27 July 96 also in *Imphal Free Press*. All Assam Lawyers Assn. souvenir, 1996.

27. International Humanitarian Law, NE Herald Tribune, 17 Feburary, 1996.

28. Human Rights of AIDS patient, Souvenir, Journalism Dept., GU, 1995.

29. Perspective of Global AIDS Law, International Conf. ILI, 1996.

30. Historical Perspective - International Humanitarian Law, ICRC, 16 April, 1996, Guwahati, also Calcutta,1995.

31. Illegal Trade in Human Organs, Freedom, July 1995.

32. Myths & Reality of Human Rights, Keynote speech, NEHRCO, Guwahati, 1995.

33. Dalit Liberation, Allahabad, 1996, *cf.* His other writings on Ambedkar.

34. Time to End the Nightmare, Time to Repeal AFSPA, 58, *Freedom*, 24, Oct. 96.

35. Hot Spots - Taking HR seriously, ASHRC, 3-6 October, 1996.

36. Contemporary debate: Violence against HR in India, keynote address, New Delhi, 10 Dec, 96.

37. On Immediate Revocation of AFSPA, 58, Memo, NHRC, ND, 13 May, 1997.

38. Right of Children in North-Eastern States in a Situation of Ongoing Armed Conflict, National Institute of Public Cooperation, Guwahati, 28-29, Jan. 1998 (chaired on 29.1.98).

39. Indigenous people's perception, NECOHR, 1997, Guwahati.

40. Right to life, Human Security and Border Security, (presidential address) HR Seminar, Lakhipur, 10 May, 1998.

41. *Mee-Oibagee Haq,* National Research Centre, Imphal, 1999.

SUPREME COURT VERDICT

NPMHR VS. UNION OF INDIA, WRIT PETITION (CRL) 550 OF 1982

Before J.S. Verma, CJI and other 4 judges
27 November ,1997

Excerpt

56. The learned Attorney General has placed before us instructions in the form of a list of "Do's and Don'ts" these

are issued by the Army Head quarters from time-to-time. The instructions contained in the said list which must be followed while acting under Armed Forces(Special Powers) Act 1958 are in these terms :

"Lists of Do's and Don'ts while acting under Armed Forces (Special Powers Act, 1958)"

Do's

1. Action before Operation

(a)Act only in the area declared, 'Disturbed Area' under Section 3 of the Act.

(b)Power to open fire using force or arrest is to be exercised under this Act only by an officer/JCO/WO and NCO.

(c)Before launching any raid/search, definite information about the activity is to be obtained from the local civil authorities;

(d)As far as possible co-opt representative of local civil administration during the raid.

2. Action during Operation

(a)In case of necessity of opening fire and using any force against the suspect or any person acting in contravention to law and order, ascertain first that it is essential for maintenance of public order. Open fire only after due warning.

(b)Arrest only those who have committed cognizable offence or who are about to commit cognizable offence or against whom a reasonable ground exists to prove that they have committed or are about to commit cognizable offence.

(c)Ensure that troops under command do not harass innocent people, destroy property of the public or unnecessarily enter into the house/dwelling of people not connected with any unlawful activities.

(d)Ensure that women are not searched/arrested without the presence of female police. In fact, women should be searched by female police only.

3. Action after Operation

(a)After arrest prepare a list of the persons so arrested.

(b)Hand over the arrested persons to the nearest Police Station with least possible delay.

(c)While handing over to the police a report should accompany with detailed circumstances occasioning the arrest.

(d)Every delay in handing over the suspects to the police must be justified and should be reasonable depending upon the place, time of arrest and the terrain in which such person has been arrested. Least possible delay may be 2-3 hours extendable to 24 hours or so depending upon a particular case.

(e)After raid make out a list of all arms, ammunition or any other incriminating material /document taken into possession.

(f) All such arms, ammunition, stores etc. should be handed over to the Police, State along with the seizure memo.

(g)Obtain receipt of persons and arms/ammunition, stores etc. so handed over to the Police.

(h)Make record of the area where operation is launched having the date and time and the persons participating in such raid.

(i) Make a record of the commander and other officers/ JCOs/NCOs forming part of such force.

(k)Ensure medical relief to any person injured during encounter, if any person dies in the encounter his dead body be handed over immediately to the police along with the details leading to such death.

4. Dealing with Civil Court

(a)Direction of the High Court/Supreme Court should be promptly attended to.

(b)Whenever summoned by the Courts, decorum of the Court must be maintained and proper respect paid.

(c)Answer questions of the Court politely and with dignity.

(d)Maintain detailed record of the entire operation correctly and explicitly.

Dont's

1. Do not keep a person under custody for any period longer than the bare necessity for handing over to the nearest Police Station.

2. Do not use any force after having arrested a person except when he is trying to escape.

3. Do not use third degree methods to extract information or to extract confession or other involvement in unlawful activities.

4. After arrest of a person by the member of the armed forces, he shall not be interrogated by the member of the armed force.

5. Do not release the person directly after apprehending on your own. If any person is to be released, he must be released through civil authorities.

6. Do not temper with official records.

7. The Armed Forces shall not take back a person after he is handed over to civil police.

57.The instructions in the list of "Do's and Dont's" which must be followed while providing aid to the civil authority are as under :

"List of Do's and Dont's while providing Aid to Civil Authority"

Do's

1. Act in closest possible communication with civil authorities throughout.

2. Maintain inter-communication if possible by telephone/radio.

3. Get the permission/requisition from the Magistrate when present.

4. Use the little force and do as little injury to person and property as may be consistent with attainment of objective in view.

5. In case you decide to open fire,

(a) Give warning in local language that fire will be effective.

(b) Attract attention before firing by bugle or other means.

(c) Distribute your men in fire units with specified Commanders.

(d) Control fire by issuing personal orders.

(e) Note number of rounds fired.

(f) Aim at the front of crowd actually rioting or incitingto riot or at conspicuous ring leaders, ie. do not fire in the thick of the crowd at the back.

(g) Aim low and shoot for effect.

(h) Keep Light Machine Gun and Medium Gun in reserve.

(i) Cease firing immediately once the object has been attained.

(j) Take immediate steps to secure wounded.

6. Maintain cordial relations with civilian authorities and para military forces.

7. Ensure high standard of discipline.

Don'ts

8. Do not use excessive force.

9. Do not get involved in hand-to-hand struggle with the mob.

10. Do not ill-treat any one, in particular, women and children.

11. No harassment of civilians.

12. No torture.

13. No communal bias while dealing with civilians.

14. No meddling in civilian administration affairs.

15. No military disgrace by loss/surrender of weapons.

16. Do not accept presents, donations and rewards.

17. Avoid indiscriminate firing.

18. The learned Attorney General has submitted that instructions provide an effective check against any misuse or abuse of the powers conferred under the Central Act on an officer in the armed forces in as much as contravention of these instructions is punishable under Sections 41, 42 (e), 63 and 64 (f) of the Army Act 1950.

Part-III

Enlarged Legal Discourse

15

Law - Science Discourse

Enlarged

The communal autonomy of legal regime and the exaltation of universal reason by science are no longer incompatible values in the globally wired inter-netted twenty first-century-global society, as both of them are found to have been holistically integrated in the domain of knowledge.

There is no permanently settled term like — 'modern' and modern science. Law-science enterprise operates in *continuum*. For our convenience, centuries may be used to measure the benchmark. Science internalises morality and responsibility in its true essence, while the temptation for demonising its inner essence could be as strong as the basic instinct of fear, jealousy, insecurity and aggressiveness.

Law not merely provides a normative framework for the expression of the science-essence, but it also enunciates the super-eminent principles of every civilization. Scientific and technical rationality may characterise the 21st century world - outlook, yet futuristic studies do not at all rule out the presence of conflicts and rival power-centres, which could turn to be an ugly face of Law-science interface. However, we can safely turn towards the pretty side of the interface and remould our world - outlook accordingly.

The discourse continues century after century in order to re-define the multi dimensional man and his performance in history as well as his ever increasing and shifting idioms of rationality. Scientific rationality is a cultural expression ahead of its time, with whose illumination intelligent man discovers the truth within the province, humankind can ever expand.

Rationality

Human rationality is a function of his cultural achievement; so is the scientific human-rationality. The discourse between legal regime and scientific enterprise operates within the ever-shifting framework of integrated human rationality. A scientific truth changes as soon as an established scientific law is de-constructed by another more acceptable law. It happens in the negation of centuries old Aristotle's law of human heredity based on blood, by Rosalin Franklin Watson-Crick's DNA concept. The obscurantistic location of human mind somewhere near the breast or the cardiac territory has been negated by neurobiological, histological and bio-chemical profile of the brain.

Synaptic memory molecules, synthesised Ribonucleic acids in the brain, peptide revolution are the growing concern of the molecular neuro-biologists. Japan is constructing huge neural computer of the sixth generation by entirely duplicating the human neural and brain architecture. Unlike the small human brain, its size could be huge and uncomfortable, yet it could be achieved. Nanotechnology in the next century can easily miniaturise it so that we can keep the second brain in a carry-bag for any unforeseen contingency.

Similarly, new Physics supplants new scientific truths in place of the older truths. It could be cosmology or, particle physics or, quantum mechanics. Heisenberg's quantum-indeterminacy principle contradicts the backbone of physical sciences — the principle of determinism and the law of causality. Legal and scientific rationality interact within the shifting framework of human rationality, which after all is a cultural vocabulary of a certain epoch. A final truth or a final law of biology or physics is evasive as human mental and conceptual construction because finality is nowhere circumscribed. Albert Einstein wrote in New York Times, (September 1950)

> "Science is the century-old endeavour to bring together by means of systematic thought the perceptible phenomena of this world into a thoroughgoing an association as possible. To put it boldly, it is the attempt at the posterior reconstruction of existence by the process of conceptualization."

To Einstein, value-judgement is external to science. He wrote-

> "For science can only ascertain what is, but not what should be, and outside of its domain value judgements of all kinds remain necessary "(A symposium, 1941).

Legal science or, enterprise has within its province, on-going human efforts to assess the perceptible social phenomena and also a process to provide a normative statement on the human conduct in regard to other perceptible and social phenomena. The 20th century and the-next-century socio-legal studies would be based on scientific attitude. Scientific rationality would provide a viable explanation for man-nature interaction; human rationality apparently functions autonomously, yet it is inseparable from the wider cosmic and natural rationality, of which it is an important component.

Bertrand Russel states about science :

> "And it is part of scientific attitude that the pronouncements of science do not claim to be certain, but only to be the most probable on present evidence "(Russel , The Basic Writings, 1961, p.642).

Among all the scientific statements made about science in the 20th century, Russell-Einstein statements carry convictions, as two of them are widely accepted as the representative conscience and intellect of the present century. Legal and scientific enterprise has to appreciate epistemology, axiology, free - enquiry and the polemic about determinism. Science as such cannot be classified in isolation save for convenience, as the scientific epistemology is an integrated whole and holistic in its approach. However, value-laden science could be trisected into developmental or utilitarian science, which is an instrument of de-constructing obsolete bedrock of human civilization and is a constructive tool, 'Demological or Militarised science' which is rather a powerful tool of satans, devils, conquerors, colonisers, racists and hegemonist-cliques and 'Puritan or, abstract or, epistemological or, value-free science' that entertains science itself as a human pursuit, in other words — science for the sake of science.

The third one is vulnerable to demonological science, which is the science - arm of political and military power. Legal enterprise and global mechanisms acting together can considerably reduce its vulnerability. For centuries, the holy church had conducted continuous inquisitions against science as perfidy; now the inquisition has ceased to exist, since science itself has enlightened the holy church or obscurantist beliefs of any denomination. The ecclesiastical inquisition is succeeded by military-state in quisition, disguised thinly under the false facade of non-violent state, liberal democracy and global peace-keeping. Non-violence has been tactically used as a facade by brown chauvinists in South Asian drama in the 20th century, till they threw out the facade in May 1998 by blasting nuclear weapon tests and by snarling at for the kill in a new arms race.

The post-cold war order is gradually substituted by another cold war for global trade. The poly-centric world has several contenders for power viz., Japan, United States, Germany, China, India, the dormant Russia, Asian tigers, Brazil and European Union. They attempt to exploit patent laws under WTO by using science and legal regime towards imposing power-structure of their own choice and definition. The law-science discourse may be given a new twist in order to legitimise new forms of national or regional hegemonism within an innocuous framework, called 'globalisation' and 'global village' — a euphemism of the 21st century technological neo-colonialism of the weaker nations and population groups of the planet. India has not opted out of this brand of race, although it is a past master in presenting soothing terminology like non-violence and non-violent state. No state had ever been non-violent in history. Science has become currency of power and law, the explicit language. Scientific rationality has been subservient to legal rationality.

The world-outlook in the next century would be informed by the scientific revolutions of the present century at its fag-end. Futurological studies have partly lifted the emerging profile.

John Naisbitt in his 'Global Paradox' has forecasted tele-communication revolution, travel industry, new opportunities, global freedom and democracy in the 21st century. Alvin and Heidi Toffler in their 'War and Anti-War' (1994) note that peace may break out in the next century notwithstanding the relentless war process, new war and anti-war forms. Alvin Toffler in his 'Powershift' (1991), while defining the global power equation within Tokyo-Washington-Berlin triad, like Mikhael Gorvachev in his politbureau speeches in the *perestroika* season, has signalled the incoming info-regime and the emergence of brain-based economy in lieu of brute force economy.

Futurologists of the former Soviet Union had been partly skeptical of the technological determinism in the technotronic era. Post-industrial science and economy have been the academic concern of American and Western think-tanks. The Third world obsession lies with technology transfer, R & D and their concern for a dignified role and place in the WTO framework, wherein patenting of bio-diversity and other scientific inventions would remain a witty game of social Darwinism. Futurologists do not rule out conflict in the next century. How to rationalise the conflict - discourse in the legal regime, informed by a higher order of scientific knowledge remains the pertinent question. Science has revolutionised human consciousness in an unprecedented way in a century and yet the scientific revolutions are taking place in this age and the next century. The present day scientific revolution would be considered primitive after one or two millennia and we do not put a full stop in science, because it is becoming the new morality of mankind notwithstanding the rise in Fundamentalism.

Futuristic studies have sharpened the legal and scientific congnition of 20th century-man, who perceives the next century with the help of tools available with him. Legal rationality has to assess and evaluate the rationality of the new STR (scientific and technological revolution) in the context of broad human rationality, of which survival, security, and development are the constants. The new STR-rationality envisages three major threshold areas, out of several collateral scientific explorations.

Firstly, the new bio-technology revolution has shown the road maps for molecular biology, genetic engineering, recombinant DNA, polymers, green and energy revolutions and technology for achieving sustainable development, among others. Major branches of science are found increasingly developmental in perspectives. The philosophy and regime of Laws would be dramatically changed.

Secondly, the bio-medical technology is radically transformed by Human Genome project, IVF (*in vitro*-Fertilization), surrogacy, organ grafting, designer babies, reproductive technology, cloning, and molecular neurobiology, among others. Legal concepts will no longer remain the same in harnessing them judiciously.

Thirdly, the province of new physics is exotic enough to explore unusual terrains in silicon valley, automation and robotics, sixth generation and neural computers, nanotechnology, cybernetics, cyborg (still a fiction), information highway, telecom-revolution, space stations and space colonies, among others. The inner, cultural essence of man has been dramatically altered and his rationality has been equally overturned. Beliefs are substituted by thought and curiosity for evidence.

The human consciousness is no more the same as it had been in the past. Even in the recent past, Darwin has overturned the firmly established theory of creation. Before Darwin, there was no human choice other than accepting theory of creation and consequential Spanish inquisition and even in this primitive 20th century, we have more than one choice — creation theory or, theory of evolution. The choice is going to proliferate in the next millennium.

However, primitive jungleman organised in September 1995, with fair accuracy and military precision, mass-hypnotic event — Milk sucking Hindu deity in order to demolish human intelligence and regain their lost priestly magic. The old world order has to give in to a new world order.

Rationality of bio-tech revolution

STR-rationality cannot insulate an autonomy outside the reach of legal and social rationality, which also are qualitatively enhanced by the rationality of STR (science and technological revolution). The law-science interface is best explained by their harmonious inter-relationship. These are subject to all human choice and deliberately chosen human enterprises. The bio-technology revolution of this epoch and the subsequent epoch is evaluated with this relativistic perception.

The adventurous Human Genome project, undertaken by the scientists is targeted in revealing the genetic secrets of man thread by thread. The mysterious hand of the Almighty is going to be lifted from His genetic hold over man and man is going to be mysterious himself thereby usurping the place of the Almighty (Did he or she exist at all?). The institutions so far held to be sacred and divine are not going to withstand the bio-technology's ideological offensive. The old belief system is going to be de-constructed and replaced by technological rationality of another age. SBH (Seuqencing By-Hybridisation) technology, developed by Argonne national laboratory scientists (near California, USA) can decipher the human genome a thousand times quicker than the traditional means, with the help of a biological 'superchip'. Mapping of the one lakh or more human genes could be done easier and faster than ever. The possibility is that Bible and other texts have to be re-drafted, or re-constructed as they can no longer sustain the amusing story they are telling.

Legal regulation of human reproductive technology has been made in developed countries in their preliminary forms. Human reproductive technology and its impact on women is the subject of inter-disciplinary study of World

Federation of Mental Health. In mid-1980s, UNESCO has commissioned the International Social Science Council to survey the impact of bio-medical sciences on human rights.

In 1994, the University of Pennsylvania has succeeded in altering the 'Germline' of human reproductive lineage. The Pennsylvania scientists destroyed the sperm-forming cells of a mouse and re-populated the tests with cells from another mouse. Application of the technique to human organs is a possibility. IVF technology was developed in 1978 by uniting a sperm and egg in a laboratory petri-dish. Only 17 countries enact laws on embryo-research and IVF (*in vitro* Fertilization). In a case - Davis vs. Davis, USA, 1989 — the battle was for the custody of frozen human embryo. Louisiana state in the USA has given the status of a judicial person to a human embryo in 1990. In India, only after completion of 3 months, an embryo is considered to have acquired life. Jurisprudence is going to be substantially altered with every bio-technology revolution.

David Rorvik's story about cloning of a millionaire, as published in 1978 was not to be fully believed till Dr. Jerry Hall and his colleagues in George Washington university successfully fertilised a human egg, divided it into a two-cell-embryo, separated the cells and allowed them to grow as separate and identical embryos. In cattle cloning, an embryo being separated into 8 cells and implanted in the uterus of surrogate mothers resulted to the birth of 8 offsprings. The Vatican and moral regimes have been outraged by the IVF in the 1980s as because their first premise no longer holds true and valid. What the Vatican would defend is uncertain. The capability to clone man has been reached but for the legal restraint of the capability.

In 1990, British parliament has enacted that a particular form of cloning called — 'Nuclear substitution' is illegal and Human Fertilization and Embryology Authority has regulated embryo research. German Embryo Protection Law in 1990 renders cloning of human embryo a punishable offence. In France, embryo research is guided by a national consultative committee. In case the legal regime does not prevail upon embryo research and human cloning, STR rationality may totally wipe out our five-thousand-years-old myth about God, determinism and the entire God-based superstitions.

The result-pope, pagans and priests will be again unemployed. Can the STR or technological rationality fill in that vacuum remains an interesting polemic for all rationalists and the rest. In the USA, statutes restrict the use of reproductive technology and judicial response on artificial insemination of unmarried persons has not given a clear indication, whereas nearly half of the American states limit artificial insemination to married women. Several of the reproductive technology are not yet viably conceived by the Indian law-biotechnology enterprise. Medical termination of pregnancy is allowed by the law. Hindu bigots accept it, but Muslim bigots are skeptical. The believers on their own differ among themselves, because as living fossils they belong to 5000 years B.C. by living in the 2000 A.D. A poor chap would worship the cow as Nandini and he may not change, because he believes and knows not what he should believe in. He could even shatter the state with his belief. They represent a passing phase in humanity.

Kidney robbery and large scale racket have been detected in Bangalore, Bombay and Delhi. Unsuspecting poor persons have been trapped for generous blood donations and their kidneys are immediately robbed of by Indian nephrologists, who have been allegedly paid an exorbitant price for each kidney robbery, by the Shaikhs. The Transplantation of Human Organs Act 1994 defines brain death and permits living donors from amongst relatives of the recipient or through the authorisation committee. The positive side of the Indian law is that it would benefit one million patients and the other side is the fear for legalised robbery through legal and technical loopholes.

The problem is not of technology nor of nephrology alone, but is about the mind-set of the professionals to rob of the man in the street. Medical negligence and patient's suits against medical practitioners have frequently come up before consumer-law tribunal. The technical rationality has been contaminated by vile consciousness and vulgar economic demands of Western market. Science may fulfil human need, but it should not be an impediment to freedom and dignity to life. The Mafia elsewhere has laid its hands over human organs.

Genetic engineering and DNA technology has a positive role to play in several aspects of man-nature relationship. DNA probing of the underpants of a rape victim by the FBI in the USA led to genetic evidence and conviction of the criminals. (USA vs. Two Bulls, USA, 1990). In cases relating to parenthood, the DNA evidence could be used. Legal regime would find the DNA technology to be dependable. The negative picture could be the possibility of demonising the bio-technology by way of devising genetically altered insects which can devastate selected crops or, by way of sponsoring genetically engineered super-plagues or, inventing race-specific weapons, which can permanently liquidate a specific race or ethnic group or monoculture from the surface of the earth. American futurologists foresee these possible abuses. Legal rationality has to prevail upon these grim possibilities.

Pat Roy Mooney states that northern gene-banks had already stored 93% of the plant genetic materials of the South. WTO (World Trade Organisation) bears a special responsibility towards the judicious preservation of the germplasm and biodiversity of the underdeveloped South. Injudicious use of the economic and technological rationality may lead to re-colonisation of the under-developed world by the smart nations in the 21st century under the cover of unregulated globalisation and market economy. Science could be used for the easiest re-colonisation of simple or indigenous societies.

Bio-technology can give clean technology for fighting industrial pollution and can float microbe to fight out environmental degradation. UNESCO international commission conference, held in New Delhi in early 1995 has given priority to education to fight out economic stagnation, and environmental degradation with the instrumentality of science, research and communication technology. International agreements provide for reduction of CO_2 emissions and regulation of biotech-farming.

The other side of the biotech-rationality could be envisaged. Giant agro-chemical conglomerates and MNCs come up with enormous market access to the disadvantage of marginal farmers. With the rise of *in vitro* revolution and intelligent robots in Japan, farmers and industrial hands would remain unemployed. Tests are being carried out in ZTL (Zentral Tierlaboratorien) in Free University, Berlin which accommodates as many as 80,000 animals notwithstanding protests made by social activists for the protection of animal rights. Radiation tests on human bodies have also been carried out recently in the USA and human experimentation had in all possibility been conducted in connection with the Manhattan project in the USA prior to releasing atomic bombs in Japan in 1945. Indian scientist Chidambaram and ultra-nationalists claim in 1999 that India can prepare neutron-bomb. Race continues.

The basic human rights have to be surrendered to the irrational demands of bio-technological scientists on occasions and also to the political or economic expediency of the rulers. This form of rationality infringes upon the basic human essence and consciousness. Law-science interface would have to assess the de-humanising rationality, as evolved out of expediency and technological determinism. UNESCO and United Nations made preliminary declarations towards humanising science and techonology, yet a concerted global blue-print charting the road - map of science for the next century still remains out of sight.

Techno-tronic rationality

Human consciousness and rationality in the post-industrial era has been considerably enhanced, since scientific temper, free enquiry, independent judgement, creative and innovative thoughts along with the freedom of conscience coupled with *'right to dissent'* are acquired by common men and elites. State, church and religion stood strongly against the propagation of these values till the other day and how many conscientious leaders and scientists had attained ignominious martyrdom for exercising independent judgement is yet to be taken into full account. The 20th century STR and new physics at the threshold of the 21st century have been experimenting on a wide range of fields starting from Nanotechnology of the future, space farms-stations , intelligent robots, neural computers compatible with the human brain and energy systems to cosmological province like the ever-shifting calculation of Hubble constant, which would reveal the birth of the universe. By taking our galaxy as a reference point, galaxy moves away from our point. The figure obtained after dividing the speed of a galaxy by its distance from our home galaxy provides the Hubble constant.] Cepheid stars are set to bear Hubble constant of 50 to 100 km/s, Mega-par-sec. The age of the universe are calculated by professional cosmologists . The culture and consciousness of man are revolutionised. 'Time' observes that the 20th century "overthrew our inherited ideas about logic, language, learning, mathematics, economics and even space and time"(17: p. 28).

The small instance of Hubble constant is cited in order to appreciate the human ability in this age. By sitting in a hill-top at Pasadena, the professionals rewrite the *Janamkundli* (horoscope) of the universe. The primitive human mind and superstitious mind-set is placed to rigorous testimony. The search for scientific truth continues and the social truth would also be shaped in its image. For the twilight zone, we have to bear with scientists A to E, who teach *chemical evolution of life* in class - room and reject it the moment he leaves the lecture-hall. The classical divine law is on the defensive.

The Cartesian rationality has been abandoned along with Newtonian classical mental process. Non-static character of universe, the behaviour of the sub-atomic particles in the form of energy pattern, dual character sub-atomic particles, the use of hidden and local variables, approach to probability and holistic methodology, the equation of Chinese *'Yin'* and *'Yang'* principles in the mystical areas of new physics, the charm for unification theory or , a 'theory of everything, as Crease and Mann so calls in their book, "The second creation ", coupled with Heisenberg's indeterminacy principles in the quantum theory and the quantum-relativistic approach to GUT, among a host of others, are the obsession of the next century professional physicists around the world. Human philosophy and consciousness would no longer remain where they are at present, once the nature's top secrets are gradually uncovered by her children. Many social beliefs and institutions that are going to be replaced by a new rationality of the 21st century which would be better understood as 'old rationality' in the vocabulary of the immediate 21st or 22nd century generation. In this context, Albert Einstein spoke:

> "Here knowledge of truth alone does not suffice ; on the contrary this knowledge must continually be renewed by ceaseless effort, if it is not to be lost, it resembles a statue of marble which stands in the desert and is continually threatened with burial by the shifting sand." (Albany, NY. October 15, 1936).

Artificial intelligence is sharply contending with the human intelligence. At what point of time AI would leave human intelligence behind is a question suitably left to the progeny of the 21st century. The only consolation is the belief that the child should not be wiser than the parents.

DARPA—Pentagon's Defence Advanced Research Projects Agency — is reportedly having a long term objective for devising a system capable of making one million logical inferences per second.

Japanese MITI had sponsored Fuchi's fifth generation computer. Japan works for constructing a neural computer by replicating the human neural circuit in its wholeness. Human neural rationality has to compete with the future artificial intelligence. Demonised computer science like the West German computer spies had access to nuclear data SDI by breaking into as many as 430 computers.

Cyber-war has already been started by electronic hackers and cruis-virus made its presence already. The info-highway, as envisaged as of now would have its highway criminals in the absence of a legal regime. Citizen's right to privacy and classified state secrets could be infringed upon, by unscrupulous hackers and secret services. Science always loses her privacy, unless law protects her modesty. Science, left unprotected by the legal regime may play truant in the politician's permissive red light area. Apocalyse could occur any moment.

Intelligent robot-culture, which Japan has evolved with advanced technology, would help automation in an unprecedented way, but the human labourers are gradually losing their place, position and resources. By using nanotechnology, surgeons may insert tiny cameras inside the chest and molecular-manufacturing with the help of nanotechnology would alter the medical, histological profile of man. Space stations, space colony, space farms and space travel would completely overturn human superstition about heaven-hell, divinity and cosmic consciousness. Should anybody sponsor Ayotollah Khomeini or for that matter any Ayotollah or priest, who worships the moon, for a lunar landing with Neil Armstrong, his preaching and belief about heaven and heavenly gods would have to be changed. Human rationality at this age has to alter gradually in commensurate with the revelations of STR. Methane-hit slabs, collected from sea-bed may explain Bermuda triangle mystery.

Fossil fuel like petroleum is going to be exhausted by the middle of the next century. Alternative energy systems are explored before the energy reserve is totally dried up. Fuel cells, which are based on separation of Hydrogen and Oxygen like electrolyte solution yield electricity and water. In California, hospitals, hotels and offices are run with fuel cells. Energy, environment, economic stagnation, global warming up and sustainable development are in the current global agenda. The new global trade order — WTO — along with other global economic institutions or, institutional economics have profound concern over the iniquities, perpetuated by high-tech and post-industrial nations.

As Toffler state, brain force economy is going to replace the brute force economy and scientific knowledge would be the new form of capital in the new order. How far could the ethical regime co-exist with the rationality of the techno-tronic era constitutes the main issue of the discourse. Preparation for such a legal regime, which can comprehend the discourse paradigm, its legitimacy, validity and above all, its effectiveness constitute the matrices of the legal rationality. Legal rationality and scientific rationality have to be found in the discourse frame-work, since both of them are interactive and mutually influential.

At the higher level, physics transcends equations and wires, advanced technology transcends the specific form of the matter and take the form of philosophical enquiry. The apparent boundary as found between Cartesian parts of the rationalism — be it legal or scientific or philosophical — rationality melts down and the domain of rationality becomes the same subject of discourse. It is also true that the approach roads, road maps leading to the major domain have been found to be diverse.

Common discourse medium

Albert Einstein had repented thus in 1951 :

> "My share in the production of the atom bomb consisted in a single act. I signed a letter to President Roosevelt in which I stressed the necessity of making experiments on a large scale to check the possibilities of making an atom bomb. I was fully aware of the dreadful risk which the success of these undertakings implied for humanity.
>
> But the likelihood that the Germans might be working on the same problem with a prospect of success compelled me to this step. There was no other way for me, although I have always been a convinced pacifist." (3: p. 146)

Demonical science always leaves a suicide-note before the occurrence of the doomsday, the time when a situation becomes totally irreversible. Value-laden peace-research, therefore, attempts to pre-empt before the Satanic science turns around its dreaded face to mankind. Otto Hahn also felt himself guilty. As Plato dreamed a perfect state which is an impossibility, he thought that political science is the supreme of all sciences. The proposition is a workable statement. Kant and Socrates found virtue and knowledge inseparable. We can take a que from their idea and can render scientific or legal knowledge to be inseparable from virtues. But virtue no longer remains a prisoner of primordial definition.

Value-free science is a mechanical and lifeless frame. Value-laden science has a soul and purpose. Shifting epistemology bears with shifting axiology. Even Pope Paul II, who represents the church that had inquisitioned scientists and knowledge-workers has realised that faith and science represent different orders of knowledge. Unity of knowledge however would negates the duality as stated by Pope.

In order to ascertain scientific responsibility in relation to the security of man and nature, several movements and conferences had been organised viz., Einstein-Russel sponsored Pugwash movement, 1955 (First General secretary of Pugwash movement 1955 has been awarded Nobel peace prize in 1995), Club of Rome, 1968-75 for averting the doomsday, NIEO, 1974, Willy Brandt Report of 1980s, Rio Earth summit, 1992, World Human Rights Vienna conference, 1993, GATT conference, 1994, and UNESCO International commission conference, New Delhi, 1995 on education, among others. These global exercises project the common objective in the judicious use of science and technology for the improvement of the quality of human life and nature. Bio-social essence of Man, production relations, human essence and social relations are the concern of benevolent and utilitarian science.

Perceptions, based upon different approaches like - Theocratic model, Liberal democracy, Social Darwinism, Socio-biology, Genetic-cultural co-evolution, Existentialism, Marxism-Leninism, Frankfurt school, Technological determinism, Socrates-Kantian system, and post-industrial globalisation, market economy, among others, made attempts to construct in their own ways man- science relation, natural-social sciences relation and man's existence in a hostile environment. Herbert Marcuse, Jurgen Habermas and the critical school think-tanks have witnessed the curse of modern science and technology. A holistic approach could enlighten the wider discourse that prevails between and among the approaches or, social institutions like science and law, by keeping the human essence as a fundamental truth.

Legal discourse has access to natural law. Similarly, new physics and new biology or the STR, could be equally addressed to the law of nature. The basic human rationality informs law-science interface. Once the technological rationality is rendered to be completely independent of human basic-rationality, the basic purpose of STR is frustrated. Legal rationality surpasses the mere presence of a legal regime. Considering these paradigms, scientific premises need re-structuration and re-enunciation. Futurologists make honest efforts to visualise the unborn future, but the mid-wifery nurtures all kinds of conjectures besides *futuristic* studies, which are not currently devoid of ideological prejudices.

References

1. Bertrand Russel, The Basic Writings, 1961.
2. Sonja Bargman, Ideas and Opinions by Albert Einstein.
3. D.P.Gribanov, Albert Einstein's Philosophical Views, 1987.
4. L.P. Buyeva *et.al.* ed., Civilization and the Historical Process, 1983.
6. Ivan Frolov, Man-Science-Humanism : A new synthesis, 1986.
7. USSR Academy of Science, Science and Society, 1989.
8. Fritjof Capra, The Tao of Physics, 1977.
9. Fritjof Capra , The Turning Point, 1981.
10. Stephen Toulmin, The Philosophy of Science, 1953. *See* Nidditch also.

11. All books by Alvin Toffler, particularly Powershift and War & Anti-War, 1994.
12. All books by John Naisbitt, particularly Global Paradox, 1995.
13. Robert P. Crease, Charles C. Mann, The Second Creation.
14. Paul Kennedy, Preparing for the Twentyfirst century, 1993.
15. Available literature on Futurology and Journals.
16. Edward A. Feigenbaum & Pamela McCorduck, The Fifth Generation, 1983.
17. The century's Greatest Minds, *Time 100 Special* Issue, vol. 153 no. 12, March 29, 1999.

16

CLS in Mainstream Legal Thought

CLS — Critical Legal Studies — has provoked the American legal mind-set since the 1980s, sneaked in the legal domain of Canada, Germany, France, Britain although it remains a non-starter among the Indian jurists. While the American universities have initiated debate about the CLS by taking it as an issue deserving sufficient notice, Indian benchmark could be explored in the volatile literature of some of the jurisprudents, who in spite of retaining their traditional loyalist attitude towards the colonial legal heritage, characterise their legal thought with elementary nuances of critical mind-set.

The premise is that the mainstream Indian legal thought is witnessing fault-lines, which are not dramatic as yet, but they represent alternative scenario. Since the 1980s, the Supreme Court of India has departed itself substantially from the rigidity and woodenness that stood for decades against administering justice to the wider constituency, largely composed of the subaltern Indians. The developments, reinforced further by legislative activity, indicate a trend that shares in rudimentary form — the basic premises of the CLS debate.

The Supreme Court Judgements in the recent past indicate CLS stands for the widely used American term — Critical Legal Studies a pattern which is innovative and political.[1] It can also withstand executive arbitrariness in order to maintain independence.[2] The foreignness of Indian law has also substantiated.[3] Jurists are searching for righteousness in *Dharma* [4] in pluralistic life of the Indians. Committed judges,[5] informed of strong social commitments and energised by creativity have altered the scenario of the apex court, notwithstanding the criticism of the mainstream loyalists, who largely adhere to the pre-independence role of the judicial power. The juristic thought, as observed in the last two decades in the country has substantially departed from the one, which the British left as a legacy for decades, despite the colonial hangover.

The realists in the USA focused their studies in the behavioural aspect and decisional performance of the judiciary. The skepticism started in the 1930s with critical works of Jerome Frank and his contemporaries. He has examined the modern legal magic in his book. The critical theory had evolved out of the premises of the Realist movement. The American Supreme Court turned out to be revolutionary since 1937 in this age and it laid down historical judgement in 1954.[7] American Supreme Court, led by Marshall and Warren in different occasions integrated national policies within the judicial pronouncements.[8] The court had joined the *Machtkampf* — the national power — struggle[9] in order to assert its role in framing national policies of significance. Indian Supreme Court by its judgement given in May 1995 has enlarged its policy-making domain by advising the union government of India to adopt a uniform civil code in fulfillment of the directive principle, as enunciated in article 44 of the Constitution. There are several instances. The judiciary is widening its otherwise limited jurisdiction while addressing itself to the major concerns of a plural and federal society.

The apparently broad extent of the policy-making role of the American Supreme Court[10] is, however, limited to certain areas only. The constitutional principles, judicial power and democracy are found to be integrated.[11] Lord Denning's judgements characterise the judicial activism in the island state of UK.[12] In the Indian continent, the jurists gradually appreciate the absence of a methodology and a critical framework[13] in the process of judging the judges. The following trends emerge in the Indian legal scenario in the recent past :

1. Juristic and judicial activism;

2. Alternative approaches for determination of Justice -particularly in social and collective justice-domain;

3. Sociological interpretation of the Constitution and value-laden judicial review;

4. De-construction of technicalities and rigid forms of *locus standi* in class actions;

5. Limited judicial accountability towards marginalised citizen group and de-empowered constituencies;

6. Progressive departure from the colonial hangover and adoption of creative doctrinal formulation;

7. Intra - institutional tussle;

These judicial measures, coupled with viable jurisprudential thought gradually de-construct the colonial foundations and mind-set of justicing system in India. However, it would be too early to read more compulsively in the emerging pattern, since the mainstream legal philosophy has not qualitatively undergone a radical change.

The University Grants Commission Curriculum Development Centre, in its report given in 1990, takes note of the post-colonial situation of legal education in the country and addresses itself to the cause of attaining a just society. It observes : "The other distinguishing features of legal sciences is pre-occupation with the institutional materiality of the laws through which the struggle for a just society must be waged. The ways in which legislative, executive, judicial powers, institutions, and legal professions are designed and operate remain a special province — for critique, reconstruction and retooling — of legal science." De-construction of the existing tools and apparatus of legal education is kept as the hidden agenda of the UGC move. The report presents testimony of the fiasco of the mainstream tradition in imparting legal education to the next generation. However, it did not go very far, lest it should be de-legitimised by mainstream's prophets. Hidden and implicit contradictions, which are waylaid in the Indian mainstream legal thoughts, are being explored. In this context, the American perceptions, projections and debate about the CLS are taken as seriously as possible.

Profile of CLSM

CLS or, CLSM is the outcome of the conference, held in the Harvard University, USA in 1982, wherein one thousand participants attended. Its intellectual ancestry could be traced to the Realist movement in 1930 and the nucleus-formation in 1977. The CLSM addresses itself to de-construction of the mainstream American legal mindset and to the re-construction of its alternative blueprint. The movement, while being a conglomerate of critical theorists has not succeeded in projecting a coherent alternative theory to the mainstream legal thought. The mainstream thought itself is not more coherent save that its tributaries espouse constructivism, experimental jurisprudence, pragmatism and realistic innovations. CLS, however, embraces critical social theory as its core essence.

CLS is characterised broadly by the following common features:

(a)Critical consciousness replaces the conventional legal consciousness, based upon legal autonomy ;

(b)Legal reasoning is equated to political ideology ;

(c)Unjust socio-legal structures which are the expressions of hierarchy, subjugation, hegemony and dominance are considered to be lethal and they need de-construction ;

(d)The individual self has important role in achieving social harmony ;

(e) Existing theory of rights call for re-construction ;

(f) The need for intellectual assault on the mainstream legal tradition has been deeply felt ;

(g) Legal education, legal profession and other legal activities call for drastic overhauling or, de-construction

(h) CLS bursts in the official Marxism and Liberalism, while rejecting formalism and objectivism ;

(i) CLS makes an effort to provide an alternative blueprint of legal thought and structures; how far, it may be considered radical or could it be treated as a viable revolutionary format remains a pertinent question;

(j) Communal and Customary Law should have a place.

The CLS postulates, expositions and debates are subject of ongoing study and in this assessment, the literature is presented. The two sources of CLS are the American Realism of 1930s, on the one hand and the progressive tradition in American historiography.[15] It has attacked the entitlement procedure under law-and-economics and indicated 'concern for the politics of legal thought'.[16] While considering the mainstream American legal thought to be bankrupt, it centres on the indeterminacy of legal reasoning, and its disagreement with the ideological nexus of the actual judicial decisions.[17] The movement considers the contingency of history and the fate of humanity which is at stake.[18] It does not stand for anarchy, but for identifying possibilities to resolve the contradictions, found in the social apparatus and law.

The Critical Legal Studies (CLS) share common ideological platform with the premises of the Critical social theory, also known as the Frankfurt school, which had been constituted by German emigres who, for fear of Nazi ideology in their ancestral homeland, took shelter in the USA during the last world war.

Critical social theory provides formidable critique of positivism in social sciences and stands for emancipatory reason.[19] Individuals have to be liberated from alien structures and definitions. Among all the social theorists, Herbert Marcuse is the romantic representative of the Critical theory. He felt that Marxism does not lead to absolute knowledge and that it is to be used to study contemporary problems and historical situations. The leaders of the Frankfurt school have pointed out the need for emancipatory reason and the malaise of the contemporary technological civilisation of man.

CLS denounces the value-free models of law[21] and it makes an effort to combine legal theory with the social theory, as the CLS theoreticians affirm that law is divisive and hierarchical.[22] In an age of contradictions, the judge makes a political choice and legal education is the training for affirmation of the hierarchy.

American legal philosophy[23] since 1880 has traversed terrains of legal rules, morality, decision-making, social engineering, skepticism and sociological dimensions of jurisprudence. Post-colonial legal tradition in India is relatively nascent and all the institutions are relatively young. The colonial hangovers that deformed the ingenuity of legal thought in the country have to be phased out. The contingent question is about the search for alternative blueprints and their legitimisation through the existing structures and process. These possibilities cannot be fully exploited within the existing material, physical system and ideological structures and hence, the need for a critical attitude to be nurtured in the fertile mind-set. The CLS has been evolved out of the impending juristic necessity of a contemporary civilisation.

The concept of examining law as an autonomous field of study is substituted by a relational theory of law [24] that explores the 'interaction between legal relations and other forms of social relations'. It is represented by CLS in the USA, *Critique du Droit* in France and British Critical Legal Conference.[25] CLS assumes that the liberal legal system is based upon contradictory visions of human nature.[26] New phrases used by the CLS scholars ridicule the terminology, adopted by the conventional legal discourse.

American CLS theorists centre around keypoints[27] viz., gap between paper rights and real rights, legal response to the ruling class interests, legitimisation process adopted by the class and denial of participation to American citizens e.g., in the making of economic decisions. The faith is that if an idea cannot withstand critical scrutiny, it should not be adored.

Entropy or second law of thermodynamics is increasing in the legal system and law gives legitimacy to the *status quo*.[28] Powerful factions use the legal process as a mere smoke-screen for the instrumental purpose of positive law.[29] CLS circles conceive the judicial review to be political and congressional elite has imposed legislation upon the passive majority.[30] CLS like the modern art makes people angry and leaves hunger unsatisfied.[31] It is commented that CLS stands for radical social change, but its focus on *praxis*[32] is questioned. It does not merely mean the study of ideology, but the exponent's desire to alter the consciousness that the exists between capitalist domination and modern legal consciousness.[33] This attitude deviates from the traditional province of social sciences, as the exponents like to transform the legal consciousness. The CLSers want to reduce the 'risk of judicial tyranny'[34] without outlawing judicial review in the constitutional theory, as judicial review controls the legislative tyranny.

Harvard law professor Roberto M. Unger is a key person in the CLS movement. As a result of varying responses to the CLS, even the Harvard faculty has suffered vertical divide into supporters and opponents of CLS. Media took elaborate notice of the CLS polemic, which has borne dramatic effect. These intellectual events are not expected to happen in the Indian legal circles, who had been largely accustomed to delivering monologues and priestly oracle from the peak. Pluralism merely exists on paper like the under-utilised or never-utilised paper rights, which the CLS abhor vehemently. Unger has evolved through his major works on CLSM, a concept of super-liberalism, enlarged or deviationist doctrine, context transformation, role jumbling and ideas about organic groups and intelligible essence as well as negative capabilities.[35] Roberto Unger could have been influenced by the message of the Chinese cultural revolution and modern pop songs, considering his detachment to the old values, old ideas and old world-outlook. He assumes the role of a red guard in rejecting outworn ideas, where as outworn ideas survive among the masters.

His elaborate thesis on the 'Critical Legal Studies Movement'[36] cites the practice of politics, criticism of objectivism and formalism, explains the four categories of rights and deviationist doctrine. He writes : "To imagine and establish a state that had more truly ceased to be hostage to a faction, in a society that had more truly rid itself of a background scheme of inadequately vulnerable division and hierarchy, we might need to transform every aspect of the existing institutional order."[37]

Unger's Knowledge and Politics (1975), Law in Modern Society (1976), Passion (1984), 3 volumes on Politics (1987) and CLSM (1983) considered as a whole, elevates him nearly to the status of Spinoza, Dante and Virgil by his supporters, while his detractors would pull him down to populism. Herein lies the romanticism of CLS, which projects a new vision of organic groups (society) and individual and collective empowerment. William Ewald[38] criticize him that he is mistaken in premising 'that logic is ideologically tainted' and his attitude towards liberalism. Unger's messages like - *'Trashing is scholarship'*, *'Everything is Politics'* and *'Law is nonsense'* provoke scholars who would hole him up somewhere in the leftist camp. Cornel West[39] attacks Ewald and states, "The edifice Ewald believes he has dismantled is not a palatial mansion in which CLS dwells but rather an old decrepit doghouse abandoned by Unger long ago." Unger's anti-foundational vision is said to have created epistemological break. In India, Krishna Iyer's incoherent flourishes act as poor substitutes.

Contemporary jurisprudence gives adequate space to rights-debate. CLS attacks the liberal perception of rights and expose how 'mere power becomes legitimate right'.[40] CLS retains radical political objectives and dismisses the 'standard legal scholarship' and 'proposals for legal education' and the 'ruling ideas of contemporary legal system'.[41] Duncan Kennedy, another prominent CLSer attacks the ideological content of legal education ; in his words, "Teachers teach non-sense when they persuade students that legal reasoning is distinct, as a method for reaching correct results, from ethical and political discourse in general (i.e. from policy analysis)".[42] He states, — "Law is an aspect of the social totality, not just the tail of the dog - Because it is part of the equation of power rather than simply a function of it, people struggle for power through law,...[43].

CLSer R.W.Gordon states,[44] "Law, like religion and television images, is one of these clusters of belief and it ties in with a lot of non-legal but similar clusters that convince people that all the many hierarchical relations in which they live and work are natural and necessary." These belief structures are contingent and moulded by power elites. In India, some of the national Law Schools pass on British colonial thought and class- Legal education to resurrect a ruling class to the progeny of the ruling class. The National Law School at Bangalore is ideologically bankrupt, and acts as a hard task-master to produce gendermerie for the Indian Bourgeoisie. It cannot so critical.

Trashing is a word used by CLS, but others call CLS as trashing.[45] CLS representative[46] prefers altruistic vision of standard to political philosophy of individualism. The mainstream jurists like to retain the rigidity of the structure, while the CLSers like plasticity of the structures.[47] The rival ideological approaches against the retention of structures turn out to be subject of debate.

Modalities of argument present the ideology of constitutional law.[48] Tushnet[49] proposes to supplement the liberal tradition of judicial review with republican tradition, considering the fact that preferences and choice have to be admitted. Women rights are within politics[50] and women have concern over reproductive choice.[51] CLS reaches out to

International law as well, notwithstanding its primary concern over municipal laws. CLS recommends the removal of the stagnation52 of International law. CLS draws attention to Martin Luther King's denial of repressive ideologies[53] and his alternative vision of the commumity[54], which amalgamates theory and experience.

CLS provides an alternative vision to what the mainstream legal philosophy had bequeathed to the legal ideologues, law persons and jurists of Western legal system. Both dogmatic and official Marxists as well as the heavyweights of the western liberal tradition have suspected of the CLSers as belonging to their respective opposite camps, while CLS assaults both the tenets. It makes forays into the epistemological bedrock of the mainstream thought, the false consciousness, as received by the community and individuals about the apparently sacrosanct legal autonomy, which otherwise is a function of the powerful manipulative elite, the alienation of legal science from social science and the structure that legitimises injustice, hierarchy, subjugating, hegemony and colonisation.

By probing deeper into the roots, law falls within the game plan of politics and the market denies equal access to one and all. Similarly, the hegemony is shifted down to legal education and legal profession through the same carrier that perpetuated hegemony and denied significance of the individual personality. CLS provides for de-construction of these unjust structures in order to reconstruct harmony and responsibility. The CLS imagery in the mindset of Indian jurists and law-persons or, the power elite is not yet very succinct and obvious, although Indian legal order and structures are far from being just and non-oppressive. However, occasional and symptomatic outbursts — largely incoherent and inaudible — come out of the vocal chords of a couple of legal opinion-makers who can scratch, but cannot more the mountain.

Reflective imagery

Juristocracy[55] is a formidable component in the power struggle in the community in the context of *Machtkampf* of a broader canvass. The judiciary, as the author notes, is not as much neutral as it is made out to be. It does not have a constituency to call its own, yet it may also be said that its constituency transcends the demarcated political constituencies, which are delimited for electoral purposes exclusively. Indian Supreme Court changed its colours, and its judicial responses since the 1980s, have been found to found pro-active, as it rectifies the executive aberrations which are disadvantageous to the class action of the underdogs. However, the apex court is caught occasionally playing to the gallery. It also reflects the national politics in some of its activist roles.

PILers among the Supreme Court judges since the 1980s made efforts demonstratively that gross public injuries be judicially rectified, but the judicial reliefs are peripheral considering the widespread, deep-rooted social injustice. A prominent PILer, who had done substantial work is Krishna Iyer, a former judge of the Supreme Court. His judgements were of far-reaching consequences and his legal philosophy is described in his books - 'Law, Freedom and Change' (1975), 'Justice and Beyond' (1982), 'Law and Religion' (1984), 'Human Rights and the Law' (1984), and 'Indian Justice - Perspectives and Problems' (1984), 'The Dialectics and Dynamics of Human Rights (1999)' among others. He made efforts to evolve value-oriented jurisprudence, democratise justice by discarding the cult of the robe, create sociological interpretation of the Constitution, and to accept processual justice. His concept of social rights against the Western version of naked liberty is innovative. He writes, "Law is not an end in itself but a means to justice, legal engineering being directed to the realising and securing of social justice".[56]

In his assessment, the symptoms of the legal dis-order are merely manifested by group violence, ideological terrorism, student revolt, labour struggles, political protests, civil disobedience and destruction of public property. The primary evidence of CLS are found in the less-than-coherent and dis-organised format, as structuralised by Krishna Iyer. He projects an alternative vision to the rigid, neo-colonial, feudal, casteist, racist and unjust structures, foisted upon the people by the power elites. Yet the coherence of a CLS, vindication and open-ended de-legitimisation of the structures and the much-wanted-ideological rigours are not yet organised by the jurists and academicians. It looks like a one time waiver to the escalating injustice, perpetuated by the minority power elite, many of whom are the inheritors of the evil legacy, which survives by way of compromise and patchworks in the bargaining game of power in a win-win situation.

Indian legal architecture is feebly responding to the changing value-perceptions of this age. The response pattern is largely reformist in nature, far short of being revolutionary in content, conviction and commitment. On several occasions, it is patchwork and casual. The pattern could be a precursor of a full-blooded CLS philosophy; or, the possibility of market-manipulation of the trend can not also be ruled out. The apex court bears its class character and it has not yet recruited eminent law professor, as the politics of the bar is or leftists very strong and well-organised.

Indian legal mind, while adhering to the mainstream conservative thought for political and historical reasons, is no longer un-malleable. The sociology of law and paternalism[57], profound idea of social justice and its tenets[58] and the fortitude to unmask the masquerading justice[59], reinforced by the pro-active Supreme Court's strategic support[60] indicate the psychic readiness of the Indian legal mind to accept change against the stoic presence of the mainstream legal thought, which had outlived its purpose. CLS steps in at the threshold of legal philosophy at the fag-end of the twentieth century, whi‹ had witnessed strong surrogate presence of British positivism, being locked up in the dock while awaiting for the legitimate trial.

References

1. *Supra*. Ch. on Judicial Activism and also Upendra Baxi , Indian Supreme Court and Politics, 1980

2. Gumanmal Lodha, Judiciary : Fumes, Flames & Fire 1983
3. Rajeev Dhavan, ed., Marc Galanter's Law and Society in Modern India, 1989
4. Rajeev Dhavan, Dharmasastra and Modern Indian Society ; A Preliminary Exploration, in *Journal of the Indian Law Institute* (JILI hereinafter), Oct-December 1992, p.515
5. Rajeev Dhavan, ed., Judges and Judicial Power, 1985
6. Jerome Frank, Courts On Trial, 1949
7. Leo Pfeffer, The Supreme Court Speaks, 1967
8. Naorem Sanajaoba, Law and Society, 2001, 1991, pp.61-70
9. Henry J. Abraham, The Judicial Process, 1978, Ch. VIII, p.315 ; *cf. f.n.*i. *Supra* for details.
10. Lawrence Baum, The Supreme Court, 1992, p.253 *et. seq.*
11. John Agresto, The Supreme Court and Constitutional Democracy, 1986, p. 161 *et. seq.*
12. Lord Denning, The Due Process of Law, 1993
13. Rajeev Dhavan, *et. al*, Judges, op. cit.
14. UGC, Report of the Curriculum Development Centre in Law, Volume I, 1990, para 2.10, p.12
15. Mark Tushnet, Critical Legal Studies : An Introduction to its Origins and Underpinnings, Journal of Legal Education, 505(1986), p.506
16. *ibid.* p.509
17. Allan C. Hutchinson Patrick J. Monahan, Law ,Politics and the Critical Legal Scholars, Stanford Law Review, January 1984, p.201
18. *ibid.*, p. 227
19. David Frisby, The Frankfurt School, in John Rex ed., Approaches to Sociology, p. 209
20. Douglas Kellner, Herbert Marcuse and the Crisis of Marxism, 1984, p.9.
21. Lloyd, Introduction to Jurisprudence, p. 710
22. *id.*
23. Martin P. Golding, Jurisprudence and Legal Philosophy in Twentieth Century America, in *J. Legal Educ.* (1986) p. 441 *et. seq.*

24. Alan Hunt, The Critique of Law : What is 'Critical' about Critical Legal Theory, in Journal of Law and Society, Spring, 1987,p.16
25. *ibid*. p.5
26. J. Paul Oetken, Form and Substance in Critical Legal Studies, *Yale Law Journal*, 1991, p.2212
27. Reviews. Critical Legal Studies, *Modern Law Review*, May 1984, p. 364
28. John Stick, Book Review of A Guide to Critical Legal Studies by Mark Kelman, in Columbia Law Review, Vol.88 ; 390(1988) p. 425
29. Cornell Law Review, Vol. 75 : 83, (1989) p.100
30. *ibid*. p. 95
31. David Luban, Legal Modernism, Michigan Law Review, Vol. 84: 1656, (1986) p. 1657
32. Ed Sparer, A Friendly Critique of the Critical Legal Studies Movement, *Stanford Law Review*, January 1984, p.554
33. David M. Trubed, Where the Action is : Critical Legal Studies and Empiricism, *Stanford Law Review*, Jan. 1984, p. 591
34. Mark Tushnet, Critical Legal Studies and Constitutional Law, in *Stanford Law Review*, Jan. 1984, p. 635
35. Lloyd, *op.cit*. pages 583-6, 639-45, 709-16
36. Roberto Mangabeira Unger, The Critical Legal Studies Movement, *Harvard Law Review*, Jan. 1983, p. 562
37. *ibid*. p. 591
38. William Ewald, Unger's Philosophy : A Critical Legal Study, *Yale Law Journal*, April 1988, p. 689
39. Cornel West, CLS and a Liberal Critic, in *Yale Law Journal*, April 1988, p. 758
40. Allan C. Hutchinson and Patrick J. Mahan, The "Rights" Stuff : Roberto Unger and Beyond, in *Texas Law Review*, 1989 p. 1483
41. Hugh Collins, Roberto Unger and the Critical Legal Studies Movement, *Journal of Law and Society*, Winter, 1987, p. 37
42. Duncan Kennedy, in Lloyd, *op. cit*. p. 801
43. ibid. p. 803
44. R.W. Gordon, in Lloyd,*op. cit*., p. 795
45. Mark G. Kelman, Trashing, in Stanford Law Review, Jan. 1984, p. 292-7
46. Christopher T. Wonnell, Problems in the Application of Political Philosophy to Law, *Michigan Law Review,* Oct. 1987, p. 131

47. Lawrence Lessig, Plastics : Unger and Ackerman on Transformation, *Yale Law Journal*, 1989, p. 1173
48. Philip Bobbitt, Is Law Politics, Review Essays, *Stanford Law Review*, May 1989, p. 1305
49. *ibid*. p. 1239
50. Elizabeth M. Schneider, The Dialectics of Rights and Politics, *New York University Law Review*, October 1986, p. 623
51. *ibid*. p. 634 ;
52. Phillip R. Trimble, International Law, World Order and Critical Legal Studies, *Stanford Law Review*, February 1990, p. 823
53. Anthony E. Cook, Beyond Critical Legal Studies; - Dr. Martin Luther King, Jr., *Harvard Law Review*, March 1990, p. 987
54. *ibid*. p. 1033
55. N. Sanajaoba, The Emerging Juristocracy, *Gauhati University Journal of Law*, 1990 Volume, pp. 35-48
56. Krishna Iyer, Law, Freedom and Change, p. 46
57. Hari Chand, A Sociological Approach to the study of Constitutional Law, JILI, 19, 1977, p.1; Peter Sack, Legal Technology and Quest for Fraternity, 32, JILI, 1990, p. 294 Chhatrapati Singh, The Ideological Roots of Legal Paternalism in India, 24, JILI, 1, p.84 ; Jagat Narain, Law and Human Mind, 23 July,1981, p.1 ; Upendra Baxi, Conflicting conceptions of Legal Cultures and Conflict of Legal Cultures, 33, JILI, 1991, p. 173; Chhatrapati Singh, The Dialectics of Law, 28, JILI, 1986, p. 36 ;
58. E.S. Venkataramiah, Some Thoughts on Social Justice,25, JILI, 1983, p. 289; P.M. Bakshi, East and West: The Legal Systems and their Convergence, 26, JILI, 1984,p. 222 ; Sasheej Hegde, Limits of Law Reform, 29, JILI, 1987, p.153; Peter Sacj, Law Reform, 30, JILI, 1998, p. 309; Parmanand Singh, Social Justice for the Harijans, 20, JILI, 1978, p. 355; Jagat Narain, Judicial Law Making, 27, JILI, 1985, p. 198
59. Alice Jacob, Nehru and Judiciary, 19, JILI, 1977, p. 169; Anirudh Prasad, Imprints of Marshallian Judicial Statemanship of Indian Judiciary, 22, JILI, 1980, p.240

    Cf. Upendra Baxi, Judicial Discourse : Dialectics of the Face and the Mask, 35, JILI, 1993, p.1. Baxi writes, " In the discourse of the law, justice is merely an aspect of power....In the law, then, we may expect at the very best not the *power of justice* but *justice of power*....The calculus of power influences the design of legal justice."(p.3) He repeats St. Augustine's classic statement : *"What is State without justice but a band of robbers?"* The Fabian socialist legal ideologues, however, are nowhere near de-construction of unjust institutions. They insist upon melodrama of cosmetic reforms.

60. Pramanand Singh, Judicial Socialism and Promises of Liberation: Myth and Truth, 28, JILI, 1996, p. 336 ; D.N.Saraf, Limits of Judges' Domain: Some Policy Considerations, 30, JILI, 1988, p.45. *See Journal of the Indian Law Institute*, Vol. 40 (1998), Special issue on Human Rights.

17

Post - Modernist Legal Knowledge

Post-independence India does not make a complete break with the British colonial institutions. Whatever the General Electric Company does, it is for America and whatever the colonial institutions do, it is for India. Indian legal consciousness is moulded in this model.

Institutionalised transfer of legal knowledge through the professional law schools and promotion of legal consciousness through the inter-active social milieu are ongoing process, which call for periodic assessment and qualitative upgradation in the context of changing human civilizations. The modernised politico-legal institutions would have suffered from cultural lag, should we leave them, where they are and not where they ought to be. Hence, the need for post-modernist provocation arises so that legal consciousness and knowledge imparted so far through the multiple media including the social and law school resources, would periodically pass through critical re-appraisals.

Where critical attitude towards the institutions and ideas are found missing, the cultural lag may widen itself to the extent of reaching a crisis stage at a certain point of reference. The Bar Council of India resolves to update under-graduate law syllabi in 1998 ; the substantive law remains the same, however.

The present multi-disciplinary concern reaches out to modernist approaches like the concern over law and society, law and technology, theoretical experimentation, right to development, green (environmental) rights, law vis-a-vis the market economy, democracy, family and power equations, among others. Vulnerable sections are given attention. The modernist structures transcend law's conventional provinces and do not merely confine to providing, retaining and regulating the ordered society through justicing, legislation, and bureaucratisation.

The conventional domain, however, makes physics and medicine possible, geography, literature and mathematics a reality and the entire intellectual exercises, inventions and discovery safe. Even the mightiest cosmological architecture as well as the tiniest spark of sub-atomic particles do not run into random Brownian motion, as because they too follow their own physical and materialistic laws. Human laws do not differ much in essence and purpose either from these laws. However, the human laws need continuous upgradation and qualitative transformation through critical appraisals.

The modernist structures and theories had substantially transformed the idiom, vernacular and the reach of law towards anti-colonial machineries, economic egalitarianism, welfare statism and also towards communalisation of the legal domain at varying levels. The structural responses have progressively sensitized the de-colonisation process, vindication of the national rights and widespread national recrudescence - the visible demonstrations of which have rallied before our own eyes in the most unbelievable theatricals like break-up of the mighty Soviet Empire into fifteen independent nation states, the transformation of Yugoslavia into five independent countries and the painless break up of Czechoslovakia into two Czech and Slovak republics.

One can see the ethnic and nationality unrest in Burma, India and Sri Lanka within the Asian geography, which are not devoid of deep-rooted structural questions. The post-modern institutions, continental and global structures and ideology definitely respond to a certain world-outlook and *zeitgeist* — the spirit of the time, the teleology of which cannot be conveniently undermine and encapsulated into straight-jacket political categories of an obsolescent epoch. Legal knowledge cannot be quarantined from these issues.

Every epoch carries with her a definite spirit, performance-potential, and a lexicon of semantics of its own. That is why the laws of Manu, the laws of faith and the laws, as understood in the Bible had been found to be true exclusively within the respective epochal framework, they had been connected with, and the post-modernist laws uphold their necessary legitimation and validity on their own rights. The process seems to be irreversible and forward-moving. Several radical theories of the past had stripped off their radical complexions, which stigmatised them, as they are gradually internalised into the contemporary value-system.

The victims of civilisation, the vulnerable groups within the society and the children of lesser gods contest the marginalisation-theology of the dominant races, population groups and the power elites. The conflicts have expression in violence and it reaches out even beyond violence, in world wars. Violence originally starts as soon as deprivation, denials and sufferings are endorsed by the society; the responses from the vulnerable groups as well as the victims of the laws, which are far from being pleasant, constitute the real counter-violence. Violence is very much in the need of a re-definition and elaborate cognition. Fidel Castro in his famous, 'History will absolve me ' speech during his trial in 1953 spoke with a skeptical refrain :

> "Furthermore, if there is in this world a people that utterly abhors favouritism and inequality, it is the Cuban people. To them, justice is symbolised by a maiden with a scale and a sword in her hands. Should she lower before one group and furiously wield that sword against another group, then to the people of Cuba—the maiden of justice will seem nothing more than a prostitute brandishing a dagger. My logic is the simple logic of the people."

Legal education and legal consciousness, while being a component of the holistic social consciousness, has to be critically evaluated in spite of adhering to untenable dogmatism and determinism or even the fatalism. The CLSM

(Critical Legal Studies Movement) as discussed in the preceding chapter has, therefore, nurtured a critical socio-legal philosophy, which deprecated the American legal education, American legal profession and also preferred an alternative to either Marxism or Liberalism.[2]

The CLSM advanced criticism, self-criticism, role-jumbling, context-smashing, constitutionalism of the permanent mobilisation, radical political goals and added new concepts like organic group, intelligible essence, empowered democracy, dis-entrenchment, negative capabilities, destablization rights, market and solidarity rights within the rights regime.[3] As much as Marxism and Liberalism with human faith claim to emancipate MAN, so much is the claim of the CLS. The CLS movement strikes directly against dominance, hierarchy and hegemony. Critical attitude is a reliable and dependable approach for a generation, which dislikes a sudden, unpredictable system-holcaust or an untenable crisis. Post-modernism in legal consciousness and legal studies is accompanied with critical world-outlook and critical attitude towards the dominant ideology and theories. The consciousness is neither partisan nor segmental but holistic. As an example, the Bahujan Samaj Party claims that the minority rules the oppressed majority in India.

Hegemony[4] of elites or dominant class is a negation of the democratic scheme of human dispensation. Antonio Gramski hits out at the intellectuals. In his words :

The intellectuals are the dominant group's "deputies" exercising the subaltern functions of social hegemony and political government.[5]

Casteism is not the monopoly or thriving market of Vedic puritanists and racial obscurantists. Only leaders like Dr. B.R. Ambedkar and people of his like—the post-modernists could contest it in both theory and practice. Theory and practice constitute the totality of the knowledge structure. Dominance and hegemony negates democratisation at the very root. 1. Alvin and Heidi Toffler, War and Anti-war, 1994 Mao Dze Dong, therefore, wrote in 1937:

> Marxists hold that man's social practice alone is the criterion of the truth of his knowledge of the external world. What actually happens is that man's knowledge is verified only when he achieves the anticipated results in the process of social practice (material production, class struggle or scientific experiment).[6]

> V.J.Lenin wrote — " Without a revolutionary theory there can be no revolutionary movement." It is applicable to legal ideas equally.

The power elite have given legislative seal to several welfare-norms, as prompted by their vision of a new liberal society, only to be shelved from the necessary enforcement. The bureaucracy, the executive and above all, the power-elites are not prepared to transform the legislative norms or even the constitutional norms to operative social norms. The end-result is a big hiatus found between the values, goals, norms and the realities.

Milovan Djilas in his 'New Class' had given evidence of a new class emerging out of the classless communist society. The man who happened to be the next in the political hierarchy to J.B. Tito in Yugoslavia had, therefore, been imprisoned. The communist *apparatchik* and the bureaucracy had their own lion's share in the mismanagement of the former Soviet Union and the eventual break-up. C. Wright Mills writes in his book, 'The Power Elite',[7] that the American elite, who has acquired institutional means of power and communications is now in 'command of instruments of rule quite unsurpassed in the history of mankind.'

Cliques, coteries, extra-constitutional centres of power, dynasty-based democracy are no longer values foreign to the practising democrats in India. The laws which emanate from the oven of the cliques and coteries and the degraded democratic institutions could be either elitist or class-oriented. The legal consciousness created in this context has to be distanced from the prevailing social consciousness. The modelling and working of the institutions should respond to the parameters, intellectual goals and needs of the informed social consciousness which also advances. The universities and law schools are the academic instruments of power-elites. Bertrand Russel[7a] observes, "Institutions such as universities largely remained in the grip of the dogmatists..."

Massification of law and politics is a democratic exercise, as the mass participate in the nation-making, national re-construction, revolutions and the historical movements. In this context, Muammar Al Qathafi deprecates the fraud, committed in the name of democracy elsewhere. He writes in his 'Green Book' :

> The mere existence of a parliament means absence of the people, but true democracy exists only through the participation of the people, not through the activity of their representatives.[8]

> If, however, the parliament emerges from a party as a result of winning an election, it is a parliament of the party and not of the people.[9] Thus it becomes clear that representation is fraud. Assemblies formed by a method of appointment or hereditary succession do not fall under any form of democracy.[10]

The theory of political obligation, consent, dissent and representation, among others, do not merely remain in the academic work, as they are instrumental in legitimization of the norms, creation of legal obligations and sanctions in the event of violation of the legal norms.

Human institutions are subject to constant supervision, re-modelling, re-institutionalisation or if need arises, to de-construction. It may be noted that when M.K. Gandhi found his party alienated from the mass, he wanted to distance himself from his party. The mass has been alienated. The empathy that we work up emotionally towards serving institutions, may totally negate the very purpose for which the institutions had been designed and created.

Post-modernism is post-structural and post-ideological. The bedrock of justice has also been constantly re-defined. At one time, burning of widows in the east and witches in the west was supreme justice, which at present are conceived by one and all as supreme injustice. The empirical evidences overwhelmingly support the shifting notion of justice in space-time continuum. Law and justice stand on shifting human premises and values, which are mediations of deeper conflicts found in the milieu progressive societies. Legal knowledge devoid of justice as paradigm, and its transmission is a threat to the entire system.

Comparative legal ethnologists, cultural and historical anthropologists had already agreed to the idea of legal evolutionism, whereas the radical Marxists had demonstrated the concept of break and quantum leap in the evolutionary line of human history. Theories of crisis and catastrophe better explain the latter human phenomenon. Human history and to be specific, the legal and political history, need not follow a unilinear direction.

The cosmic ocean devours many events thereby demonstrating the catastrophe of one kind or another modest deconstruction of institutions which pale before such colossal drama. In the process of defining justice through the mythical experience, *Srimad Bhagavad Gita*[11] explains the de-construction ideology on a colossal scale :

> Verily, as the many torrents of rivers flow towards the ocean, so do those heroes in the world of men enter Thy fiercely flaming mouths. (Ch. XI, 28)

> The Blessed Lord said : I am the mighty world-destroying Time, here made manifest for the purpose of unfolding the world. Even without thee, none of the warriors arrayed in the hostile armies shall live. (Ch. XI, 32)

At the micro-level, reconstruction of institutions is a possibility as much as de-construction of the machineries could be a reality. Legal knowledge and consciousness follow the dialectical process, which is brought about by the transformation of values, their negation or by the emergence of a new set of values. The immutability criteria of natural law had already been substituted by a possibility of accepting realigning values. Values are the shifting premises of the respective generations, which while responding to the demand of the civilization, find intrusion in strategies and developmental concepts. Even the scripture is critical.

Bible does not sustain the unsustainable. It says:

> A healthy tree cannot bear bad fruit, and a poor tree cannot bear good fruit. Any tree that does not bear good fruit is cut down and thrown in the fire.[12]

Jesus warned the teachers of law - the Pharisees:

> How terrible for you, pharisees! You love the reserved seats in the synagogues, and to be greeted with respect in market places.
>
> How terrible for you :
>
> You are like unmarked graves which people walk on without knowledge of it.

Legal knowledge in India

The formal institutionalised legal studies in India had drawn sufficient attention of law reformers and sufficient quantity of reports have generated alternative blueprints for legal education reforms.

The reports — both official and unofficial — had advocated for reformists measures viz., adoption of socially relevant legal education[14] , need for a national policy and national council of legal education,[15] qualitative upgradation of teaching and research in the discipline of law,[16] delivery of legal services to the rural poor and the disadvantaged groups, [17] and modernisation and de-colonisation of the law curriculum,[18] among others.

Some of these reports had given more thrust to the need and potential for growth of the elitist law schools. The remaining subaltern law schools may not come out of the entrenched GNP or, debt-trap, which characterise the developmental models of the third world economy. The consumers of justice cannot, however, be discriminated against, although the law schools remain either bourgeois-oriented or, elitist. Legal knowledge and legal consciousness would not be made hierarchical and hegemonistic. A critical attitude to the delivery of legal knowledge, justice and system-evaluation has to be cultivated amongst the law-reformers, law-persons and other human resources.

One should be prepared to rethink the post-modernist provocations and the premises that generate provocations. Elitist legal education, imported by the power-elites for the perpetuation of their class-interests and legitimisation of class-justice cannot be expected to deliver the goods to the dis-empowered and emasculated mass, who had been deprived of justice for a long time.

References

1. Fidel Castro, History will Absolve Me, 1978, p.71.
2. *Texas Law Review, Standford Law Review* 1984, Special issue.
3. Roberto Mangbeira Unger, Critical Legal Studies, Movement *Harvard Law Review,* January, 1983 Volume 96.
4. Antonio Gramski, Selections from the Prison Notebooks, 1989 see chapter on State and Civil society.
5. *ibid.* p.12.
6. Mao Tse Tung, Five Essays on Philosophy, p.3.
7. C.Wright Mills, The Power Elite, 1959 pp. 18, 23,69, 283.
7a. Russels Unpopular Essays 1950 p. 125.
8. Muammar Al Qadhafi, The Green Book, Libya, p.7.
9. *ibid.* p.9.
10. *id.*
11. Swami Swarupananda, Srimad Bhagavad Gita. 1989, p.256.
12. Good News for Modern Man, The New Testament, Bible Society of India, 1975 p.17.
13. *ibid.*, p. 182; see also pp. 15, 25, 62, 123, 372, 380, 457,467.
14. University Grants Commission, Towards a Socially Relevant Legal Education, 1979, New Delhi. The consolidated report studies 10+2+3 legal education, state of pedagogy, National Service Schemes, among others.
15. All India Law Teachers' Association, Report of the Committee on Reforms in Legal Education in the 1980s, Delhi University, 1979,

the AILTA report recommends major structural reforms in legal education.

16. University Grants Commission, Status of Teaching and Research in the Discipline of Law, 1981. The report emphasizes infrastructure requirements of L.L.M. studies and Ph. D. in the Law Faculty. Subsequent CDC Report of 1990s is utopian ; 90 percent of Indian Law Schools do not have even the minimum infrastructure.

17. National Law School of India & International Commission of Jurists, Geneva, 1990, Report of Asian Seminar for Law Schools, on Delivery of Legal services for rural poor and other Disadvantaged groups. The report highlights the need for coordination of the profession, law school, media, governmental agencies and NGOs.

18. University Grants Commission, Report of Curriculum Development Centre in Law, New Delhi, 1990. Vol. I &II. The spirit of reform as advanced by the CDC is more of archival and elitist significance, as even the top law schools and universities in India are not in a position to materialise the utopian objectives in the absence of total governmental support. The GNP and GDP percentage of allocation in India's context would have to be multiplied twenty or thirty times, in case the report is to be literally implemented.

However, the author feels that within the available resources, some modest reform measures could be implemented, notwithstanding the prolonged neglect of legal education by the Union and State governments. In 1998, Bar Council of India has modernised its curriculum by prescribing 28 papers and giving emphasis on practice. The sustaining laws, however, are of British colonial vintage.

18

Futurology and the New Order

Futurology that is futuristic is a new discipline that empowers the policy-makers to anticipate possible outcome of the present interactive and evaluative process and to organise or, even reorganise the paradigms. A brainchild of human and physical sciences, it reaches out to all creative activities, including the shaping of the new orders. Every new order ripens into the old order and that continues.

Recollect the future and predict the past (time warp), Crystal-gazing and Nostradamus might be paradoxical, but futuristic studies of events, processes, behaviours and phenomena could be made scientific. High-tech societies of the ancient world, like the one China evolved two millennia ago, simply crumbled down, as the Chinese could not develop an important instrument of thought — the 'hypothesis', which still remains the greatest gift of Greece to the West and subsequently to the rest of mankind.

The vision unfolds with the abundant hidden possibilities, which the 'hypothesis' opens up to the time-warp. The capacity to design vision, exploit the basic instinct of creativity and formulate central assumptions is essential for futuristic studies. When the HDV forecasts meteorology as the latest 16 M machine or Cray 14 could do, ESP kind of intuition has not been Credible. More and more lives could be saved in terms of millions or, so in Bangladesh or coastal areas with the help of advance-warning system, as provided by even the primitive 20th century hightech apparatus of today. This is one instance out of several capabilities of modern man, who might be bracketed along with the stone age people, a millennium hence. If we logically extend the might of information regime of this stage of development, we can gaze at the distant outline of probabilistic results, behaviours, phenomena and trends, which could be connected with the 4Ms that matter most to us all — Man, Matter, Mind and Machine.

Systems are objects of system analysis, when we consider the rational and the irrational systems. The former could be subjected to scientific system-analysis and the latter may be brought under trial and error modes of enquiry. The CNS (Central Nervous System) that functions within an organised brain is like a self-organising info-system. The governing principles applicable to the CNS are more or less the same in regard to the subsequent generations of neutral computers, which are yet to be fully developed: Centralised and coordinated info-regimes of the contemporary society or, future societies are simulated replication of the above mentioned biological and meta-biological machine systems. Behavioural studies of these diverse, but homologous systems are significant in futuristic studies.

Forecasting and prediction could be either rational or purely intuitive. Intuitive scriptural predictions like the *'Qayamat'*, the *'Mahapralaya'*, the 'Resurrection' or the 'Apocalypse' constitute a set, distinguishable from Malthusian essay of population-resource-imbalance or, Marxian design for a classless world-order or, contemporary concern for what we would like to label as info-global village, based on a just and equitable world order. Intuition may be conceived as an activity of the self-organised subconscious, unconscious mind-set. It may also find philosophical access to 'Determinism', 'Pre-Determinism', 'Precognition' and 'Fatalism' and even appear as an irrational domain.

Whereas scientific analysis is fondly used in the case of the second set of predictive designs, intuition remains the corridor of communication between an undefined source and an assumed consequence, that can bear evidence. Rational process differs from an irrational process, as the latter is seemingly unverifiable. Error is possible in both the activities due to interventions. Futuristic studies are intended to be a rational, scientific and analytical activity. An expected trend, may, however, be reversed, should a significant variable changes dramatically or, an element of change affects the activity. Magic effect is not contemplated in futurology, as it is understood today. 'Content-analysis' and 'system-analysis' are also used by futurologists. Naisbitt group in USA studies 6,000 daily papers and journals in order to prepare or assess a possible trend. Available resources are fully utilised while visualising a trend.

In a strong bid to win the last world war, Americans explored several possibilities including the 'content analysis' of daily papers, which provided value-laden information. In order to enable themselves to shoot down erratic enemy warplanes, the Allied scientist invented Cybernetics. Manhattan project could be said to be an excellent example of information-coup, unlike the highly transparent and visible Pearl harbour provocation. Defence researches on common civilian themes like genetech (1 : 1958), biotechnology, cloning genome, transgenesis on the side of the new biology and electronics, high-technology, superconductivity, cryogenics, next generation AI (Artificial Intelligence, 2 : 1992) and particle physics etc. on the side of new physics could have been processed in secrecy. Several branches of contemporary scientific information remain forbidden-knowledge. Silicon valleys of post-industrial societies remain prohibited areas. Information does not easily escape to developing societies in the way they are desired to be.

However, information piracy is also as old as the profession of espionage, which transcends any accepted human morality. Nearly 200 futurological journals are being published in USA and the West. Conventional and orthodox lines of thinking are not fully matching with the futuristic paradigms. Nuclear scientists currently develop 'simulation technology' in lieu of actual tests. The list would be fairly long (34: —)

As regards the different methods and approaches to thinking, convergent and dogmatic thinking is replaced by perceptive, strategic, divergent, creative and lateral thinking. Fantasy plays the central role in futuristic studies. So much is creative thinking.

Western mind

Old assumptions can not completely explain new doctrines, and principles, notwithstanding the agreement of the inference with the original self-evident postulates. The logical coherence alone can not save the invalidity of postulated ideas. Karl Popper has, therefore, espoused the falsifiability of theories. Self-evident truths are basic premises, advanced in the canvas of the spirit of time and specific cultural-attainment. That is why self-evident truths are also negated and contradicted.

Reason and rationality functions as cultural parameter in this context. Reason, is after all, what we call reason. It could be a non-reason too. We start and end up with central assumptions. The info-global village is visualised as an integrated whole. The rise and fall of civilizations are recurrent themes for historians like Arnold Toynbee. Hydrological civilisations four millennia ago had easily faded away with the change of river-bed and shifting of water-level. Information and technology of an epoch can not always serve another epoch.

Paul Kennedy in his work 'Rise and Fall of Great Powers' (3:1987) explains how Dutch, Portuguese, Spanish, French and English colonial sea powers have now been succeeded by Japan, USA and *'Festung Europa'* of E.U. He further postulates in his subsequent treatise, 'Preparing for the Twenty First Century '(4:1993) two anti-thetical trends, represented by world-wide political fragmentation and economic globalisation. Besides, the United Nations corroborates de-colonisation process the world over and justifies the installation of NIEO. The Uruguay round of GATT gave birth to another global trade-order in the form of WTO(5:1994).

The issue is whether we require new central assumptions or, we still fall in certain set patterns or, Gestalt in the movement of history. The philosophy and science of history gives testimony to the existence of set patterns — the unilinear movement of human society. The cyclical theory and the theory of leaps, catastrophe, chance and jerks. The last is not a pattern but an event, which breaks up the continuity. We call it revolution. Revolutions happen in science, technology, thought, culture and society. Even religion is a revolution of a bygone age—partly obsolete in this age of technology.

No better evidence of the recent trends is given then by the post cold-war global phenomena — like Rio Earth Summit 1992, Vienna World Conference on Human Rights 1993, GATT Final Act 1994, emergence of WTO 1995, emergence of nearly 20 independent countries out of former Soviet Union and Eastern Europe and rise of the Pacific-rim in the world economic horizon. There is a possibility of democratizing and restructuring the United Nations. NIEO should not be a forgotten legacy, as long as iniquitous and unjust distribution of economic wealth remains a global fact. Asymmetry tends towards symmetry and the cycle continues.

The Asian and Pacific rim scenario deserves to be watched out. Indian re-interpretation of Nostradamus is self-assuring in the sense that India stakes its claim as a regional power, notwithstanding a dominant presence of China, which, to some of the China-watchers in the West, is generating its potential of emerging as the economic power-number-one. Abdul Kalam believes that 'India can still emerge a major developed country' and science would affect 'all walks of economical and social life.' (35: —) Super-powerism — be it Euro-centric or, Sino-centric or, otherwise, had been repudiated by Mao Dzse Dong in his three world thesis.

Contemporary futuristic studies are value-laden. Collective right, responsibility and obligations as seriously considered in the info-global village, sacrosanctity of human rights, sustainable development, protection of environment, concern for animal and plant rights, global interdependence and info-global-village are emergent values of this age and civilization. Values shift as much as the meanings of justice shift in different epochs. When we consider 'value-shift', as significant, Toffler considers 'powershift' as decisive. He has his own American perceptions.

Soviet futuristic studies on the Marxian world-order remain a polemic, following the political decline of the Soviet empire before our own eyes. The mishap or, even one mishap, owing largely to inner-contradictions, cannot entitle one to hastily jump into major conclusions. Marxian dialectics and argumentation survive the Soviet Union. However, the classical definitions can not elaborately explain info-based labour, value, alienation and international relation. It appears that a re-enunciation is preponderant, specially at a time when colonialism and imperialism has changed colours, only to be substituted by new-forms and prototypes of dominance and hegemony. Communist China retains political communism, while restructuring its command economy. Its technology and vision also shifts thereby bringing new order.

The predictors prepare their own judgements before they lay hands on forecasting. Economic liberalists envisage the rise of the Pacific rim, China and India. Colonel Qadhafi in his 'Green Book' and its commentary, predicts that the Blacks (*Afrikanners*) would rule the world one day. He calls it Black power. It reminds us of the Mediterranean (centre of the world) or, Euro-centric concept of the world, which is similar to Chinese world view of the past. While Japan, USA and Germany-led E.U. contend for economic leadership of the world in the next century, China perceives that the next century would belong to her. India with all her inherited sub-terranean faultlines and disjunctiveness too cherishes dreams of greatness and her presence in the global scenario.

The rise and fall of successive world orders viz., the pre-Christian era, Chinese and Indian orders, the subsequent Islamic millennium and the present Western millennium, just to cite a few, render every world order to mere passing phases. Legal regimes - national and global are the articulated political expression of these orders. An infallible permanent legal order or normative-prescriptive human order can not be imagined.

The resource-mobilisation and equitable re-distribution of the orders are carried out by the legal regimes. Primacy of one power or, the American exceptionalism as it is being made out today is a total misnomer. However, nations are in the race. Futuristics is a technique to enhance the quality of the human race of the nations.

The concept of insulated legal and constitutional autonomy is an outdated relic. The legal enterprise is a vital component of the entire futuristic exercise. The enterprise, while being an attribute of the new order, also shapes the format and dynamics of the order.

The West forecasts, the combination of gene therapy with immunotherapy by 2000 A.D., introduction of video post cards by 2005, of cars equipped with anti-collision radar by 2007, identification of genetic root of all diseases by 2015, human colonisation of Mars by 2044, making of thought recognising computers by 2025, use of nuclear fusion to generate electricity by 2040, making of self-reproducing microscopic robots by 2044 and extension of human life span to 140 years by 2500A.D.(34 : 18). Despite possible errors in years and details, the next millennium would throw up some new materials, concepts and so on that would alter the human outlook. The order would generate ideas of interdependence and self-reliance.

American futurologist Alvin Toffler's triology postulates an accelerating future, third-wave revolution in the post-industrial society and acceptance of the changes to come. His 25 assumptions as given in his book "Powershift" furnish, among others, that conflict is an inescapable fact, equality of power is an improbable condition and that "Knowledge" is even more undistributed than arms and wealth. Soviet futurological works, published by Progress and Novosti before 1991 break-up suffer from over-ideologisation of the otherwise credible database. The more ideologised the objective data are, the higher is the probability of suspecting the futuristic studies. Books devoid of ideological tilt are hard to find with.

The fate of the former Soviet Union can be equally met by other powers, as it happened in the past. The Western futurologist are not above their own Western interest in designing their futuristic studies, yet they do not suffer from the terror of regimented data, as transparency characterise their methodology. John Naisbitt describes the shifting of industrial society to information society, of national economy to world economy, hierarchies to Networking and from North to South in 1980s (6:1984, 1990). The 1990 trends as he assumes, include powerful drive of tele-communications, worldwide free trade, environmental attention and obsolescence of war. Naisbitt forecasts unprecedented freedom and democracy, tele-com revolution and new opportunities for Asia and Latin America in the next century. (7 : 1995). Paul Kennedy postulates new challenges in Biotechnology and new industrial revolutions in the 21st century (4:p.137). In 1960 Arthur Clarke had forecasted the emergence of artificial intelligence that would surpass man's in 2080 A.D. The list of central assumptions could be enlarged corresponding to man's achievements in science and expansion of vision.

Trend studies could be made on the basis of hard evidence. Rationalised and realistic science-fiction works of today may become a visual reality tomorrow. In the same way as the Hindus and Arabs invented 'zero' and as Newton and Leibniz explored calculus, even a new medium of mathematical expression may possibly be designed or, created in order to compensate the infirmity of contemporary mathematics. Ramanujan wanted to unravel the mystery of infinity. The moment it is unravelled, the mystery would be totally de-mystified. In social sciences too, the mystery of human mind, consciousness and basic instincts call for fuller explanation despite man's access to the least line of resistance to the unknown entity, which is largely a creation of his intellect and ignorance. Evasion is not science, whereas a valid explanation could be thoroughly scientific.

Russian Mind

Before the break-up of the former Soviet Union, Russians had their own futuristic studies, which in some aspects may be relevant even after the break-up. Science in the year 2000, post-atomic civilization, the space-age (8:74-268), critique of neo-eugenic project (9: 241), future space activities and image of the year 2000 as seen in futuristic models (10: 281), paradoxes of the bourgeois civilization (11: 6), a new synthesis of man and nature, development of psycho-physiological abilities (12: 280) and formation of one science through integration of science and social progress (13: 252) remain Russian futuristic perceptions which could be unfolded in years to come.

Russian futurological works like George Shakhnazarov's futurology Fiasco (14: 1982), The Coming World Order (15 : 1984) and "The Destiny of the World (16 : 1979) analyse the interaction of the global forces, criticise the theory of convergence and examine the crisis of capitalism. The coming world order, as the Russians perceived, would be a just human society beret of the power-monger. However, power remains a reference point of man in his versatility. How can we resurrect it judicious is an issue that may figure in the future agenda.

Although futurology started with the Ossip Flechtheim's essay in 1943 and Alvin Toffler's lessons in 1966, Government of India had opened its futurology panel in 1978 - 1981. Seth-Harva method is popular in India. The Indian method follows five steps including preparation of future scenario and study of its policy-implications.

The Western, Russian and Third world's deep concern for man and his cosmic relation would remained a sensitive issue till the boundary of space or depth of the atom are assessed in a millennium or beyond in the ongoing process of unlocking the mystery of the universe. CDF Collider Detector at Fermilab found the mass of "Top Quark" as 176 billion electron-volts and D; Zero group found it as well Quark Physics just begins. The building blocks have to be deciphered.

Carl Sagan is a man to melt down today's fiction to tomorrow's scientific fact. The future evolution of human brain (17 : 197), search for extra-terrestrial intelligence (18 : 314), shores of cosmic ocean (19 : 19) figure in his vision. In his book 'Contact' (20 : 327) which is novel unlike the other non-fictions, Carl Sagan projects his future vision through the medium of story-telling. What, after all, is science at the beginning? A fiction that comes true. Rationalised, phantasization and intuitive perceptions, based upon exploring resourceful possibilities are what we understand as futurology. The romances of UFO-logy may not survive longer than the unveiling of the facade, which mystifies the unidentified objects. That is why United States of America has undertaken the 'Project Blue Book' [21 : 324]. Politics and law run the government, which in its turn, runs the sciences. The converse would be hardly true in this science-society interface.

In the process of mankind's journey towards the third millennium, Albert Einstein would remain a reference - person of twentieth century's material and scientific achievements. In his address, delivered at a celebration of Max Plank's sixtieth birthday (1918) before the Physical Society in Berlin, Einstein had remarked, "In the temple of science are many mansions, and various indeed are they that dwell therein and the motives that have led them thither."

"The supreme task of the physicist is to arrive at those universal elementary laws from which the cosmos can be built up by pure deduction. There is no logical path to these laws; only intuition, resting on sympathetic understanding of experience, can reach them" he said. The first few decades of the third millennium is a curtain-raiser for the emergence of info-global village, silicon valleys, speaking and thinking neural computers, society of robots, bio-tech and genetic revolutions, successful genome-project, man-machine-matter dialogues, new material and technologies like polymer, superconductivity, cryogenics and super-highway cosmic colonisation. The level and technology of info-communication technology would leap into a new height. The political consequence would be the possibility of adopting direct democracy the world over; however, the possibility might be totally reversed, should the info-imperialism or info-colonialism ever happen in the global order. Power and morality may remain polarized in the future. The new order has to create new morality.

The new agenda (better call it old agenda — two-three centuries hence) would incorporate dynamic alteration of the traditional nuclear family and traditional social bonding, culmination of racism, casteism and similar imposed hierarchies, realignment of political and economic powers, re-structuration of nation-states interspersed with occasional historical discontinuities, breaks, redefinition of man's position, power and role in the new environment. Possibly in that age of cosmic gateway, among others, catastrophe and disasters always loom at large, specially in the countries housing nuclear arsenals; even a break of chance or mishap may convert the contemporary super-powers into republic of ashes and insects. West knows it, but cannot realize this. Only total nuclear disarmament guarantees their leading position and survival. Agenda-setters should see that the entire evolution is not totally reversed and we do not return to the first few seconds of primitivity or time-zero, because of imprudent greed and irresponsibility. A democratic, transparent info-society can remove the alarmism and address itself to a just message. In the event of re-colonisation, human rights could be vanquished or eroded.

Trend

Apart from optimism, info-global village undertakes information avalanche from around the world, which in the absence of strategic info-management may even lead to info-pollution, computer-aided crimes of unprecedented magnitude. The profiles of bio-tech revolutions, new physics, proximity-space conquest and colonisation, man-machine equations, among others, step into the gateway of the Third millennium. The 21st century would also be recalled as a primitive age at the end of the third millennium, in the same way as we look back into the discovery of fire, wheel, gunpowder and press. The drama, would progressively unfold till our domestic star crosses Chandrasekhar limit, provided genetic disasters and accidents do not disrupt the genetic-integrity of homo-sapiens and other species. A dark shadow always follows every feat of human achievement, like the invisible side of the moon. Judicious use of science, imagination and resources by the earthlings would promote their self interest. Knowledge and science should not be overstretched to a point from which a return may be next to impossibility. Hence the need to reiterate Russel-Einstein's statement in the Pugwash movement in 1950s.

We assess the scientific benchmark with cautious optimism. A few visible high watermarks of contemporary R & D, S & T are being noted in the above context. Third generation intelligent robots remain so as to replace the pageant of human, industrial proletariat, whose pre-eminence is partly in threatened. Robot census in 1988 is as follows :

Japan	-	176,000
W.Europe	-	48,000
USA	-	33,000
Rest of world	-	23,000
Net	-	2,80,000

(Source - 4:1993, p.88)

Robotics-leap forward would boost-up the economy of Japan and developed countries, but the fate of human workers remains rather uncertain as robotics culture enters into large scale utilization. Chinese programme 863 gives a turning point in high-tech, since 1987 in the field of bio-tech, space-tech, laser tech, info-tech, energy and advanced materials. Wang Daheng, Wang Ganchang, Yang Jiachi, Chen Fangyun are the leading scientists behind the Chinese futuristic programme — '863'. 15th National Congress of Chinese communist party held in 1997 has set new targets in S & T frontier. It may further increase the GNP and GDP. China could be another superpower in the near future.

The commercialisation of knowledge is on the rise. It is true that plagiarism, piracy, mindless imitation may influence the non-original and uncreative mind of scholars, researchers and copycat scientists in third world, yet patentability of inventions should be judiciously used.

Edward de Bono in his 'Serious Creativity' (22:1992) laments that many brilliant people plagiarise ideas and concepts without acknowledging the original authority. It is a valid point to be noted, since even nuclear secrets had been stolen by nations and scientists. Indian Patent Law 1970 maintains a cool balance to protect knowledge, ideas and invention. It is amended in 1999 to match with WTO. GATT final act 1994 and its creature WTO,1995 has espoused legalisation and large scale patentability of scientific inventions, sealed national safeguards through licensing and limited patenting of third world explorations (5:1994). MNCs and G-8 would, be the undisputed beneficiary of the model of commercialisation of knowledge and intellectual property in the post-cold war and WTO era. P-5 of the UN and G-8 hold the leverage of decision-making in this age. The new order is fairly imbalanced and the global divide continues.

Unless the WTO, functions in conformity with the objectives and paradigms of NIEO, a possible re-colonisation of the least developed countries by the knowledge-rich countries not be ruled out. American leadership in 1994 adheres to the American interpretation of 'technology transfer' of the earth summit and biodiversity convention as a voluntary conduct of the West. Henry Kissinger projects the need for American leadership the 21st century, while mystifying American values — excellent as well as malignant (23:1994); however, he cannot undermine the significance of the half-awakened sleeping Asia. Technology transfer is not be possible except on Western conditions and prerogatives. WTO has to be seriously engaged in future to curb and eliminate aberrations, Western prejudices and preferences which are detrimental to the rest of the world.

John Naisbitt observes that 'information society is an economic reality' and also that nearly 7,000 scientific articles are written in each day. Knowledge or, info-explosion may even occur, in case the colossal magnitude of generated knowledge is not streamlined, classified, regulated and utilized with strategic interest. An innocuous, ill-prepared planner, national builder, opinion-leader or, scientist may be a victim of information avalanche, drowning and info-quake. Naisbitt writes, "In the computer age we are dealing with conceptual space connected by electronics, rather than physical space connected by the motor car". Scientists (social, physical or technological) have to deliver intellectual property to the knowledge-hungry society. Cyber-democracy can replace representative form of democracy.

In empirical or, experimental sciences, third world scientists may not be in a position to give a lead to Japan, U.S.A. or E.U., yet they are in the rat race, so long as they are in the profession of knowledge-generation and knowledge-delivery. In the 21st or, 22nd century, education should be capable of re-empowering the human resources so that they may cope with the increasing demands of the next millennium. Third world Nobel laureate Abdus Salam and his Trieste-circle felt that the third world scientists and knowledge-workers may join the global race in the province of theoretical sciences. Third world should evolve and design its own perception of the incoming future by keeping aside the copy cat image of advanced countries.

In social sciences, the emigre Germans evolved Frankfurt school during the last war while remaining as fugitive-immigrants in the USA. The Frankfurt school has been critical of the 'uni-dimensional man' and the diseased technology-based civilization in this age (24:1984). But the malaise has been overlooked by the consumer society.

Human knowledge and intuition having been diversified for convenience, through institutions of learning and research, might not abandon the basic premise of the unity of knowledge. The magnificent hall of knowledge having a hundred door and a thousand crevices does not at all lose the basic unity of the hall and its uniqueness entity.

The civilizational principles are carved out by the law-persons, statesmen, scientists and the humanists, from out of this pool of unity of human knowledge. Superior civilizational principles survive the occasional stages like reforms, revolutions and even armed conflicts between nations, whereas the inferior values gradually recede in the tunnel of the past till they evaporate in extinction.

These principles are the universal currency of security, equality, development, peace, stability and interdependence. The new order has to represent them.

Asian mind

The third millennium like the last two millennia may witness alternative power-states in succession and decline of some of the incompatible powers. Paradigms of incompatibility may be examined by altering the variables. However, Japanese phenomenon is fascinating for the simple reason than resource-poor and naturally incompatible land of the rising sun (Nippon) is likely to continue to be the economic power number one of the world or in top slot in the future. It is the largest creditor of the world, while USA remains the largest debtor.

Japanese MITI (Ministry of International Trade and Industry), Ministry of education, unique corporate management (25:1981) and national ethos characterise Japanese leadership and power-position, which is the envy of resource-technology-rich USA and its alliance. It may stimulate resource-poor states and the countries as well. The under-lying deeper secrets are, however, yet to be revealed. MITI plans to leap from the use of 100 parallel processors in the 5th generation AI to 10,000 parallel processors in 6th generation at a cost of 770 million dollars for one decade. Fuchi's KIPS (Knowledge Information Processing), adoption of PROLOG and knowledge-engineering through an expert system has indicated signals of success (26:1984). The third millennium may witness a high level of artificial intelligence and even surpass it in some areas, because the CNS (Central Nervous System) is not immune from duplication.

'Creationism' is an absurdity — pure and simple and the third millennium logic may raise a reverse ethics like this: why and when Man created his God ! A primitive Albert Einstien may still argue on the basis of Jewish faith that dice did not play God by breeding super human beings. Jean Daussdt remarks, "Most American scientists are in argument with us. Certainly, James D. Watson is in agreement" (27 April, 1994). Toffler's 'Powershift' indicates the new trend like info-tactics, info-wars, and info-agenda which are based on hard data. The info-global village has already experienced smart card, electronic money, universal product code, data protection laws, electronic- highways, high-speed data network, datamation, info-monopoly, computer spies, meta-software, expert system and computer hackers.

Computer-terrorism like narco-terrorism could be equally disastrous. USA alone classifies 20 million documents as secret a year. Info-piracy and info-catastrophe are also the other possibilities. Another hazard is the info-imperialism, which could surpass the Leninist version of the classical imperialism. Toffler—Alvin and Heidi in their book 'War and Anti-war' (28:1994) interconnect society, economies, war and morality in their own perception of the 21st century. *Perestroika* and *Glasnost*, as enunciated by Mikhail Gorvachev, are and would be equally applicable to all open and transparent governments and also to the UN structure.

Citizens do possess 'right to privacy' and 'right to information' in judicious doses. The USA has enacted Freedom of Information Act 1966 and India is carefully evading its responsibility to enact such a law. Both the citizens rights could be equally threatened by unscrupulous use of computers and by the intrusive national info-regimes. Unless info-regime is democratised, info-operation and info-imperialism may usher in.

Areas of Japanese dominance are identified. Global exports of high technology products in 1980 and 1989 are as follows :

Micro-electronics

1980	**1989**
1. U.S.A.(18.3%)	1.Japan (22.1%)
2. Japan (13.2%)	2.U.S.A. (21.9%)
Robotics/Machine Tools	
1. W.Germany (25.8%)	1.Japan (22%)
2. U.S.A.(14.1%)	2.U.S.A.(21.9%)
Telecom Equipment	
1. W.Germany (16.7%)	2.Japan (24.7%)
2. Sweden (15.3%)	2.W.Germany (9.5%)

Computers

1. U.S.A.(38.6%)	1.U.S.A.(24%)
2. W.Germany(11.5%)	2.Japan (17.5%)
Scientific Equipment	
1. U.S.A.(28.3%)	1.U.S.A.(25.2%)
2. Japan (7.1%)	2.Japan (12.9%)

U.S.A. leads in aero space and Germany in organic chemicals

(*Source : Paul Kennedy, 1993 p. 153*).

Print-media and journals speculate that the USA has an inbuilt psychosis that Japan may lead the West in Bio-tech revolution and artificial intelligence. USA intermittently threatened Japan with its unilateral-trade-protection weapons like Super-310 and Special-301 etc. and has also created NAFTA — an American trade bloc, notwithstanding the framework of GATT and WTO. The Japanese corporate management is envied by the West. Several Western authority including Paul Kennedy notes that the IQ of average Japanese is 117%, while that of white Americans and Europeans flicker around 100%.

It is reassuring that 34 of the world's largest 100 companies are Japanese, despite Western self-protectionism and installation of fortress Europe. Bio-tech revolution can be the closest rival of new physics, medical, human genetic and neuro-biological sciences can be completely revolutionised by the genetech upsurges. The possibilities are wide and open. Genetically-engineered microbes may operate as ecological mine sweepers. Trans-genetic animals may be created, proteins may be restructured, *in vitro* production may be widely used. *Nano technology* may be undertaken and DNA labs may come up. A trendsetter could be found in Human Genome Project, 1983, which is becoming successful and would unravel the mystery of man. To a committed scientist or, an ordinary person with scientific attitude, theories of universe and chemical evolution of life explain origin of life without subscribing to false beliefs and superstitions, planted in human mind just five millennia ago.

Indian scientists released TIFAC report in 1996 for harnessing S & T in the 21st century. The government has undertaken nuclear weaponisation since 11 May, 1998. With this venture, she has won mixed responses. What the future, holds for nuclear India would be interesting, considering its economic growth, HDI and weapons race in South Asia. Global dissemination of information and knowledge may play an important role in redefining some of the categories of human perception, thought, philosophy and world outlook. As cited earlier, WTO may set a new trend for commercialisation of intellectual property, which is largely the domain of the post-industrial states. Conflict between and among the least developed, developing and developed societies may be sharpened, until and unless the global info-village ushers into a just, equitable world order (29:1995). Is mankind prepared to avert disasters and catastrophe, largely of his own making is a pertinent question.

Futuristic studies should not be led by dogmatism and ideological rigours. A judicious assessment of the trend, potential and possibilities will remain significant within the province of human ingenuity. P.M. Narasimha Rao's lecture in Harvard University on 17 May ,1994 is teleologically futuristic. He said, "Monocultural absolutes are, or ought to be, on the way out in world affairs. Institutions like Harward face this intellectual challenge, since you are the trend setters. I attach great importance to this because no society can act in the absence of a trend"(30:1994). Universities have to set and evaluate trends in all the faculties.

When we study the global order, peace-keeping and preventive-diplomacy were the two major concerns of the UN secretary general Boutros Ghali. Kofi Anan takes up the thread at the UN from his predecessor. The writer would like to cite Heidi & Alvin Toffler's work " War and Anti-war"(31). The two husband and wife futurologists smell non-equilibrium of the global system, its non-linearity and hyper-connectivity (326). They note that tribal hate spread far and wide and the existing intellectual weapons of peace making are out of date (31: 2)). Like Mao Dze Dong, they reiterate 'that the war to end the major wars are in the need. Neither the 21st century nor the third millennium would be devoid of conflicts. The fear is that the eight nuclear weapon powers including Israel, India and Pakistan may close the curtain either by accident or mistake.

Asian powers are on the rise, as they have the largest human resources and natural resources. China and India stake claims as viable powers. China's claim as the super power of the next century is taken seriously, since China has already become world leader in biotechnology, super conductivity, laser optics and carbon isotopes and it has averaged 9% growth per annum for the last one and a half decade. If China would surpass Japan by achieving dollar 6 trillion economy by the year 2050 (32) is a valid question. Pacific including Indonesia, Koreas, Taiwan, Thailand, Singapore and Hongkong etc. may replace the pre-eminence of North Atlantic sooner or later (33)

Futurologists are not above their national and emotional hangovers. Only a fair and comparative data study would provide a balanced picture. American futurologists project American perceptions and their sub-consciousness. So do the rest.

The new order

The steady rise of the Pacific rim countries — the Oriental bloc in the next millennium has been a subject of concern for the Atlantic rim people — the Western bloc, which has dominated the second millennium after Christ and prepares to govern The third millennium.

The increasing political devolution and decentralisation, compounded by the eminent role of science and technology and the eventual, increasing economic interdependence of the countries has been instrumental in reshaping the world order, which generates normative and prescriptive structures at regional and trans-national levels and legal regimes. Noam Chomsky has visualized an unequitable order in the new order.(37 —)

The concept of bi-polarism or, cold war has been substituted by multiple centres of power or, multipolarism, notwithstanding the of the surviving military superpower. The re-alignment of forces is an ongoing process.

The alternative structures as envisaged include Samuel P. Huntington's vision of the clash of civilizations (36: 312), Henry Kissinger's vision of rise of six macro-states in the midst of post-nations, Alvin Toffler's perception of the Washington-Tokyo-Berlin Triad, which retains Beijing or Delhi at the backyard and other similar Western-oriented futuristics.

The micro-states and small countries, which are late beneficiaries of the science and technology could not endorse the above vision of the regional powers as their ultimate destiny in literal terms, as the fear for re-colonisation looms at large in the cyber-space and the incoming cyber-democracy. An unequal world legal order or, economic and political arrangement, which is the first sin in the 'equality doctrine' would not remain stable and will not withstand the legitimate aspirations of the subjugated nations and weak states. Nature seeks symmetry; so does the world order.

References

1. Features on Genetic Engineering at large. See N.Sanajaoba,GENE-TECH—SOCIO-LEGAL DIMENSIONS, a keynote address to the world congress on law and medicine, New Delhi, 1985
2. N.Sanajaoba, Fifth generation artificial intelligence and 3rd generation of human rights, UGC human rights seminar, Law department, GU, 2-4 May 1992
3. Paul Kennedy, The Rise and Fall of Great Powers, New York, 1987
4. Paul Kennedy, Preparing for the Twenty-first century, 1993; *See* World Focus, The New Millennium, Oct.-Dec., 1998
5. N.Sanajaoba, World Trade Organisation, 1995, PSN, MAPS, 1994, last issue Imphal
6. John Naisbitt, Megatrend 2000, 1990; *Cf.* his book Megatrends, 1984, Asian Megatrend, 1996

7. John Naisbitt, Global Paradox, 1995: almost all the published works of Alvin Toffler are also used as source materials in this chapter
8. B.G.Kuznetsov, Philosophy of Optimism, Progress, 1977
9. I.Frolov, Global Problems and the Future of Mankind, 1982
10. N.N.Inozemtsev, ed., Global problems of Our Age, 1984
11. A. Kukarkin, The Passing Age, Progress, 1979
12. Ivan Frolov, Man-Science-Humanism : A New Synthesis, 1986;
13. M.G. Chepikov, The Integration of Science, 1978
14. Georgi Shakhnazarov, Futurology Fiasco, 1982
15. Georgi Shakhnazarov, The Coming World Order, 1984
16. Georgi Shakhnazarov, The Destiny of the World, 1979
17. Carl Sagan, The Dragons of Eden, 1986
18. Carl Sagan, Broca's Brain, 1983
19. Carl Sagan, Cosmos, 1983
20. Carl Sagan, Contact (a novel), 1986; *See also* novels by Asimov too. Rest of the works of Sagan are non-fiction.
21. Brad Steiger, ed., Project Blue Book, 1987
22. Edward de Bono, Serious Creativity, 1992; A critical reading of Bono's works provides unconventional thoughts
23. Henry Kissinger, Diplomacy, 1995. See his other works
24. Douglas Kellner, Herbert Marcuse and the Crisis of Marxism; *Cf.* Herbert Marcuse, Negations, 1968 and other original works;
25. Richard Tanner Pascale, Anthony G. Athos, The Art of Japanese Management: Japanese Zen management use *Wa* concept i.e group harmony, use interdependent harmonious *Sempai-Kohai*(senior-junior relationship). Japanese consider *sanshu no Jingi* i.e. the three sacred objects as sword, Jewel and the mirror; See Japan the country report, *Times of India* special report 24 pages on Japan, 25 November, 1984.
See *Time* 28.4.1997 on Japan by 2000 A.D.
26. Edward A. Feigenbaum, Pamela McCorduck, The Fifth Generation, 1994
27. *Science Reporter*, April 1994
28. Alvin and Heidi Toffler, War and Anti-war, 1994
29. N. Sanajaoba, the New World Order in the 21st century, *Assam Tribune*, 1 April, 1995
30. Samuel and Elizabeth Zodidi Memorial lecture, Harvard University, USA, 1994

31. Book Review of War and Anti-War by N. Sanajaoba, PSN of MAPS, Imphal, March 1995, p.26
32. The *Time* special report CHINA the next Superpower, May 10, 1993, pp. 14-45. *Time*, 3.3.1997 on China 2000. See *Beijing Review*, 31 March 1997
33. *Time* special report THE PACIFIC RIM, 12 February 1993. *Newsweek,* 2000 forward to the Millennium, 26 December 1994
34. *Time* Special issue, The New Age of Discovery, January, 1998.
35. Abdul Kalam and Y.S. Rajan, India 2020 A vision for the New Millennium, 1998
36. Samuel P. Hutington, The Clash of Civilizations and the Remaking of World Order, Viking, 1996. *Contra* - Edward Said's Netaji Subhas Bose oration, 19 Dec. 1997, Telegraph 1-3 February, 1998, Said deplores Hutington
37. Noam Chomsky, World Orders, Old and New, 1998.

19

Designers For Peace Diplomacy

Behind the great strides of the statesmen, and peacemakers, the spadework and networking tasks are performed by skilled visionary and political craftsmen — the diplomats. The threads of the comity of nations are knit by the diplomatic engineering skills. No worthwhile world order and legal regime is safe at the hands of injudicious political engineers. In this context, the works of Kautilya of the past, Henry Kissinger and Gromyko of the century have been revisited in this discourse. Unlike the formal legislative machineries, the diplomatic machinery legislates in both private and public. We choose three mainstreams of state-craft that moulded the world order and its dynamics.

Indian Empire

European diplomacy had self-destructed imperialism and created European nation-states after the break-up of Austro-Hungarian or, Ottoman empires. Hindustani diplomacy had not only enlarged a dozen of district size republics at Hastinapur and her immediate neighbourhood into *Bharata*, but also expanded the *Rajya* into a colossal Indian empire by continuously gobbling up hundreds of *Hindu* nations and independent countries. This is the miracle of Kautilya's *'Arthashastra'*, which had been internalised into the deep psyche and sub-consciousness. Several other schools of Indian diplomacy that prescribes *'Arthashastra'* as the standard core-text book of contemporary Indian diplomacy. L.N. Rangarajan, IFS, a practising Indian diplomat in five countries edited *'Arthashastra'* with sharp diplomatic insight and acumen.

The *'Arthashastra* , is believed to have been written on palm leaf in the *grantha* script before 1850-2300, it had been published by Dr. R.Shamasastry in 1909, and in three volumes during 1960-1965 by Dr. R.P.Kangle. The present work of a professional Indian foreign service personnel — L.N. Rangarajan has improved the clarity of the text, rendered the translation more readable and it appears to be a rearrangement of the verses. The text provides a manual for organisation of state apparatus, administration of justice and foreign policy. In the current review, the excerpts and quotes are taken from Rangarajan translation of the *Arthashastra*.

How the *Arthashastra* was instrumental in creating a vast Hindu empire out of a small Hindu state at South Bihar (*Magadha*) speaks volumes about the potency of *Hindustani* imperialism. The conqueror had his native country *Magadha*, assumed his neighbouring country *Kashi*. *Kashi* as the enemy, and *Koshala* (near Himalaya foothills) or *Vriji* (northern Bihar) as middle and neutral kingdoms. That was the original India. There were sixteen mahapanapadas or nation states as well (page 43). The imperial expansion had never looked back henceforth. The Europeans did not acquire such a lethal manual at their hands inspite of their fragile and brittle profit-based imperialism and colonialism, which had been dismantled totally by now, whereas the legacy of the *Arthashastra* survives in Indian continent — rather an empire, except in some small border states, annexed in recent years and where faultlines had been found to exist from the initial position. The *Arthashastra's* conqueror - king (read Indian state after 1947 or, *Bharata* before the Mughul consolidation of India) has to protect the citizens from external aggression. The other responsibility was the enlargement of the territory by conquest. (1: 676).

It appears that the sacred duty of the power-elite of Indian state lies invariably even in today's context, in the conquest of other states and expansionism, considering the internalisation of the *Arthashastra* in the psyche of the ruling class. The ruler of South Bihar (Magadha) in Kautilya's time had a vast empire in the mind. The area extending from the

Himalayas in the north to the sea (in the south) and a thousand *jojanas* wide from east to west is the area of operation of the king emperor (1: 742). Had there been no Himalayas to block the physical vision, the Hindu empire could have been visualised up to north pole. A Russian chauvinist leader Zhirinovsky also claims all territories up to Arabian sea as his Russian fatherland; As he does not have an *Arthashastra* on his side, his rhetoric bears no weight.

The methods of conquest of the world had also been fairly described by the manual :

> 'I. After conquering the enemy, the conqueror shall direct his attention to the king who's the middle king; then he shall turn to the neutral king;
>
> 4. The fourth way is to overcome a weak neighbour without allies, having become doubly powerful, overcome another neighbour and with the increased power, a third one and so on' (1: 744)

The conqueror (empire-builder) classifies the other kings (hereafter, read nation states or, states) in terms of *ari* (antagonist), *shatru* (enemy), *mitra* (friend), *ari-mitra* (enemy's friend), *mitra-mitra* (ally of the friend), *ari-mitra-mitra* (enemy's friend's ally) *a parshnigraha, aakranda, a parshnigraha-asara, aakrandasaa, antardhi* and neutral king/ state, *madhyama* (middle kind/state) (1: 552). Each and every state falls into a straight jacket slot — friend or enemy.

In *Mandala (*circle of kings) system, the would-be-conqueror the ally and the ally's ally constitute the first circle with eighteen elements of the circle. There are four circles of the conqueror, the enemy, the middle and neutral states having 72 constituents.(1: 559).

The Kautilyan state after having perceived the neighbours as hostile only to be annexed and guarded in the rear, evolves special techniques to deal with the confederacies and obligarchies. (see today's SAARC, SAPTA, SAFTA, ASEAN or ARF and SEATO/CENTO of 1950s. NAM could be described as contemporary India's *mandala* system in a altered context.

After annexation of new territories, the conqueror has to perform certain diplomatic obligations. 'Having acquired new territory, the conqueror shall substitute his virtues for the enemy's vices and where enemy was good, he shall be twice as good.'

> 'He shall reward, as promised, those who were traitors to the enemy for his sake; if they had exerted themselves more (than required), they shall be rewarded more than promised.'
>
> 'The posts previously occupied by the enemy's men shall be filled by the conqueror's own people or those who were in disfavour with the enemy'.(1: 741)

Conquest, annexation and take-over remaining the essential *Dharma* of a Kautilyan Hindu State, suppression and elimination of active dissent like revolts, rebellions, conspiracies and treason remains the primary task of the early Indian state, which otherwise is committed to 'ARTHA (welfare/well being) and *Shastra* (statecraft) of the loyal citizens. The scientific methods of institutionalised state terrorism are elaborately prescribed. 'Thus the kingdom (state) will continue to be enjoyed by the kings's sons and grandsons (read as ruling class), free from the dangers caused by (seditious) men (1: 167).

The programme depicting covert activities of the state (1: 499-550) would be the envy of world's creamy secret services like CIA, MOSSAD, MI-5, MI-6, former KGB (comparable to present day ISI, RAW, IB). ARTHASHASTRA is very much elaborate on the details of king's use of spies, secret agents, assassins in the covert operations. The Brahmın - Kautilya had provided the rules and mechanisms in details for murder, oppression and state-repression.

The spies had been *guda* (concealed), *samstha* (established), *tikshna* (sharp practice) and *sattri* (secret agent). The spies had to masquerade under 29 cover-up professions with as many as fifty sub-types. They disguised themselves as: ordinary citizens, holy-men, merchants, teachers, entertainers, household attendants, barbers, astrologers, *purana* reciters or, even thieves and robbers, women spies should disguise as nun, rich widow, actress, musician and lovers (1: 501). The internal security measures were equally elaborate in keeping all the ministers under interception. The modern state, however, adds high-technology, wealth and more lethality.

Diplomacy in Kautilyan concept is *'Mantrayuddha'* that is 'war by counsel' in lieu of physical warfare (1: 676). The other three forms of warfare are viz., *'Prakasayuddha'* (open warfare), *'Kutayudha'* (concealed warfare like upajapa - psychological warfare) and *'Gudayuddha'* (clandestine war without waging a battle).

'Antarvamsikasainya' — the king's own guards — are remotely comparable to Saddam Hussein's special guards or contemporary Indian SPG, who look after premiers their dynasty and their like. Contemporary Indian state is remarkably similar to Kautilyan state except the ingenuity and sophistication of modern statecraft.

The *'VIJIGISHU'*- would-be conqueror (*read* hegemonistic state in this age) should make peace with an equally powerful or stronger state but wage a war against a weaker state, after considering short term and long term advantages. The manual is intended to provide four practices in specific situations : 'relative power, deviations from the ideal, classification by type of motivation, and the influence of the intangible' (1: 543). Kautilya differed from his predecessor-teachers in prescribing the policy to be followed by weak states. 'One should neither submit spinelessly nor sacrifice oneself in foolhardy valour. It is better to adopt such policies as would enable one to survive and live to fight another day' (1: 544).

Kautilya enunciates the six basic principles of *Bharatiya* foreign policy (of expansionism):

i) a king shall develop his state i.e. augment its resources and power in order to enable him to embark on a campaign of conquest;

ii) the enemy shall be eliminated ;

iii) those who help are friends ;

iv) a prudent course shall always be adopted;

v) peace is to be preferred to war ; and

vi) a king's behaviour, in victory and defeat, must be just. (1: 547).

The six methods of hegemonic Bharatiya foreign policy in Kautliyan terms are embodied in : *'Samadhi'* (making peace), *'Vigraha'* (hostilities by means of open war or, secret war or, undeclared clandestine operations comparable to today's proxy wars of all sorts in Indian continent), *'Asana'* (keeping quiet), *'Yana'* (war preparation), *'Samsraya'*(seeking protection) and *'Dvidhibhava'* (dual policy literally comparable to British method of divide and rule, adopted 1500 years after Hindu rulers had practised successfully). Rangarajan presents Kautliya's six foreign policy methods :

1. Making peace is entering into an agreement with specific conditions (i.e., concluding a treaty). A king (read state) shall make peace when he finds himself in a relative decline compared to his enemy.

2. Active hostilities are waging war. A king superior to his enemy in power shall attack him.

3. Being indifferent to a situation is staying quiet. When a king considers that neither he nor his enemy can harm the other, he shall remain quiet.

4. Augmenting one's power is preparing for war. A king with special advantages shall make preparations for war.

5. Getting the protection of another is seeking support. A king depleted in power shall seek help.

6. Dual policy is making peace with one king and war with another. A king whose aim can be achieved (only) with the help of another shall pursue a dual policy (1: 563).

"When an aggressor is on the point of attacking, the weak king (read state) has three choices : he can make peace (with the aggressor), try to avert the attack (by diplomatic *mantrayuddha*) or wage secret warfare. He shall (try to) win over the sections favourable to him in the aggressor's camp by means of conciliation and gifts and prevent treachery in his own camp by sowing dissension and use of force" (1: 668).

The weak state could use the circle of kings to his advantage. All kings (read states) whether allied or not shall be cautioned that, after destroying the weak king (state), the aggressor (hegemon) would turn against them and that it was in their own interest to help the weak king (1: 670). The versatile role, perception and obligations of a weak state when besieged and occupied by the aggressor are also elaborately discussed by Kautilya. Lying low on being defeated (of India's war with China, 1962 on India's failure to negotiate with Macmohan line-border dispute, as proposed earlier by China) and acting with fairness on defeating enemy (cf. India's release of 95,000 Pakistani POW's after 1971 India's war of liberation for Bangladesh against Pakistan) give testimony to the omnipresence of the Kautilya in the MEA and South Block.

The Arthashastra presents the manual of different kinds of war meticulously. Psychological warfare is one of the components (cf. now conducted by electronic and print media, among others). Hindu imperialism (*Vijigitsu*) used soothsayers, readers of omens, astrologers, puranic experts (read *pandits* and *vedantists*), intitutionalists, and clandestine agents as propaganda machinery. 'An agent, in the guise of a holy man shall take refuge in a popular temple of the city and by his performances of magical tricks gradually win over the principles and use them to out manoeuvre the enemy' (1: 731). We cite a local example too : — the holy men-agents, high-tech holy men relentlessly allure the vulnerable and susceptible sections even today; use of holy-men in the expansionism of the Vijigitsu is a very old and established practice. They render the native absolutely defenceless before they are colonised and put down forever.

Kautilya like his predecessors elaborately prescribes the methods of demoralising besieged people. A modest example is given : 'Agents shall be concealed in tunnels or inside images in temples and fire sanctuaries and the king shall while worshipping carry on conversations with the deity' (1: 533). Note : 'Ganesha' sucking milk on a particular day at a particular time as scheduled in all temples in 1995 is a poor invocation of Kautiliyan method : Some more miracles could also happen like WWW Internet oracles of deities; they may use laser and others to advance their mission.

Statecraft

The *Arthashastra* under review incorporates besides two chapters — Introduction, the Kautiliyan state and society , eleven parts viz., introductory sections, the State and Its Constituent Elements, the King, the well-organized State, treasury, sources of revenue, accounts and audit civil service regulations, the departments of the Government, law and justice, covert operations, foreign policy, defence and war plus notes, appendices, maps, verses and index. The *Arthashastra* preserves *'Dharma'*, *'Artha'* *'Moksha'* and *'Kama'* of the hindus and by extension to non-hindus as well. The manual has a purpose to serve.

> 'The source of the livelihood of men is *artha* (wealth), that is to say, the territory (and inhabitants following various professions) is the wealth (of a nation). The science by which territory is acquired and maintained is *Arthashastra* - the science of wealth and welfare'(1: 100).

The classical work edited by Rangarajan, which embodies the precious state-of-the-art statecraft of the Hindustani regime is a manual for political science, economics, social sciences, constitutional law, administrative law and international law. 'Wealth alone enabled the creation of more wealth' (1: 73). 'The root of wealth is economic activity and lack of it brings material distress' (1: 177). The *Arthashastra*, however, omitted education and health in its welfare concept. In the 20th and 21st century, education and health are considered to be one of the top national agenda in developed world. Two departments viz., Ministry of educational MITI in Japan are directly instrumental in raising Japan to the status of economic superpower. In 1999, India ranks 132 in the HDI — Human Development Index.

The *Samahartr* (Chancellor) and *Samnidhatr* (Treasurer) were responsible for economic and fiscal management. *Dharmastha* - the judge upholds justice and *dharma*. In brief, Kautiliyan state was a highly organised state. The fear is that it was overzealously regimented, the populace despite its social welfare objectives.

The *Arthashastra* being edited, translated and rearranged by a retired high level professional, practising Indian diplomat has been recast in the idiom and vocabulary of this age. Rangarajan has elaborately summarised Kautilyan diplomacy elsewhere in the book, while demonstrating the continuing relevance of the manual to the peace-builders around the world. Peace is yet to break out. Undoubtedly, the Indologists, Sanskrit schools and Indian power-elite or, ruling class had made its internalisation and knowledge a part of their intellectual tradition. Even by Pavlovian reflex action, statecraft, or even hegemonic instincts of the *Arthashastra* are assimilated in the psyche of the high-caste ruling power-elite. The marginalised or underdogs, who have been indoctrinated to settle for a humble way of life, submission withdrawal and resignation had been for millennia, are kept intellectually defenceless against the Kautilyans. Many people around the world are so much deeply entrenched in the oppressed from life so that they visualise any alternative way of life as totally uncertain and risky. The classic would enlighten one and all about statecraft, domination, hegemony, laws, economy, and justice of a resourceful, civilised section of people from the modest, who spread their sway from Gangetic belt to a vast territory of Indian continent.

The application of these crafts with necessary variations may be read into modern India's engagements with big and small countries in India's *Mandala* viz., Indo-Bhutan Treaty, 1949, Indo-Nepal Treaty 1950, Tashkent Agreement 1965, and Indo-Soviet Military pact 1972; Indo-Burmese Secret protocol 1952 for appeasement of Burma by disclaiming Kabaw valley of Manipur, Indo-Bangladesh Water Agreement 1997; Indo-Myanmar Border Trade Agreements 1966; Shastri-Shrimavo agreement 1964 and Rajiv Gandhi-LTTE pact, Sri Lanka 1987, just to cite a few, (see also-Gujral Doctrine). Kautilya's continued relevance has been re-affirmed time and again by India's South Block and official think-tanks. But Kautilya's negation lies in post-1960 modern state's behaviours, whose rationality transcends naked *'realpolitik'* and moved towards some form of symbiotic discourse. The hawks in MEA, however, would still insist upon sustaining regional cold war, and a nuclear arms race after Pokhran-II by invoking nuclear deterrence.

Treaty-making is a part of Kautilyan foreign policy. 'A wise king will make one neighbouring king fight another neighbour and having thus prevented the neighbours from getting together, proceed to overrun the territory of his own enemy' (1: 582). A wise king (read state, at present) would prevent the rise of a situation that would harm the allies (*cf.* NATO, NAFTA, ASEAN, OIC, APEC or, SAARC of the contemporary age). 'The best ally is one, who has the following six qualities : an ally of the family for a long time, constant, amenable to control, powerful in his support, sharing a common interest able to mobilise his forces quickly and not a man who betrays his friends'(606). Kautilya has classified ten types of allies. They are (i) an ally who, identifies himself with the conqueror, (ii) an ally who is likely to grow in power, (iii) a very weak ally, (iv) a fickle ally, (v) a perfidious ally (who should be crushed before crushing the enemy), (vi) an indifferent ally, (vii) a weak ally, (viii) an unscrupulous ally, (ix) an ally in calamity and (x) an ally attacking the enemy, affected by a calamity(1: 610). I.K. Gujral doctrine attempts to build up his unilateral neighbourhood doctrine without necessarily looking for reciprocal bilateral responses. It could be perceived as a component of Nehru's *Panchashila*. However, India's stature as a hegemon in South Asia is gradually perceived by her neighbourhood as the days of India as a peace-monger have receded.

Indian hegemony which preceded the European hegemony and colonialism in South Asia by a millennium would have been an impossibility but for the Kautilyan prognosis and statecraft, which has been fully integrated to the psyche of the ruling class and successive power-elites. Ironically, Mr. Mountbatten (they call themselves as Lord that is also used to denote God) did what the great Kautilyan wished. How they built up imperialism by wiping out states in the continent falls within Kautilyan's four methods of subjugation of nation states — *'sama'*, *'dana'*, *'bheda'* or *'danda'*.

The weak (state/country) shall be controlled by *sama* (conciliation) and *dana* (placing with gifts) and the strong by *bheda* (sowing dissension) and *danda* (force)- Dissension (British divide and rule 1500 years later) is a strong point for hegemony. 'Dissension is sown by demanding wealth, troops, land or inheritance (from the subjugated king) on behalf of a neighbouring king, a jungle chief, a protector or an unjustly treated prince (of the subjugated king's family) (1: 611). Kautilyan studies would easily reveal the way dissension is sown in contemporary civil society.

Although hegemony, expansionism, imperialism is the forte of Kautilyan diplomacy since the days of Chandragupta till Sardar Patel and his hegemonistic clique led by V.P. Menon, the emerging world order has to set aside some of the Kautilyan paradigm.

Soviet Union

Reconstruction of peace and development in the post-war world would have been an extremely difficult job without the first rate diplomats and statesman's presence in the scenario. Of the two super-powers, that existed before the 1991 dramatic termination of the cold war, the Soviet Union was the one which by rising from a scratch, played a counter-balance to the principled American hegemony. A key player in Soviet Unions diplomacy was Andrei Gromyko, who by working with all the Soviet leadership without a break from Stalin to Gorbachev and by actively negotiating for world peace with as many as fourteen USA secretaries of state and nine American presidents, left a diplomatic space of his own in the peace-management. The MEMORIES, written by Gromyko, 1990 while being drafted on the line of an autobiography describes his personal experiences in the Soviet diplomacy. He bothered most for peace with a human face and brought the Soviet Union to a respectable leadership of the underdogs and millions of colonies.

Tony Benn's introduction is a curtain raiser to 19 chapters of MEMORIES including 'In the aftermath of revolution', 'Potsdam', 'The arms race', 'Europe', 'The East and Africa', and 'From Nixon to Reagan'. The excerpts herein after are from Gromyko's book. The Soviet foreign minister, who became president of the USSR at the fag-end of his fifty years of hectic diplomatic career, relinquished voluntarily the presidency with an address delivered on 1 October, 1988 in the Great Kremlin Hall: ' To perfect the political system and to achieve the creation of a socialist state based on the rule of law will demand enormous efforts' (2:445). MEMORIES by Gromyko, 1990 does not regard American paradigms like isolationalism, Monroe doctrine, Marshall plan, containment (of communism), brinkmanship, Clintonian 'enlargement' as bedrocks of world peace and freedom. The approaches are fundamentally different.

He admits the horrendous Stalinist repression, unlike the bad communists elsewhere who equate Stalin with sainthood. Stalin did the massive repression through the farcical 'semblance of legal process' conducted by Vyshinsky (2: 409). Stalin the proletarian dictator 'slept all day and worked at night, starting at two o'clock in the morning.' (2: 411)

At the initial stage of the last world war, the Soviet foreign policy aimed at building up anti-fascist co-operation and liberation of European nations (2: 49). Ultimately, it paid dividends. Roosevelt administration treated Soviet Union as victim of fascist aggression (2: 76) and worked intimately with Stalin against the fascism of the Nazi, who practised Aryan racial supremacy to dominate the world. Aryan racism is essentially crude, brutal and de-humanizing.

The Soviet Union interpreted American democracy as a 'democracy of the military-industrial complex and the Pentagon's arms race is big business' (2: 92). Had the Americans built up arms race merely to counterbalance, the speculative Soviet threat to American principles (read national interest), they should have dismantled NATO and defence-related trade-blocs immediately after the closure of the 'Warsaw' pact and there is little justification to retain it after the end of cold war with the collapse of Soviet Union in 1991. Gromyko constructed this proposition in the work.

In 'Tehran and Yalta' (see ch. 6), Stalin, Churchill and Roosevelt agreed to end Nazi Germany's violence, to convene a United Nations conference and they released the final document — 'Unity in the organisation of Peace as in the conduct of war' (2: 119). Gromyko's work is a re-statement of his personal experience, unlike the circumscribed text books of sedentary authors. Potsdam is different from Yalta (ch. 7). Harry Truman's unscrupulous statement is cited : 'If we see that Germany is winning the war, we should help Russia, but if Russia is winning we should help Germany, and let her kill as many Reds as possible', (2: 123). With three atomic bombs in his hands, Truman wanted to dictate terms to Soviet Union. Stalin was not Truman and Gromyko describes leaders who could shape the events :

> 'Outstanding personalities are the product of conditions in a particular Time. On the other hand, these people can and do influence the course of events and the development of society' .(2: 127)

In the 1950 Korean episode, Stalin, chose to make an emotional decision (for once) by ordering the Soviet Council to abstain from the meeting inspite of Gromyko's suggestion to attend the meeting and exercise veto against US's design. Gromyko choose to be right. The great unifier of Soviet Union and communist party was a 'harsh man who did not count the human cost of achieving his aims, and who created a monstrously arbitrary state machine that sent multitudes of innocent Soviet people to their deaths' (2: 134). Khruschev did not miss the opportunity to de-Stalinise Soviet Union. Gromyko was also a party to it. Much to the disbelief of the historians, the Soviet Union acted differently in the split of Germany. Gromyko wrote : 'All Germans, where ever lived, should remember that the Soviet Union never wanted the dismemberment of Germany. It was the USA and Britain who at the three power Allied conferences proposed tearing of Germany apart'(2: 145). The West wanted that post-war separations should benefit the Allies except the Soviet Union.

The body languages at Potsdam were expressed in different styles — Stalin was calm and steady and Attlee speaks scarcely at conference. Churchill in the earlier occasion never used prepared text, made short statements and stretched individual words. Truman's smile was not a smile, as it gave false impression and he read prepared text and notes passed on to him. (2: 146)

The principle of unanimity among big five - also known as — veto in the Security Council — was largely a contribution of the Soviet Union (2: 149). The capitalist bloc would always carry out their decisions in the Council by permanently superseding Soviet opinion, in the absence of the unanimity principle. Effective powers had also been shifted to the Security Council from the General Assembly, on the pressure of the Soviet Union. By June 15, 1997, India's South Block wanted to buy off a permanent UN Security Council by paying 40 million dollars.

At the beginning, American people appreciated the role of Soviet union in the war, but the concept of evil-empire (Reagan's vocabulary) has been gradually evolved by American administration. "Dulles invented the idea of 'brinkmanship', which he regarded as an advanced way of conducting external affairs and which he embraced until the end of his life"(2: 222). Adlai Stevenson resisted Soviet proposal for disarmament (2: 175) and the arms race continued (see ch.9). The USA had been on the course since 1941. 'The USA put two billion dollars into making three bombs, 150,000 people were employed; and two new towns had to be built in secret'(2: 183). Gromyko recalls 'Albert Einstein's repentance — If I (Einstein) had known that Hitler was not going to be able to develop the atom bomb, I would never have supported the American atomic research programme'(2: 184).

A first-rate Soviet diplomat - Mr. Gromyko describes the foreign policy. 'A country's foreign policy has to stand on the solid foundations of an efficient economy and a reliable defence force.' American President Reagan in September 1984 saw in the Soviet Union a threat, which leaves to him to choose 'between surrender or death' (2: 393). America's principled policy, as loudly enunciated by veterans like Henry Kissinger, was calculative. 'Behind all this lies the clear calculation that the USSR will exhaust its material resources before the USA and therefore will finally be forced to surrender' (2: 394). The Soviet Union did not capitulate, but it collapsed three years after Gromyko's death. The West saw red-syndrome even in Charlie Chaplin and Marylyn Monroe (2: 89-87). Her death is wrapped in mystery.

Americans behaved like boxers in their quest for supremacy. 'In diplomacy, there is a healthy tendency to compromise, whereas in sport, and especially in boxing, there is absolutely no such inclination'(2: 425).

Among the first rate diplomats, a few names are prominent. V.M. Molotov 'occupies a special place in the history of Soviet diplomacy' (2: 403}. Politburo laid down the guidelines of foreign policy; Stalin's view was decisive and the rest was handled by Molotov, who had profound influence on Stalin, (2: 404). But powerful persons like Molotov, Melenkov, Kaganovich or, Bulganin had been expelled from party(2: 405). Stalin's axe-man Beria was done to death later on.

Gromyko considered Kissinger as a 'capable, even a highly capable, man' in foreign affairs (2: 367). He, however, suspected Kissinger's judgements', consistency which offended both logic and history. 'Even so, for almost the entire period of his tenure as secretary of state, Kissinger practised the technique of applying pressure on the Soviet Union wherever possible, whether in Asia, Africa, the Middle East or anywhere else, as a way of forcing us to make concessions' (2: 369). Pointing his finger at Mr. Henry Kissinger and Ronald Reagan, Gromyko cites Roman philosopher Seneca's statement : "When a man does not know which harbour to head for, no wind is fair" (2: 370).

British prime minister Macmillan's tenure was characterised by cold war and arms race. Soviet delegation to the UN was led by Khruschev. It was September 28, 1959 at the UN, where Macmillan was talking about East-West relations. The delegates were listening intently. Suddenly, at the point where Macmillan started using especially strong language against the Soviet Union and her friends, Khruschev bent down, took off his shoe and started hammering it on the desk in front of him, the sound of the shoe on the bare wood resonating around the hall, while he shouted : 'The Soviet Union is for universal disarmament -'(2: 202).

Mr. Gromyko reminisced his personal meetings with chairman Mao Tse Tung, who had studied ancient Chinese philosophy, liked good joke, but became a different person immediately when a difficult political question arose (2: 323). Sino-Soviet rift has been interpreted in different way by persons of varied persuasions. Gromyko wrote about Mao : 'Mao was conciliatory assuring me : 'China will never cause relations with Soviet to worsens and we will march shoulder to shoulder with you in the struggle for peace' (2: 320). However, Gromyko would have liked to play down Chinese insinuations at a later stage, about Soviet social expansionism and hegemony. His studied silence on the subject is well taken.

The Guevara's speech as the head of Cuban delegation on 11 December, 1964 in a full-packed General Assembly of the United Nations condemned 'US interference in Cuba's internal affairs and the US blockade'(2: 236). 'After dinner, Che and I had a tete -a- tete. He told me :'I'm going straight from New York to a distant land, to help the people there in their struggle for a dignified life and freedom'(2: 237). After three years, Che had been done to death in Bolivia by enemies of freedom. The long arms of the CIA reached any where, any time.

MEMORIES describes what diplomacy actually stands for

> 'When I talk to non-diplomats I often sense that they think of diplomacy as the attempt to outwit one's partners in talks, or to make especially apt remarks, to sparkle with sudden or come up with unfamiliar quotations. This is far from the reality. I therefore plan to demonstrate here that the work of an official representative abroad requires many different skills, but first and foremost the ability to analyse problems as they come up and to present them clearly to others in all their essentials.' (2: XX).

As these words come out from the horse's mouth, Mr. Gromyko, deputed as ambassador to London in 1952 started to read as much as he could about Britain, all documents in archives, list of books and journals published in Britain (2: 415). This is not a new thing, since the study hours of leading statesmen of the world are longer than those of many of the book-worms or, even scholars. An American president in 1964 raised his speed reading to 2,000 words per minute. As cited above, Stalin's working hours spread over from midnight to next morning. The architects of world order had vision, conviction and unusual efforts.

Colonial question

Soviet diplomacy and foreign policy has been consistently anti-colonial and anti - imperialistic. Its contribution to the liberation of one hundred and forty countries from out of or in addition to the fifty odd UN members in 1949 is simply historic and significant. Demagogues would ridicule the emergence of nations as evil aberrations. It is far from true; in the light of the war-time rise of national liberation movements in colonial and dependent countries, a solution to the problem was urgently needed.

The USSR was in favour of granting these countries their independence, while many of the Western powers, especially Britain, were naturally for retaining colonial rule (2: 155). USA followed suit. No new world order can sustain colonies.

The USSR firmly resolved to support giving independence to the colonies, where waves of national liberation movements were on the rise since 1945. Italy's colonial possessions had also been raised in Foreign Ministers meeting in London in September-October 1945(2: 195). Since the defeat of fascism in 1945, by the 1980s, a large number of African countries gained independence (2: 340). ' the leaders of the Indian national liberation movement, Tilak and Gandhi, took a close interest in the evolution of Russian thought'(2: 308). Nehru's hatred for colonialism and imperialism gave an assessment of the international situation (2: 309).

Unlike the Western and American stand towards Palestinian national question, Gromyko considers US and Israeli obstruction to the formation of Palestinian state as a contravention of UN resolution of 1947(2: 334). He, in conformity with the Soviet practices on Kashmir question, maintains cultivated silence in the MEMORIES, on the contravention of UN Security Council resolution of 1948. For India's sake, Soviet Union had to make a caveat to her consistency in national questions. Soviet stand in favour of Polish national question had been consistent (2: 143). He plays defensive in regard to Soviet interventions in Hungary, Czechoslovakia and Afghanistan. Every good communist can appreciate the 1977 Soviet Constitution and its implications.

'Eisenhower doctrine', officially announced in 1957 sought American right to use armed forces to impose her will in the Middle East. 'The doctrine (which overtly and covertly, was widely followed) envisaged opposing national liberation movements' (2: 217). Universal de-colonisation (*sic*.unfinished task in South Asia) has been the result of relentless and uncompromising Soviet efforts, which Nehru has firmly supported on the floor of the United Nations in 1960. 'In the end, the Assembly adopted the declaration on granting independence to the colonial countries and peoples. This historic decision has been initiated by our country'(2: 311). Soviet Union did not support liberation movements. Ironically, in the North-East.

Gromyko came to know Krishna Menon during the UN debate on Kashmir question, which had not been resolved despite Gromyko-Menon discussions. Menon's defence of India's interest in Kashmir was a classic and a dramatic event. 'Menon found it hard to do his work in this atmosphere (*sic* working of American capital), but he stuck it out. His speeches at the UN tended to be long and they took a lot out of him. After one such speech, he collapsed from exhaustion and had to be carried out on a stretcher'(2: 312).

MEMORIES depicts the personal — partly official — account of a first rate diplomat of the socialist world about the Soviet conduct in diplomacy, foreign affairs in crucial periods of the twentieth century. It is a Soviet counterpart of Henry Kissinger's DIPLOMACY in their divergent perceptions. Gromyko states: 'International affairs naturally predominate in my memoirs, because I spent so much of my life involved in them'(2: 455). The Soviet efforts for de-colonisation and destruction of imperialism bore the hall mark of Soviet people and leadership, yet the task has been partly unfinished even at the threshold of the twenty-first century. Around fifty independent states may emerge in the 21st century to join the world order.

MEMORIES, while being a first hand account, is interesting, useful and important for all shades of earth watchers and peace engineers. The collapse of the Soviet Union, which he missed to witness, was historically determined, but the ideology survives the inevitable process of restoring the original building blocks of the Union. The credit goes to Gorbachev.

United States

In the post-nation and post-industrial society, the cold war had faded away. Multipolarity of some kind — rather, a soft undefined sort of unipolarity has ushered in and the new world order emerges in an era, when contending power-centres come into play at the centre-stage. Way back in the Hindustan of Chandragupta Maurya in the pre-Christian period, nations had been brought into the *mandala* network with the *Arthshastra* as the beacon light of diplomacy. In the next century, the present world order with the US as a reference point is likely to continue, however, states have to play their own roles. Henry Kissiniger's unusual book 'Diplomacy, is a work to be seriously taken by *pundits* of peace studies, global diplomacy and persons who shape the course of history. In this thick of complex international relations, he sums up his book with a proverb'. 'Traveller', says a Spanish proverb, there are no roads. Roads are made by walking.

A Harvard university professor in 1961 at the time, when Vietnam and Cuban policy had been hammered out by the US, a nobel laureate in 1973 for the peace, Kissinger is one among the rare personalities, who shaped history either from the green room or across the table after the show of muscles in the operation areas, where the Americans held sway. It could be Middle East, US retreat from Vietnam or, ending the Chinese isolationism or Brezhnev doctrine. He had a role in these events.

The new world order would see the US not as a top policeman of the world, but it would occupy the most visible place in the order. The American role in expansion of democracy, market and human rights regardless of the frontiers has been defined by him, as the obligation of a value - laden American exceptionalism. While covering up innumerable American crimes in pulling down governments, nations or premiers, who America considers to be inconvenient or simply disposable, DIPLOMACY projects the US as an angel for peace and human freedom. The unpalatable facts of history do not find a mention in this enormous volume of history of power-equations and the national game-plans. However, the work is a rare embodiment of the sequences of international orders — successful or otherwise since Richelieu's *raison d'etat* to Wilsonianism and henceforth, to the contemporary multi-polarism. Although, the work furnishes one of the best definitions of globalisation and peace in American version, the other unsuccessful or, inoperative versions have been described elaborately. To that extent, understanding the new order with Kissinger's as a primary manual would pay dividends to earth-watchers.

In between the first chapter 'The New World Order' and the last chapter 'The New World Order Reconsidered' - are sandwiched the critical chapters on Theodore Roosevelt or Woodrow Wilson, Concert of Europe, Napoleon III and Bismarck, Realpolitik, European Diplomacy before the First World War, Hitler, Stalin's Bazar, Roosevelt, Stalin, Churchill, Cold War, Korean War, Suez Crisis, Khruschev's Ultimatum, Vietnam, Nixon's Diplomacy, Detente and End of the Cold war, Reagan and Gorbachev, among others. He observes :'In the twentieth century, no country has influenced international relations as decisively and at the same time as ambivalently as the United States' (3: 17). The excerpts herein are from Kissinger's treatise.

New World Order

'The international system of the twenty first century will be marked by a seeming contradiction : on the one hand fragmentation and on the other growing globalization. On the level of the relations among states, the new order will be more like the European state system of the eighteenth and nineteenth centuries than the rigid patterns of the Cold War. It will contain at least six major powers — The United States, Europe, China, Japan, Russia, and probably, India — as well as a multiplicity of medium sized and smaller countries' (3: 23).

Three types of nations are interacting in the new world order; they are — 'ethnic splinters from disintegrating empires', 'post-colonial nations' and thirdly, 'continental type states', which will constitute the basic units of the new order (3: 807). President Clinton's theme of 'enlarging democracy' aims at strengthening the market-based democracies and 'free-institutions'. 'In the post-Cold War world, the United States is the only surviving super power with the capacity to intervene in every part of the globe. Yet power has become more diffuse and the issues to which military force is relevant have diminished' (3: 805). He does not envisage the other equations of power.

Kissinger and for that matter, US's official think-tanks are aware of the American shortcomings. 'Geopolitically, America is an island off the shores of the large landmass of Eurasia, whose resources and population far exceed those of the United States' (3: 813). Eurasia or, Asia may be on the rise, despite his downsizing them.

US perceives Russia as the 'heartland' essential to any world order and China as an essential component of American foreign policy projections. 'Of all the great, and potentially great powers, China is the most ascendant. The United States already is the most powerful. Europe must work to forge greater unity. Russia is a staggering giant, and Japan is wealthy but, so far timid. China, however, with economic growth rates approaching 10 per cent annually, a strong sense of national cohesion and ever more muscular military, will show the greatest relative increase in stature among the major powers'(3: 829).

US is perceived to be the world leader; however, the indices are undergoing enormous paradigm-shift. 'The relative military power of the United States will gradually decline. Thus, the operation of the new international system will move towards equilibrium even in the military field, though it may take some decades to reach that point. These tendencies will be even more pronounced in economics, where American predominance is already declining...' (3: 23). 'He notes that all international systems appear to have an inevitable symmetry'(3: 26).

The work dissects the variants of diplomacy — European, British, German, French, American—- and also of the Russian, Chinese kind. The evolution of *raison d' etate* (reason of state) to *realpolitik* and balance of power or, cold war 'containment' on the one hand and Wilsonian idealism on the other hand had passed through critical tests in local, regional and world wars. *Detente* and Willy Brandt's *Ostpolitik* remained passing phases. Nixon doctrine survives, while Brezhnev doctrine has faded away. Diplomacy made a choice out of several possible options.

> 'He feels that power is too difficult to assess, and the willingness to vindicate it too various, to permit treating it as a reliable guide to international order and power without legitimacy tempts tests of strength while legitimacy without power tempts empty posturing' (3: 77).

In the context of overturning Stalin's bazar, he writes that diplomacy thus belonged to the process by which the existing order would eventually be overturned; whether it would be overthrown by a diplomacy of peaceful co-existence or by military conflict depended on the assessment of the relation of forces (3: 334).

About the choice of options Henry Kissinger comments, '... in diplomacy, the more options one side has, the fewer will be available to the other side and the more careful it will have to be in pursuing its objectives. Indeed, such a state of affairs may in time provide an incentive for the adversary to seek an end to his adversarial role'(3: 719).

The diplomatic approaches of the European powers and the US remaining very much different, the styles differed between the communist giants as well. 'Their (the Chinese) negotiating style was different from that of their Soviet counterparts as was possible. Soviet diplomats almost never discussed conceptual issues. Their tactic was to select a problem of immediate concern to Moscow and to batter away at its resolution with a dogged persistence designed to wear down their interlocutors rather than to persuade them.'(3: 727). 'Chinese leaders represented an emotionally far more secure society. They were less interested in fine drafting points than in building confidence'(3: 717).

European approaches had been varied in terms of *Raison d'etat*, Metternich style, Realpolitik of Germany, Bismarck's cabinet diplomacy, 19th century conspiratorial European style, Monologue of Hitler, Richelieu's contribution(3: 621). Since India figures in one or two lines in one or two pages only in the evolution of the complex international relations in the book, Kissinger did not care a hoot for Gandhi's serpentine manoeuvres, Jinnah's *realpolitik*, Bhutto's poor replication of Richelieu, Krishna Menon - Chagla style of monologues of wearing down the audience, Nehru's sophistication or, even Indira Gandhi's round-the-world trip in 1971 or, I.K. Gujrals's neighbourhood doctrine. These are not the cup of tea for the super powers, who can not help themselves without overlooking mole-hills.

The Harvard professor and secretary of state makes an attempt at defining the American vision in the next century. 'In the twenty first century, America, like other nations, must learn to navigate between necessity and choice, between the immutable constants of international relations and the elements subjects to the discretion of the statesmen' (3: 812). 'Whenever the balance is established between values and necessity, foreign policy must begin with some definition of what constitutes a vital interest -'(3: 812).

These choices are made among others, by leaders and leadership circle. To him, 'All great leaders walk alone. Their singularity springs from their ability to discern challenges that are not yet apparent to their contemporaries'(3: 370).

Humiliation of a great country is a diplomatic offence. It happened to Germany as will 'Great Powers had succeeded in turning a secondary Balkan crisis into a world war. — The Concert of Europe failed miserably because the political leadership had abdicated'(3: 216). At the end of the first world war, 20 million lay dead; the Austro-Hungarian empire had disappeared, unlike these great wars, the small wars also defeated great powers. He writes : in the context of Vietnam : ' The basic equation of guerrilla war is as simple as it is difficult to execute : the guerrilla army wins as long as it can keep from losing; the conventional army is bound to lose unless it wins decisively. Stalemate almost never occurs. Any country engaging itself in a guerrilla war must be prepared for a long struggle'(3: 629). In his version, America had a cause of containing communist Vietnam; but the super power, had after demolishing nearly the entire human race in Vietnam, to make an ignominious and desperate retreat. USSR made the same retreat in Afghanistan before it broke up. Super powers stretch long arms till their fingers are burnt. In post-Kissinger era, the USA has revised the NATO doctrine in making military intervention in Kosovo in 1999.

'By definition, a negotiation is about trading concessions'(3: 744). In the post-1919 Paris conference, where Germany and Russia two strongest European nations had not been represented, most of the discussions centred around territorial questions. Patience and time was required as the committee members sat through not less than 1,646 meetings(3: 232). Negotiation itself is a complex and patient process. American people and the global public opinion wanted that US army should come back home after decades of occupation of Vietnam. But the American retreat could not materialise overnight.

Under Nixon administration, Averell Harriman and Cyrus Vance, Johnson's negotiators and Le Duc Tho of North Vietnam had continued private (means) secret talks. Le Duc Tho with his impeccable politeness, after finding that the balance of forces were in favour of Hanoi maintained that 'wars were fought for political objectives'. Kissinger was involved in the process since 1961 in his status as a low level official. He comments about Tho's negotiations style that Le Duc Tho handled the American psyche as a skilled surgeon might operate on his patient; the Nixon Administration was obliged to fight on so many fronts that it only rarely had the opportunity to conduct an offensive diplomacy(3: 687).

American Exceptionalism

The US assumes its role as a giver of values, principles in terms of democracy, individual freedom, market and human rights. So, it makes a common cause with every one by sending troops, unlike China who never sent its troops outside China. The US considers the Atlantic alliance as a necessity for the West and conceives pacific community a mere speculation. Kissinger like other Americans, claims American exceptionalism in the world. They consider themselves as chosen people. The US-led world order suffers from this paranoia.

The singularities that America has ascribed to itself through out its history have produced two contradictory attitudes towards foreign policy. The first is that America serves its values best by perfecting democracy at home, thereby acting as a beacon for the rest of mankind; the second, that America's values impose on it an obligation to crusade for them around the world. Kissinger imputes them to the USA.

'The United States had been presiding over world affairs since the end of the Second World War in a manner not previously available to any nation'(3: 602). Even during cold war, America thought on this line. 'As an approach to foreign policy, Wilsonianism presumes that America is possessed of an exceptional nature expressed in unrivalled virtue and unrivalled power' (3: 809). American righteouness is, however, disputable, since several governments had been dismantled by American services and wars, proliferated outside the American soil; because as we have seen that America would conduct world wars outside its soil. This is also American exceptionalism, which Kissinger likes to omit.

The West finds issues after the end of cold war and Europe face two contemporary challenges(3: 823) and the balance of power (3: 182) has been now discarded.

China is on the rise and the super power — Soviet Union had been reduced to its building block. DIPLOMACY makes an assessment of its fall from American perspective. the theory of American exceptionlism is simply narcissistic.

'The former Soviet Union was a military super power and at the same time an economic dwarf. It was also possible for a country to be an economic giant but to be militarily irrelevant, as was the case with Japan' (3: 23). Expansionists in South Asia or elsewhere may note that : 'the irony was that after a certain point, expansionism no longer enhanced Russia's power but brought about its decline' (3: 176).

Communism, as Kissinger saw, collapsed partly as a result of its own sclerosis, partly because of the pressures from a re-invigorated West' (3: 752). Gorbachev precipitated the demise of the system. The West can not wash its hands clean in the Soviet-break up. 'The most significant provision of the Helsinki Agreement turned out to be the so called Basket III on human rights, (Basket I and II dealt with political and economic issues, respectively). Basket III was destined to play a major role in the disintegration of the Soviet satellite orbit'(3: 759). Reagan-doctrine survived with the death of Brezhnev-doctrine.

'China is on the road to super power status. At a growth rate of 8 per cent, which is less than it has maintained over the 1980s, China's Gross National Product will approach that of the United States by the second decade of the twenty first century. Long before that, China's political and military shadow will fall over Asia and will affect the calculations of the other powers however restrained actual policy Chinese may prove to be'(3: 826). Kissinger does not admit of Japanese or, Chinese exceptionalism.

He comments about India — As for India, the major actor in South Asia, a newcomer nation state, its foreign policy is in many ways the last vestige of the heyday of European imperialism, leavened by the traditions of an ancient culture. 'Absorbed by the struggle to feed its vast population, India dabbled in the Non-aligned movement during the Cold war. But it has yet to assume a role commensurate with its size on the international stage'(3: 26). It is true that in spite of feeding 50 crores of starving Indians, the rulers of India spends the largest chunk of poor tax payers money for expansionism; but Kissinger was a diplomat who wanted that India should fail in India's war of Bangladesh liberation in 1971, that dismembered a Pakistan.

The Soviet Union and China acted as the mastermind behind the end of colonialism and exercise of self-determination of nations. The US had its role in shaping the international order by facilitating self-determination. Wilson, Roosevelt and Khruschev remained as the key figures for self-determination. 'America's criteria for international order was democracy, collective security and self-determination'(3: 221). Kissinger writes: 'In America's view, it was not self-determination which caused wars, but the lack of it; not the absence of a balance of power that produced instability but the pursuit of it'(3: 222). In 1942, America stood for end of British imperialism, India had been benefited by this American stand. 'Roosevelt's advocacy of world wide self-determination was a challenge to the British Empire'(3: 399). When the US realised that its involvement in Vietnam was absurd 'leading senators entered in the fray. Mansfield declared : 'We are in the wrong place and were fighting the wrong kind or war'(3: 672). Unlike the third world expansionists, the Americans could realise their mistake at least and do not justify their mistakes as some of the colonial-minded policy-makers in South Asia continue to do. The poor South Asia is now in arms race following Pokhran blasts in May 1998.

He envisages the new world order that would see American leadership, American concern for the Pacific community, although the Asian nations unlike the European nations in the Atlantic alliance, can not be easily coalesced. One can witness the rise of China. The statesmen of the world work out the designs in the structure for peace and diplomacy. The days of imperialism are over and the days of a few empires could not be sustained. The US abides by Wisonianism, one of the major components of Wilsonian doctrine is self - determination. DIPLOMACY upholds Wilsonianism and not merely the *realpolitik*.

'The responsibility of statesmen, however, is to resolve complexity rather than to contemplate it'(3: 113). He writes that intellectuals 'analyse the operations of international systems; statesmen build them. And there is a vast difference between the perspective of an analyst and that of a statesmen' (3: 27). 'His role is defined by his recognition of the relationship when it does exist and he is to create a network of incentives and penalties to produce the most favourable outcome'(3: 717).

The statesmen face problems too. 'Statesmen always face the dilemma that, when their scope for action is greatest, they have a minimum of knowledge. By the time they have garnered sufficient knowledge, the scope for decisive action is likely to have vanished'(3: 294). He passes through a test. 'A statesmen's test is whether he can discern from the swirl of tactical decisions, the true long term interests of his country and devise appropriate strategy for achieving them'(3: 109).

However, every leader who is ahead of his time is also a problem upto himself or to the environment. Kissinger's perception about leadership is clear : 'A leader who gets too far ahead of his society will become irrelevant. A great leader must be an educator bridging the gap between his visions and the familiar. But he must also be willing to walk alone to enable his society to follow the path he has selected'(3: 382).

Out of his 11 major works, DIPLOMACY is his *magnum opus*. The work describes the complicated history, diplomacy and interrelationship of the nations and states by keeping America as the beacon - light. We can disagree with him on many of his premises : yet we have to agree that the relationship of the nations in the world evades a final definition. The next century would witness pluralism and multiple power centres, notwithstanding Kissinger's American narcissieism and ebullient arrogance yet Henry Kissinger has deep insight in the order.

Epilogue

What diplomacy means to the empire and nation-builders has been drafted by Kautilya, Gromyko and Kissingers. The system-analysts try to assess the relevance of their works in the new world order. The institutions have a role to play. Samuel P. Huntington writes in his book 'The Clash of Civilizations and the Remaking of the World Order' that most of the principal international institutions date shortly after World War II and are shaped according to

Western interests, values and practices and as Western power declines relative to that of other civilizations, pressures will develop to reshape these institutions to accommodate the interest of those civilizations (5: 317)..

Towering statesman like Mikhael Gorbachev would accept the prevailing contradictions. He writes in his 'Selected Speeches and Articles' 4: "The modern world is complicated, diverse and dynamic, and shot through with contending tendencies and contradictions. It is a world of the most difficult alternative, anxieties and hopes. Never before has our home on earth been exposed to such great political and physical stresses." (4: 346) Gorbachev observes that there should be constructive and creative interaction between states and peoples on the scale of the entire world.

Paul Kennedy is equally critical: even after the cold war, we inherit a troubled and fractured planet. The problems deserve the serious attention of the politicians and public alike (6: 349).

The horizon is not totally free from the mist and war-clouds. Samuel P. Huntington writes, "A global war involving the core states of the world's major civilizations is highly improbable but not impossible"(5: 312).

Henry Kissinger ascertains the responsibility thus — "Intellectuals analyse the operations of international systems; statesmen build them... The analyst runs no risk. If his conclusions prove wrong, he can write another treatise. The statesman is permitted only one guess ; his mistakes are irretrievable."

In lieu of a conclusion, the author conceives that a just world order would continue to remain ought-to-be : the trends demonstrate that states and people with vision can still work out an order that would guarantee equality, partnership and common future.

References

1. L. N. Rangarajan, Kautilya the Arthashastra, Penguin Books, 1994
2. Andrei Gromyko, Memories from Stalin to Gorvachev, Arrow Books, 1990
3. Henry Kissinger, Diplomacy, Simon and Schuster, 1995.

Further readings

4. Mikhail Gorbachev, Selected Speeches and Articles, Progress, Moscow, 1987 p. 341-462, Report to 27th Congress
5. Samuel P. Huntington, The Clash of Civilizations and the Re-making of World Order, Viking, 1996 p. 301-322 — The Future of civilizations
6. Paul Kennedy, Preparing for the Twenty-First Century, Indus, 1993, p. 329-350, Ch. 14
7. Strobe Talbott, ed., Khrushehev Remembers, Vikas, 1975
8. J.H. Elliott, Richelieu and Olivares, CUP, 1991
9. V.K.Gupta, Kautilyan Jurisprudence, New Delhi, 1987, p. 217-256, International Law
10. J.Bandyopadhyaya, The Making of India's Foreign Policy, Allied, 1991, p. 192-282
11. J.N.Dixit, My South Block Years, UBSPD, 1997
12. John Spanier, American Foreign Policy Since World War II, Tata Mcgraw-Hill, 1989
13. Robert Dallek, the American Style of Foreign Policy, Alfred Knof, 1983, p. 154-282, Cold War Parochialism
14. Progress, Soviet Foreign Policy Vol. I-II, 1981
15. James N. Rosenau, The Scientific Study of Foreign Policy, 1980
16. James N. Rosenau, The Study of Global Interdependence, 1980
17. Selected Readings of Mao Tse Tung, 1971
18. Selected works of Deng Xioping, Beijing, 1984
19. Selected works of Zhou Enlai, Beijing, 1981

Annexure-I

UNITED NATIONS

International covenant on civil and political rights **4 August,1997**

HUMAN RIGHTS COMMITTEE

Consideration of reports submitted by states parties under article 40 of the covenant

Concluding observations of the Human Rights Committee

INDIA

1. The committee considered the third periodic report of India (CCPR/C/76/Add. 6) at its 1603rd to 1606th meetings on 24 and 25 July, 1997 and subsequently adopted, at its 1612th meeting (sixtieth session), held on 30 July, 1997, the following observations.

A. INTRODUCTION

2. The committee welcomes the third periodic report of India, although it regrets the delay in submitting it to the Committee. While noting that the report provides comprehensive information on the constitutional and legislative norms applicable in India in the field of human

rights, and makes reference to the Committee's previous comments during consideration of the State party's second periodic report, as well as to a number of court decisions, the Committee regrets the lack of information therein on difficulties encountered in implementing the provisions of the Covenant in practice. The delegation acknowledged in some measure these difficulties and it provided the Committee with detailed and comprehensive written and oral information in the course of the consideration of the report. In this regard, the Committee appreciates the cooperation which India has thus extended to the Committee in the discharge of its mandate.

3. The information submitted by a wide range of non-governmental organizations also assisted the Committee in its understanding of the human rights situation in the State party.

B. Factors and difficulties affecting the implementation of the covenant

4. The Committee recognizes that terrorist activities in the border states, which have caused the death and injury of thousands of innocent people, force the state party to make measures to protect its population. It stresses, however, that all measures adopted must be in conformity with the State party's obligations under the Covenant.

5. It notes, moreover, that the size of the country, its huge population, the massive poverty and the great disparities in the distribution of wealth among various social groups affect the advancement of rights. The persistence of traditional practices and customs, leading to women and girls being deprived of their rights, their human dignity and their lives, and to discrimination against members of the underprivileged classes and castes and other minorities, and ethnic, cultural and religious tensions constitute impediments to the implementation of the Covenant.

C. POSITIVE ASPECTS

6. The Committee notes with satisfaction the existence of a broad range of democratic institutions and a

comprehensive constitutional and legal framework for the protection of human rights. The Committee also welcomes frequent references to provisions of international human rights instruments by the courts, in particular the Supreme Court.

7. The Committee welcomes the establishment of the National Human Rights Commission in 1993 and the respect which the Government of India accords to its recommendations. The Committee notes that the Commission has been given powers, limited though these are, under the Protection of Human Rights Act, to inquire into complaints of human rights violations, to intervene in court proceedings involving allegations of human rights violations or otherwise dealing with human rights issues, to review constitutional and legal norms and the conformity of laws with international human rights instruments, to make specific recommendations to the Parliament and other authorities and to undertake activities in the field of human rights education. It also welcomes the recent setting up of human rights commission in six states including Punjab and Jammu and Kashmir, and of human rights courts in several other states of the Union.

8. The Committee also welcomes the establishment of the National Commission for Scheduled Castes and Scheduled Tribes and the National Commission for Women in 1992, and the National Commission for Minorities in 1993. These commissions have initiated some improvements, in particular in the levels of education and in the representation of the various groups concerned within elected bodies and other authorities.

9. The Committee welcomes the lapse, in 1995, of the Terrorist and Disruptive Activities Act (TADA), under which members of the security and armed forces enjoyed special powers in the use of force, arrest and detention. It also welcomes the related review of cases under this Act, following which a number of cases were dropped, and the directives given by the Supreme Court to deal with questions of bail under the TADA, though a number of cases still require to be dealt with.

10. The Committee has noted that positions in elected bodies are reserved for members of scheduled castes and tribes and that a constitutional amendment has reserved one third of the seats in elected local bodies (Panchayati Raj) for women. The Committee also notes the introduction of a bill to reserve one third of the seats for women in the federal Parliament and in state legislatures.

11. The Committee welcomes the restoration of elected legislatures and governments in all states within the Union, including Punjab and Jammu and Kashmir, as well as the holding of federal parliamentary elections in April-May 1996. In addition, the Committee welcomes the constitutional amendment giving a statutory basis to Panchayati Raj - village self-rule institutions - and the enactment of the Panchayati Raj (Extension to Scheduled Areas) Act of 24 December, 1996, which are designed to increase participation in the conduct of public affairs at the community level.

12. The Committee further welcomes the declared intention of the Government to introduce legislative measures to further freedom of information.

D. Subjects of concern and the Committee's recommendations

13. The Committee, noting that international treaties are not self-executing in India :

> Recommends that steps be taken to incorporate fully the provisions of the covenant in domestic law, so that individuals may invoke them directly before the courts. The Committee also recommends that consideration be given by the authorities to ratifying the Optional Protocol to the Covenant, enabling the committee to receive individual communications relating to India.

14. The Committee, noting the reservations and declarations made by the Government of India to articles 1,9,13,12,19, paragraph 3,21 and 22 of the Covenant:

> invites the State party to review these reservations and declarations with a view to withdrawing them, so as to ensure progress in the implementation of the rights contained in those articles, within the context of article 40 of the Covenant.

15. The Committee notes with concern that, despite measures taken by the Government, members of scheduled castes and scheduled tribes, as well as the so-called backward classes and ethnic and national minorities continue to endure severe social discrimination and to suffer disproportionately from many violations of their rights under the Covenant, inter alia inter-caste violence, bonded labour and discrimination of all kinds. It regrets that the de facto perpetuation of the caste system entrenches social differences and contributes to these violations. While the Committee notes the efforts made by the State party to eradicate discrimination :

> it recommends that further measures be adopted, including education programmes at national and state levels, to combat all forms of discrimination against these vulnerable groups, in accordance with articles 2, paragraph 1, and 26 of the Covenant.

16. While acknowledging measures taken to outlaw child marriages (Child Marriage Restraint Act), the practice of dowry and dowry related violence (Dowry Prohibition Act and the Penal Code) and sati — self-immolation of widows - (Commission of Sati Prevention Act), the Committee remains gravely concerned that legislative measures are not sufficient and that measures designed to change the attitudes which allow such practices should be taken. The Committee is also concerned that giving male children preferred treatment persists, and deplores that practices such as foeticide and infanticide of females continue. The Committee further notes that rape in marriage is not an offence and that rape committed by a husband separated from his wife incurs a lesser penalty than for other rapists. The Committee therefore recommends :

> that the Government take further measures to overcome these problems and to protect women from all discriminatory practices, including violence. Additional information should be provided in the State party's next periodic report on the functions, powers and activities of the National Commission for Women.

17 The Committee is concerned that women in India have not been accorded equality in the enjoyment of their rights and freedom in accordance with articles 2, paragraph 1, 3 and 26 of the Covenant nor have they been freed from discrimination. Women remain under-represented in public life and at the higher levels of the public service, and are subjected to personal laws which are based on religious norms and which do not accord equality in respect of marriage, divorce and inheritance rights. The Committee points out that the enforcement of personal laws based on religion violates the right of women to equality before the law and non-discrimination. Therefore :

> it recommends that efforts be strengthened towards the enjoyment of their rights by women without discrimination and that personal laws be enacted which are fully compatible with the Covenant.

18. The Committee remains concerned at the continuing reliance on special powers under legislation such as the Armed Forces (Special Powers) Act, the Public Safety Act and the National Security Act in areas declared to be disturbed and at serious human rights violations, in particular with respect to articles 6, 7, 9 and 14 of the Covenant, committed by security and armed forces acting under these laws as well as by paramilitary and insurgent groups. The Committee, noting that the examination of the constitutionality of the Armed Forces (Special Powers) Act, long pending before the Supreme Court is due to be heard in August 1997, hopes that its provisions will also be examined for their compatibility with the Covenant. In this respect, bearing in mind the provisions of articles 1, 19 and 25 of the Covenant:

> the Committee endorses the view of the National Human Rights Commission that the problems in areas affected by terrorism and armed insurgency are essentially political in character and that the approach to resolving such problems must also, essentially, be political, and emphasizes that terrorism should be fought with means that are compatible with the Covenant.

19. The Committee regrets that some parts of India have remained subject to declaration as disturbed areas over many years - for example the Armed Forces (Special Powers) Act has been applied throughout Manipur since 1980 and in some areas of that state for much longer - and that, in these areas, the State party is in effect using emergency powers without resorting to article 4, paragraph 3, of the Covenant. Therefore :

> the Committee recommends that the application of these emergency powers be closely monitored so as to ensure its strict compliance with the provisions of the Covenant.

20. The Committee expresses concern at the lack of compliance of the Penal Code with article 6, paragraphs 2 and 5, of the Covenant. Therefore :

> the Committee recommends that the State party abolish by law the imposition of the death penalty on minors and limit the number of offences carrying the death penalty to the most serious crimes, with a view to its ultimate abolition.

21. The Committee notes with concern that criminal prosecutions or civil proceedings against members of the security and armed forces, acting under special powers, may not be commenced without the sanction of the central Government. This contributes to a climate of impunity and deprives people of remedies to which they may be entitled in accordance with article 2, paragraph 3, of the Covenant. Therefore :

> the Committee recommends that the requirement of governmental sanction for civil proceedings be abolished and that it be left to the courts to decide whether proceedings are vexatious or abusive. It urges that judicial inquiries be mandatory in all cases of death at the hands of the security and armed forces and that the judges in such inquiries, including those under the Commission of Enquiry Act of 1952, be empowered to direct the prosecution of security and armed forces personnel.

22. The Committee regrets that the National Human Rights Commission is prevented by clause 19 of the Protection of Human Rights Act from investigating directly complaints of human rights violations against the armed forces, but must request a report from the central government. The Committee further regrets that complaints to the Commission are subject to a one-year time limit, thus preventing the investigation of many alleged past human rights violations. Therefore :

> the Committee recommends that these restrictions be removed and that the National Human Rights Commission be authorized to investigate all allegations of violations by agents of the State. It further recommends that all states within the Union be encouraged to establish human rights commissions.

23. The Committee expresses concern at allegations that police and other security forces do not always respect the rule of law and that, in particular, court orders for habeas corpus are not always complied with, particularly in disturbed areas. It also expresses concern about the incidence of custodial deaths, rape and torture, and at the failure of the Government of India to receive the United Nations Special Rapporteur on the question of torture and other cruel, inhuman or degrading treatment or punishment. Therefore:

> while the Committee welcomes the requirement by the National Human Rights Commission that all such alleged incidents be

reported and investigated, and that all post-mortem examinations be taped, it recommends :

(a)The early enactment of legislation for mandatory judicial inquiry into cases of disappearance and death, ill-treatment or rape in police custody;

(b)The adoption of special measures to prevent the occurrence of rape of women in custody;

(c)The mandatory notification of relatives of detainees without delay;

(d)That the right of detainees to legal advice and assistance and to have a medical examination be guaranteed;

(e)That priority be given to providing training and education in the field of human rights to law enforcement officers, custodial officers, members of the security and armed forces, and judges and lawyers, and that the United Nations Code of Conduct for Law Enforcement Officials be taken into account in this regard.

24. The Committee regrets that the use of special powers of detention remains widespread. While noting the State party's reservation to article 9 of the Covenant, the Committee considers that this reservation does not exclude, inter alia, the obligation to comply with the requirement to inform promptly the person concerned of the reasons for his or her arrest. The Committee is also of the view that preventive detention is a restriction of liberty imposed as a response to the conduct of the individual concerned, that the decision as to continued detention must be considered as a determination falling within the meaning of article 14, paragraph 1, of the Covenant, and that proceedings to decide the continuation of detention must, therefore, comply with that provision. Therefore:

the Committee recommends that the requirements of article 9, paragraph 2, of the Covenant be complied with in respect of all detainees. The question of continued detention should be determined by an independent and impartial tribunal constituted and operating in accordance with article 14, paragraph 1, of the Covenant. It further recommends, at the very least, that a central register of detainees under preventive detention laws be maintained and that the State party accept the admission of the International Committee of the Red Cross to all types of detention facilities, particularly in areas of conflict.

25. The Committee notes with concern that, although the Terrorist and Disruptive Activities (Prevention) Act has lapsed, 1,600 people remain in detention under its provision. Therefore :

the Committee recommends that measures be taken to ensure either the early trial of these people or their release. It is also concerned that there are legislative proposals to reintroduce parts of the Act and that this could lead to further violations of the Covenant.

26. The Committee expresses concern at the overcrowding and poor health conditions and sanitation in many prisons, the inequality of treatment of prisoners and the lengthy periods of pre-trial detention, all of which are incompatible with articles 9 and 10, paragraph 1, of the Covenant. Therefore :

the Committee, while welcoming the initiative to give the central Government a greater role in the administration and management of prisons, recommends that measures be taken to reduce overcrowding, to release those who cannot be given a speedy trial and to upgrade prison facilities as quickly as possible. In this respect, the Committee recommends that attention be given to the United Nations Standard Minimum Rules for the Treatment of Prisoners.

27. Concerning court procedure :

> the Committee urges the institution of reforms to the procedure of the courts to ensure a speedy trial of those charged with offences, prompt hearing in civil cases and similar urgency in hearing appeals.

28. The Committee expresses its concern at reports that fines have been imposed, without a hearing, on communities in areas declared disturbed. Therefore :

> the Committee recommends that the imposition of such fines be prohibited.

29. The Committee expresses concern at the extent of bonded labour, as well as the fact that the incidence of this practice reported to the Supreme Court is far higher than is mentioned in the report. The Committee also notes with concern that eradication measures which have been taken do not appear to be effective in achieving real progress in the release and rehabilitation of bonded labourers. Therefore :

> the Committee recommends that a thorough study be urgently undertaken to identify the extent of bonded labour and that more effective measures be taken to eradicate this practice, in accordance with the Bonded Labour System (Abolition) Act of 1976 and article 8 of the Covenant.

30. The Committee expresses concern at reports of forcible repatriation of asylum seekers, including those from Myanmar (Chins), the Chittagong Hills and the Chachmas. Therefore :

> the Committee recommends that, in the process of repatriation of asylum seekers or refugees, due attention be paid to the provisions of the Covenant and other applicable international norms.

31. The Committee deplores the high incidence of child prostitution and trafficking of women and girls into forced prostitution, and it regrets the lack of effective measures to prevent such practices and to protect and rehabilitate the victims. The Committee also regrets that women who have been forced into prostitution are criminalized by the Immoral Trafficking Prevention Act and, further, that article 20 of the Act puts the burden of proof on a woman to prove that she is not a prostitute, which is incompatible with the presumption of innocence. Therefore :

> the Committee recommends that the application of this law to women in the situation described be repealed and that measures be taken to protect and rehabilitate women and children whose rights have been violated in this way.

32. The Committee further regrets the lack of national legislation to outlaw the practice of Devadasi, the regulation of which is left to the states. However, it appears that the practice continues and that not all states have effective legislation against it. The Committee emphasizes that this practice is incompatible with the Covenant. Therefore :

> the Committee recommends that all necessary measures be taken urgently to eradicate the practice of Devadasi.

33. The Committee expresses its concern at the plight of street children and at the reported high level of violence against children within society. It is particularly concerned at reports of child mutilation. Therefore :

> the Committee recommends that urgent measures be taken to address the problem of violence against children and that specific mechanisms be set up for the protection of children.

34. The Committee expresses concern that, despite actions taken by the State party, there has been little progress in implementing the Child Labour (Prohibition and Regulation) Act of 1986. In this respect :

the Committee recommends that urgent steps be taken to remove all children from hazardous occupations, that immediate steps be taken to implement the recommendation of the National Human Rights Commission that the constitutional requirement that it should be a fundamental right for all children under 14 to have free and compulsory education be respected, and that efforts be strengthened to eliminate child labour in both the industrial and rural sectors. The Committee also recommends that consideration be given to establishing an independent mechanism with effective national powers to monitor and enforce the implementation of laws for the eradication of child labour and bonded labour.

35. Concerning the periodic report :

the Committee draws to the attention of the Government of India the provisions of paragraph 6(a) of the guidelines regarding the form and content of periodic reports from States parties, and requests that, accordingly, its next period report, due on 31 December, 2001, should contain material which responds to all these concluding observations. The Committee further requests that these concluding observations be widely disseminated among the public at large in all parts of India.

Note : The author has taken note of the fact that the observations have not been disseminated to the public as required by the UNHRC guidelines and para 35 of the conclusions.

Annexure-II

NEW DELHI DECLARATION , 1995
ACTION PLAN ON HIV/AIDS

1. Under the auspices of Ministry of Health and Family Welfare, Government of India, The Indian Law Institute and with cooperation of United Nations Development Programme, the World Health Organisation and other national and international co-sponsors, an international Conference was organised in New Delhi, India to address the issues of law and humanity and public policy as required by the advent of the HIV/AIDS epidemic.

2. The Conference was inaugurated on December 6, 1995 by His Excellency, the President of India, Dr. Shankar Dayal Sharma and addressed by Hon'ble the Prime Minister of India, Mr. P.V. Narasimha Rao and by the Chief Justice of India, Hon'ble Mr. Justice A.M. Ahmadi.

3. All three leaders of the host country emphasised the need for a concerted approach to the legal issues presented by HIV/AIDS which would not only protect society against the spread of infection, but also respect the dignity and fundamental human rights of those who are infected or who are suspected of being infected, and their families and associates.

4. At the close of the Conference, the participants resolved to adopt this **Declaration and Action Plan** as a record of their deliberations and as an encouragement to resolute action in the future.

Principles

5. The following principles were accepted as a guide to the approach which should be taken in developing laws and strategies to help combat the spread of HIV/AIDS :

5.1 All laws and policies on HIV/AIDS should be based upon sound and scientific data. They should rest upon this foundation and not upon presupposition, prejudice and stereotypes ;

5.2 In combating HIV/AIDS, it is essential and urgent as rarely before, to adopt a global approach. This includes a model global AIDS law which supports action at the local, national and international level ;

5.3 The approach, which is adopted, should respect and protect the human rights of all persons at risk of HIV/AIDS and against discrimination on the ground of HIV/AIDS. It is recognised that one of the most effective strategies for changing behaviour and ensuring against the spread of HIV infection lies in the protection of the rights of those at risk ;

5.4 Laws should be made for prevention of HIV and for protection of persons affected by HIV/AIDS which are effective and enforceable :

5.5 Law makers who have a special responsibility in responding to HIV/AIDS, must work in an interdisciplinary way with health care workers, government and non-government organisations, representatives of vulnerable groups, people living with HIV/AIDS and citizens in general who must be well informed about how HIV/AIDS is transmitted and of how the infection from same can be prevented ;

5.6. The importance of moral, spiritual and religious values in response to the HIV/AIDS epidemic should be emphasised.

Objectives

6. The role of law in the context of HIV/AIDS includes:

6.1. To protect human rights and empower individuals so that by their cooperation, the spread of the HIV infection is contained ;

6.2. To promote voluntary behaviour which will protect the health of individuals, families and children through out the world ;

6.3. To prevent coercive and punitive action against persons with demonstrated or suspected HIV infection or AIDS ;

6.4. To protect society and to promote a sense of responsibility in the face of an epidemic which poses serious threat ;

6.5. In securing the foregoing goals, the law should facilitate the provision of access to information about HIV/AIDS prevention, to health care services relevant to HIV/AIDS and to legal services to uphold and protect the rights of individuals ;

6.6. While effective laws in the context of HIV/AIDS must be just and always consistent with fundamental human rights but their ultimate objective must be to protect the individual as well as the society ;

6.7. Respect for fundamental rights must be ensured including the right to privacy and freedom from discrimination; and

6.8. To provide for the allocation of adequate resources for prevention, care and anti-discrimination efforts including support for governmental and non-governmental organisations, institutions and networks of people living with HIV/AIDS.

International action

7.1. The participants recognised the vital work that is being done in the international community to secure global cooperation in the present phase of HIV/AIDS. But more is needed ;

7.2. UNAIDS should have, as a major part of its strategy for the defence of fundamental rights in the context of HIV/AIDS and the development of standards and promotion of laws which should protect these rights, support national responses to HIV/AIDS, including those relating to legal and ethical issues ;

7.3. The other organs of the United Nations at every level should incorporate and promote programmes and activities designed to protect individuals and communities against the spread of HIV/AIDS :

7.4. The High commissioner for Human Rights_should incorporate in his programmes and in the programmes of the Centre for Human Rights enlarged strategies for promoting the co-existence of human rights of persons with HIV/AIDS and for containment of the epidemic ;

7.5. All countries should cooperate in strategies designed to promote HIV/AIDS awareness and to respond effectively to national features of the epidemic in a way consistent with local laws, policies and cultural values; and

7.6. There should be dissemination of knowledge of best practice amongst all the countries.

National action - legislative

8. The participants recognised the wide range of special areas in which, in many countries, legislation has already been enacted at the national, sub-national levels and local legislators should respond to the HIV/AIDS epidemic. In addition to this, a number of items may be provided as a check list for legislative actions, if no such action has yet been taken in the jurisdictions concerned. The participants recognised that, whereas fundamental rights are universal, legislation varies according to the legal context and local legal traditions. Notwithstanding this, they considered that

the following items should have priority attention in legislative action:

8.1 Legislation to ensure the safety of the supply of blood so that blood products, organs and tissues are accurately and safely tested before use and provision may be made for legal liability in the event that blood, which is provided, is found to be contaminated with HIV;

8.2 Introduction of anti-discrimination, equal opportunity ,privacy and confidentiality legislation designed to provide effective protection for persons living with HIV/AIDS or suspected to be living with HIV/AIDS and effective remedies for such persons ;

8.3 Removal of any restrictions on the dissemination of full and accurate information and education about prevention of HIV infection and on the availability and quality of condoms and sterile injections ;

8.4 Appropriate legislative protection for women in the context of marriage where their status increases their vulnerability to infection or to socio-economic impact of HIV/AIDS ;

8.5 The participants welcomed the initiatives, at least in some regions, of schemes for the provisions of sterile needles/syringes to prevent the further spread of HIV/AIDS amongst drug injecting persons ;

8.6 Appropriate legislative action be taken to repeal those provisions of the penal code of all countries which are contrary to modern day concepts of human dignity and human rights and have effect of impeding strategies of providing educational instructions designed to contain the epidemic;

8.7 Forbidding discrimination in employment, education, housing, health care, social security, travel, marital and reproductive rights and other privileges of people ;

8.8 Reforms in the laws relating to commercial sex workers to remove criminal stigma which interfere with imparting education to commercial sex workers and their clients, providing sex workers with alternative forms of employment to protect themselves and thereby to protect society from the spread of HIV/ AIDS.

Executive action

9. That the participants considered that there was much that could be done by governments and administration without the need for new legislation by simply fulfilling their duties to protect the communities they serve. Amongst the actions which should have the highest priority are :

9.1 The introduction of education in schools, universities and general community concerning the HIV/ AIDS epidemic, the modes of transmission and the ways in which it can be avoided ;

9.2 Prohibition of compulsory testing and screening for HIV/AIDS ;

9.3 Prohibition of isolation, segregation and quarantines;

9.4 Protection of confidentiality and privacy of people living with HIV/AIDS where contained in administrative records and the provision of administrative remedies for cases of violations ;

9.5 Provision of facilities for voluntary screening with informed consent and for pre and post test counselling of those who are voluntarily tested for HIV ;

9.6 Introduction of universal precautions for prevention of occupational transmission of HIV infection to health care workers and patients;

9.7 Introduction of sexual and reproductive health counselling and services including programmes for urban and rural population;

9.8 Promotion of mass media education, direct contact education, campaigns, counselling of relevant groups and professionals and counselling of individuals with changed behaviours to reduce the risk of infection. Introduction of education and human rights including the human rights to those persons living with HIV/AIDS infection ;

9.9 Establishment of ethical review committees to ensure ethics in the provision of health care and in HIV related research.

Judicial action

10. The participants recognised that the judiciary and law makers in common law countries have particular responsibilities in responding to HIV/AIDS epidemic. The judicial response should include :

10.1 Familiarising member of the judiciary with HIV/AIDS, the applicable statutory and common law and the need for an informed approach to the spread of virus and its impact upon the legal system ;

10.2 Prompt disposal of cases involving issues connected with HIV/AIDS ;

10.3 Judges should play a leading role in proposing and suggesting reforms of the law where necessary to ensure that the law responds in an effective and just way to HIV/AIDS.

A call to action

11. The participants considered that there was a need for a greater sense of urgency about the HIV/AIDS epidemic. The urgency must flow into the judiciary and the government into the health care system, media and to citizens in general.

12. The data provided to the Conference demonstrated an alarming increase in the spread of HIV/AIDS in the Afro-Asian region. The data should mobilise law makers throughout the region. They should throw off the shackles of complacency and adopt effective laws while at the same time avoiding measures which are ineffective. Now is the time for action including legal action.

13. The participants resolved to express their thanks to the Government of India, the Indian Law Institute and the co-sponsors for organising this conference. This was the first International Conference to address specifically the issues of law and humanity as they have a global impact in curbing the spread of HIV/AIDS.

The participants considered that it would be a futile exercise if the International Conference was to conclude and the participants were to disperse without appropriate steps being taken to follow up the work that has been done in New Delhi and to spread the message of the Conference. They, therefore, resolved to ask that there should be established both national and international Committees to address the national and international implications of HIV/AIDS from the point of view of law and humanity.

The international committee should fully cooperate with other international bodies working in this field including the UNAIDS Programme and High Commissioner for Human Rights, WHO and UNDP. Such committees should be created and further Conferences should be held in a series to continue the work of this Conference in this vital area concerned with nothing less than the well being and survival of millions.

The voice of millions who are infected and of those who are not infected but are at risk call out for an urgent action. Law makers have a role to play, in promoting an effective response to the epidemic. Out of the non-discriminatory and ethical crisis of HIV/AIDS should come a growing awareness of the role of law in responding to this global challenge and the supportive role which law makers, judges and lawyers can play to further this common cause of humanity.

14. The participants resolved as above in the belief that the crisis presented by HIV/AIDS requires urgent action by law makers at every level. Such law makers should be well aware of the fact that HIV/AIDS is not just a matter of statistics but concerns humanity in every country. The suffering of humanity demands resolute and sensitive action through global AIDS law.

Adopted
Unanimosly

New Delhi
December 10, 1995

The way of peace they klnow not;
and there is no judgement in their going:
they have made them erooked paths:
whosoever goeth therein shall not know peace.

ISAIH 59: 8

Index